FALLOUT FROM CHERNOBYL

FALLOUT FROM CHERNOBYL

L. RAY SILVER

DENEAU

DENEAU PUBLISHERS & COMPANY LTD.
760 BATHURST STREET
TORONTO, ONTARIO
M5S 2R6

© 1987

Typesetting: Computer Composition of Canada, Inc.

Printed in Canada

This book has been published with the assistance of the Canada Council
and Ontario Arts Council under their block grant programs.

Canadian Cataloguing in Publication Data

Silver, L. Ray (Lionel Ray), 1917–
  Fallout from Chernobyl

Bibliography: p.
Includes glossary and index.
ISBN 0–88879–140–2 (bound). – ISBN 0-88879-144-5 (pbk.)

1. Nuclear industry – Canada – Safety measures.
2. Nuclear industry – Canada – History. 3. Nuclear
industry – Accidents. 4. Nuclear power plants –
Ukraine – Chernobyl – Accidents. I. Title.

TK9152.S56   1987   363.1'79   C87-093231-4

*To my wife, Lynne,
for love, confidence and an idea.*

*For Chris, Keith, Steven, Tim, Jane & David,
Sarah-Jane and Rachel-Claire, Debbie & Mark
and Stephen-Thomas.
It's your world now.*

Contents

Preface

RAW ENERGY, THE FIERY PROTON cores of atoms, burned incandescent at creation time and the gods laughed. To each atom they attached an electric particle nineteen hundred times smaller than the core. This electron stabilized primal energy to elemental mass; fixed it firmly, kept it dormant, so to speak. Stripped of its electron mate the atomic core was mutable. It split or fused to spawn nearly a hundred daughter elements on earth. Unmated, frustrated, destablized, the atom's energy was awesome. Mankind was a million years learning this secret of the gods — how to control the atom's fearsome energy.

Ernest Rutherford measured the weight and speed of radium atoms. A pound of radium might contain energy equal to ten million horsepower, he said. It took a generation to refine that much radium and by then its mystique outshone its energy. The boffins tried uranium next. Radium and uranium atoms are both prone to throw off energy in fearsome bursts, to radiate like the sun. "Atom for atom the energy in such radioactivity is one hundred thousand times that in most modern high explosives," Canada's chief scientist Chalmers Jack Mackenzie told the wartime cabinet. "Although it weighs a mere twenty grams, an enriched uranium pellet in atomic-reactor fuel contains enough energy to heat a one-family home for six months or drive a car for nearly a year," Lev Feoktistov, a deputy director of the Soviet's famed Kurchatov Atomic Energy Institute, said forty years later.

Five billion years since they watched the fusion of proton cores here on earth, no more than a million years since they had seen our shaggy ancestors rub heat from sticks and strip electrons from wood to make it burn, the gods reminded earthlings that energy was not for free. It was not created here on earth, it was only transferred. "For every force there is an equal and opposite force," said Isaac Newton. There was always a trade off. The coal miner transferred his energy for fire in fuel, the sailmaker for wind power, the dam-builder for electricity. But, said the gods, so long as the sun shines and the rivers run, energy would cost sweat and tears and sometimes blood. There was no free lunch. That is the reality that shines through this Chernobyl story.

Fire accidentally sparked or tediously kindled was too hard to come by to be toyed with in prehistoric times. But about 130 B.C. Hero of Alexandria devised a plaything that turned heat energy to power. His medium was steam. Fire gave heat and the heat energized drops of water to become vapour. The atom packets in water were destabilized, you might say. They bounced more energetically as steam vapour. Hero choreographed the dancing molecules in steam, marched them through a cylinder, directed their kicks in one direction. It was enough to drive a tiny wheel. Two millenia later three Brits adapted Hero's steam engine to pump water. It kept mine depths dry and miners dug more coal to fuel bigger engines to drive trains, spin turbines, create the Industrial Revolution. That was two centuries before Chernobyl.

Chernobyl was a big steam plant. When it burst it vented the equivalent energy of 400 million kicking horses. It released atomized particles as well. The fallout from Chernobyl irradiated cancerous rays just as coal-fired steam plants spew out cancer-causing irritants. The radioactive fallout was less visible than the toxic gases that pour from conventional power-generation stations. But a world alert for signals from Bomb-test debris detected the Chernobyl fallout. They were not looking for acid rain.

This is the story of how the Chernobyl fallout circled the world, more in the mind's eye of fearful people than in actuality. Yet the fear was real. It was part of a complex of responses to the Hiroshima Bomb. The Hiroshima complex is that mix of awe, fear, guilt and incomprehension with which we buried the image of the mushroom cloud — and the genocide beneath it — deep in the recesses of our minds. For a generation activists, opportunists, politicians and vested interests ploughed those depths of the public psyche to reap a rich crop of paranoia. They claimed they were trying to cleanse the environment and ban the Bomb, to exorcise the demons from fearful, guilty minds. They did none of these things. Crud still fell from steam-plant smoke, the nuclear arsenals grew to promise extinction nine times over and the demons still danced in our heads. I had been writing of this nuclear debate for thirty-five years when Chernobyl happened. It seemed time to put it all together.

Preface

The fallout from Chernobyl raised the spectre anew in Canada. The nuclear genie first sprang from the lamp that Rutherford lit when the world of science spun on an axis through his Montreal laboratory. The Bomb was fuelled with our uranium brewed in Chalk River reactors. But so are the nuclear-fuelled steam plants that give smokeless energy yet don't explode like bombs. So, too, are gamma-ray sources brewed in Canadian nuclear-power plants. Eighty-five per cent of these gamma-irradiating isotopes used world-wide for cancer therapy, for sterilizing foods and drugs today, are a by-product of Pickering and Bruce power reactors. The gamma-beaming, cancer-treating machines, themselves, were designed at Chalk River; built in Canada. They are said to have extended the life of cancer patients in eighty countries by 13 million person-years. Those are chapters of the Chernobyl story.

The fallout was barely detectable this side of the globe but it triggered alarms and it raised questions. In Ottawa, Health Minister Jake Epp was concerned with the rain that fell on Tunney's Pasture, with radioactive salad fixings in Vancouver. At Canada's atomic control board, at the Crown nuclear companies and at Ontario Hydro, the experts asked, "How can we help?" In Moscow, Mikhail Gorbachev admitted that Chernobyl was the world's worst nuclear accident and he invited collaboration to prevent another. In Vienna, the International Atomic Energy Agency provided the forum. Three hundred and eighty nuclear experts conferred there on Chernobyl; how it happened, how another such accident could be avoided. More than two hundred news people listened, saw on-site film, queried the scientists and engineers, the medical specialists and radiation technologists. What we were told there is a part of this story.

Much of it has been written in the nuke towns of Canada. The economic and political fallout from Chernobyl touches the people of Point Lepreau, Deep River and Port Hope, Pickering and Bruce, Elliot Lake and Blind River, and in the north Saskatchewan communities around the rim of the Athabascan uranium basin. They have a vested interest in the nuclear debate and Chernobyl raised new issues in the on-going dialogue. In the fall of 1986 four Ontario Hydro engineers went to Moscow at the Soviets' invitation. The Soviets wanted to apply Hydro technology to prevent another runaway reactor; they wanted to adopt Hydro training procedures, occupational health protection, waste disposal techniques. But Hydro-Soviet trade and technology transfer was conditional on a Canada-USSR agreement. "This is an important step in achieving worldwide vigilance and cooperation in the field of nuclear safety," a Hydro spokesman told Ottawa in November. "We are thinking about it," said an External Affairs official at the year end. That chapter was still being written as this book went to press.

Fallout from Chernobyl is the story of an ongoing global industry which counted its first casualties in a generation at Pripyat in the USSR in the spring of 1986. It is a story of technological progress that delegates from some thirty nations discussed at Vienna. They determined that this progress would not end this century. Canada, which has played a lead role from the outset, will not opt out. You have a long time to live with the peacetime atom. This book may help you do so with peace of mind.

The Hiroshima complex has held us, three generations, in a tyranny of fear. It is time to dismantle it, to exorcise the nuclear demons of awe, ear, guilt and incomprehension. It is time to laugh with the gods.

Acknowledgments

MY WIFE AND I WERE IN AN economy-sized Ottawa hotel room the week following Chernobyl. We had come to town to attend an Air Force function and as usual I refreshed phone contacts on my news beat. For a decade I have covered the Canadian nuclear industry and uranium mining for McGraw-Hill's globe-swaddling *Nucleonics Week* and *Nuclear Fuel*. For much of that time I did so for the *Financial Post* as well. Habitually, we travel with my portable computer, its printer unit, a tape recorder, acoustic cups for hooking the computer to the phone, patch cords to connect recorder to computer, transcribing switch to recorder, power adapters to everything else. Who knows when nuke news will break?

It did that last week of April. "The radio said something about a nuclear accident in Russia," my wife told me. Suddenly we were festooned in electronic connections, the umbilical cord of my profession. To switch position from phone to computer keyboard in our stationary roomette meant swapping places, I to the coffee table, she to sit on the bed edge or vice versa. Patch cords were disentangled from ankles, phone cords unwound from necks, upturned furniture righted, all in the practised art of a marital minuet. Lynne monitored the news media and tracked down contacts, kept me electronically connected and emotionally unplugged, while I talked to AECB president Jon Jennekens and regulator-in-chief Zygmond Domaratski, AECL vice-presidents Gordon Brooks and Stan Hatcher, Ontario Hydro VPs Arvo Niitenberg and Bill Morison, Canadian Nuclear Association president Norman Aspin, Hugh Spence at AECB Ottawa, John Macpherson at AECL in Sheridan Park, David McArthur at the CNA in Toronto. These are the people I have talked to regularly for years. That's my business; they make it sound like pleasure. To them I am indebted for help beyond any call of duty. In the eight months that I worked on *Fallout from Chernobyl* none of these people, nor many more, turned me a deaf ear.

The list at Ontario Hydro alone is countless; from chairman Tom Campbell and president Robert Franklin to Terry Young, Michele McMaster and Tina Warren on their media desk, they responded with straight answers. So did Dennis Dack, John O'Connor, Larry W. Woodhead, Bob Popple, Tom Drolet, Robert J. Kelly, Mike Williams, Bob Wilson, Gerry Armitage and David Moysey. At the AECL Vic Snell, David K. Myers and Richard Osborne, risk assessment, radiation and environmental specialists respectively, flipped charts and culled data on my behalf. So did Geoff Knight and Bob Potvin at the AECB; Bliss Tracy, Roger Eaton, Carol Peacock and Nes Lubinsky at Health and Welfare Canada; Mark Mohr and Natalie Kirschberg at External Affairs; Brian Finlay at the Ontario Energy Ministry. People as far afield as Art O'Connor, Lyn Titus and Roland Krause at New Brunswick Power, Roy Lloyd and Don Somers at the Saskatchewan Mining and Development Corporation, came up with answers. Media man Steve Lint and various librarians at the University of Toronto could not have been more accommodating. Dave Smith, who has often hassled me at Eldorado Nuclear, answered my post-Chernobyl inquiries without hesitation. At Queen's Park George Hutchison and Guy Cote never failed to return my calls nor did their boss, Premier David Peterson, ever duck my questions. Hydro's man at the IAEA, Derry Ironside and his wife Rhoda made our fortnight in Vienna informative and productive, but best of all they let us share an evening with the Canadian contingent that serves the world at the International Atomic Energy Agency. Ron Thomas, the External Affairs man with our nuclear mission at the IAEA, gave invaluable help to us — and to the Canadian delegation collaborating with colleagues from thirty nations to make the world safer.

Especially, I owe O. John C. Runnalls at the University of Toronto, a deep debt of gratitude. He was in this business the day of the NRX accident in 1952, he advised Canadian governments for years, he developed U of T's nuclear engineering centre, he has written a good deal about the nuclear industry in Canada and he is an Ontario Hydro director. John Runnalls has been keeping me honest for years. He and Bill Morison, co-designer of the Candu reactor, waded through a draft of the first six chapters of this book to straighten me out on technicalities. Runnall's mentor was Leslie G. Cook who was studying at the Kaiser Wilhelm Institute with Otto Hahn and Lise Meitner when they took science to the edge of nuclear discovery in 1938. I am indebted to Les Cook for allowing me to use illustrations from his University of

Acknowledgments

Toronto extension course lectures in 1950. They are in the glossary.

My McGraw-Hill editors in Washington, Mike Knapik and Margaret Ryan, have been more than patient, forebearing, helpful; from Paris their European editor Anne MacLachlan made sure Lynne and I didn't sleep in the street in Vienna and she explained my pushy eccentricities to the IAEA headquarters people. There Hans-Friedrich Meyer took me in stride. Two hundred news people, all as acquisitive as I, clamoured at his door during the last week of August. No panic. Hans Meyer took our queries in order and got back to us with succinct answers. James Underhill, the Canadian Press foreign editor, accepted the stories I filed from Vienna and gently reassured this old codger three thousand miles away that they sounded okay to him. My colleagues in the Queen's Park press gallery are accustomed to my pre-senile foibles but Derek Nelson of Thomson Papers put me back on track when I drifted. Fellow fly-boy, francophone and engineer, Joe McCarthy provided translations and explanations. At the Soviet Embassy in Ottawa, attaché Igor Lobinov responded to my requests for photographs and translations that I suspect stretched his communications budget. His comrades obliged parsimoniously.

Sandra Tooze, the most scrupulous editor I have had in half a century, won me with her job at Deneau Publishers. There was a moment in history when only Sandra Tooze and my wife thought I could, and would, write this book. Both found me difficult, frustrating; an exasperating old newsman with a story to tell.

None of these people are responsible for what I have said. But all have helped me say it.

Thanks.

1

Runaway Reactor

He was going down hill at ninety miles per hour
When the whistle broke into a scream.
He was found in the wreck with his hand on the throttle
And scalded to death by the steam.

—"WRECK OF THE OLD 97," RAILWAY BALLAD, 1903

STEAM ENGINES REPLACED HORSEPOWER two centuries ago yet buggy-day terms persisted. It was simpler to think of James Watt's contraption as a horse hauling a load. A good horse could pull a 150-pound load for eight hours a day if only at two or three miles per hour. The steam locomotive went much faster, still you could throttle it down as easily as pulling on a choke strap or yanking a bridle. Even if the machine went out of control in those bygone days it was no worse than a runaway horse. But like all else, steam engines kept getting bigger.

Early Saturday morning, April 26, 1986 the operators lost control of the Chernobyl steam plant No. 4. It blew like the Southern Railway's Old 97 locomotive and the equivalent of 400 million horses got away on them. Around the world the news media referred to a "runaway reactor." Like railroader Casey Jones, operator Valery Ivanovich Khodemchuk died with his hand on the throttle. He was one of those trying to turn off this big engine when it blew. Like the fireman in that old railway ballad, Vladimir Nikolayevich Shashenok was scalded to death by steam. They found him beyond the safe confines of the control room caught in mid-stride as he and Khodemchuk had raced towards the reactor hall. "There, Valery's there!" Vladimir Shashenok

1

told rescuers before he died. There Valery Khodemchuk would remain entombed.

Of the 203 station staff and firemen hospitalized in the following hours twenty-nine died within a month. Some had been burned by a flameless fury; some were unmarked but an unseen and unfelt fire cooked the marrow in their bones. Soviet physicians moved with remarkable speed and knowledge to treat the first nuclear disaster victims in a generation. Within twelve hours doctors, physicists, radiologists, blood specialists and lab technicians were applying lore from the frontiers of nuclear medicine. Within thirty-six hours they had studied a thousand blood analyses; within days they had done more than twenty-five thousand tests on the 129 most seriously ill Chernobyl casualties. Most of the deaths were due to acute radiation sickness combined with severe burns from radioactivity. Seven died from bone marrow deficiency. This clinical data was irrelevent to Mrs. Khodemchuk and Mrs. Shashenok. Nor did the other widows find much solace in it. The next-of-kin are rarely interested in the cause of death, only in its finality.

Chernobyl shocked the industrialized world. Never mind that steampowered electric-generating plants had been blowing up for a century. Back in the 1880s explosions were so commonplace at Thomas Edison's Pearl Street New York power plant that people joked wild horses must be kicking up the electricity. Yet this multiple fatality at a Soviet generating station a century later remained world-wide news for a month. Ten times that many died of stomach infection in Angola that May; ten times as many died of cancer in Britain that month. Sixty-six times that number committed suicide in Japan, twenty-four times as many died violent deaths in Germany, 170 times more people were killed on US highways and thirty times as many Canadians died accidentally in the same period. A gun-happy American killed half as many fellow workers in an Oklahoma post office one afternoon that summer. All were as irrevocably removed from society yet none of them became postmortem celebrities.

It is noteworthy that the Chernobyl casualties were news in their own country as well as abroad. The Soviet media don't normally report accidents let alone name the victims. But these men died unusual and heroic deaths. The manner in which they died was as astonishing as the way in which Major Leonid Telyatnikov and his two lieutenants led their firemen into the lethal field radiating from the nuclear plant. They had all figured in a global news event which Mikhail Gorbachev quickly made the curtain-raiser in his *glasnost* policy of public scrutiny.

2

In any case, the evacuation of 135,000 people and 34,000 head of cattle from a thirty-kilometre zone could hardly go unremarked at home. Fallout tripped radiation detector alarms much farther afield.

In fact the Chernobyl explosion spread its own message. It sent bellwether waves into Scandinavia within a day, through Poland in three days, across Europe in a week. Spewed from the nuclear furnace, wafted high on a fiery updraft, carried far on strong winds in dry weather the unseen, unfelt rays were soon detected in a world watchful for weapon-test fallout or any leakage from local nuclear-power plants. It triggered alarms at Finland's Centre for Radiation and Nuclear Safety and at its Olkilouto nuclear power station, at four Swedish nuclear stations and at Denmark's Riso Research Centre. These alarms were designed to catch any trace of man-made radiation escaping station boundaries. The fact that the windborne contaminants from Chernobyl were detected at these Scandinavian stations, and ultimately at much more distant points, attests to the sensitivity of the instruments not to the hazard of the fallout. Canadian health authorities calculated that the Chernobyl radiation would increase the chances of the average European dying from cancer by perhaps one in a hundred thousand, the equivalent added risk of smoking fourteen cigarettes. That bit of statistical epidemiology notwithstanding, the Chernobyl disaster scared the world sick.

Chernobyl was certainly the world's worst nuclear accident. It was also the first to spread lethal fallout over a significant distance since a fifteen-megaton H-Bomb sent its deathly plume a hundred miles downwind from the US test site on Bikini Atoll thirty-two years earlier. Twenty-three Japanese fishermen, 239 Marshall Islanders and twenty-eight Americans were radioactively dusted on that occasion but only one died and just three were permanently incapacitated. The Soviet accident was the first known to cause death at a nuclear plant since a runaway reactor killed three operators in an Idaho research station in 1961. Those parameters made it newsworthy enough. But the Soviets exacerbated the non-Communist world's fearsome distrust and doomsday expectations by their initial silence. They said nothing of the Chernobyl disaster until after it set nuclear alarm bells ringing in Scandinavia. Indeed, the first government announcement was carried by *Izvestia* four days later. It was four sentences long: "An accident has occurred at the Chernobyl atomic power station; one of the nuclear reactors has been damaged. Measures are being taken to eliminate the consequences of the accident. Aid is being given to the victims. A government commission has been established."

3

Not only had a nuclear reactor run wild and caused global fallout but those frightful Russians wouldn't talk about it. Furious that the Red commissars were not meeting their news demands, the capitalist press filled the blanks with random numbers like bingo players. "2,000 Dead in Nuke Disaster," said the *Toronto Sun*. "West German and Swedish nuclear experts fear thousands may have died," the *Globe & Mail* reported. "Mass grave for 15,000 N-victims," said the *New York Post*. While the Western world was not going to give the Communists any benefit of doubt, ex-patriate politicians milked it for venom. "Tonight [we] will demonstrate our condemnation of a regime which for thirty-six hours exposed some 50,000 citizens to such doses of radiation that today they have a mere 50 per cent chance of survival," the Ontario legislature was told on May 7. By then the news media on both sides of the Atlantic were turning their anti-nuke guns on domestic targets. In Bonn, London, New York and Toronto environmentalists thrashed like moths in the TV limelight. "Close down nuclear plants everywhere," they demanded. On Tunney's Pasture in Ottawa, Canada's Health and Welfare people found traces of radiation to justify their watch. "Don't drink the rainwater," they warned trying not to sound shrill.

The Soviets themselves were overwhelmed as they fought to quell the fire at Chernobyl. "No one has ever encountered an accident like this one," Soviet Academy of Sciences vice-president Yevgeny Pavlovich Velikhov said on May 8. "Unfortunately we are still organizing a defense in depth." What the Russians feared in the first few days was a *"rasplavlaniye*, a smelting down of the reactor core." Meltdown — the melting of a nuclear reactor to an incandescent blob burning itself down through the earth — came into public parlance with an earlier accident. There had been a runaway reactor at Three Mile Island near Harrisburg, Pennsylvania in 1979. Nobody died but TMI, as it became known, blew its detectable breath far beyond the Susquehanna River. By fateful happenstance TMI coincided with the debut of a fanciful, anti-nuclear movie. With childlike simplicity, *The China Syndrome* suggested that a runaway reactor might melt its way down to the Chinese on the other side of the world. The movie was aimed at a North American audience, of course, but its concept surpassed geography.

Soviet experts were very worried that Chernobyl's molten core would explode downward to contaminate a large watershed. Fortunately, they were not distracted from fighting a worse peril — the continued release of atomized radioactive debris from the fractured top of the reactor. There was a third concern. Chernobyl had been planned to be the largest nuclear station in the USSR. Four thousand-megawatt reactors

4

were operational and two more units were to be built on the site. Reliant on such nuclear plants to meet an increasing share of electrical demand in the industrialized Ukraine, Soviet power authorities urged the engineers to do all possible to restore Chernobyl-1, -2 and -3 plants to service if, and as soon as, this could be safely done.

The Chernobyl units were based on the Soviet's prototype nuclear-power plant built in 1954. Like the world's first nuclear reactor assembled under the University of Chicago stadium a decade earlier, and like nearly sixty commercial reactors built since then in France, Britain and the Soviet Union, they are fuelled with a mix of uranium and graphite. Atomic forces in these materials interact to produce steam-making heat. The steam spins turbines to generate electricity. The process evolved from Hero of Alexandria's aeolipile (wind-driven cylinder) to the steam engine on which the British built their industrial empire. Thomas Edison applied the concept to generate electricity. Early power-house firemen stoked their boilers with coal and blew in enough air to keep it burning. Latter-day utilities fuel their generating plants with uranium and add graphite or a heavy-water moderator to stir up the nuclear fire. Regardless of the fuel Hero's basic principle remains operative: Once you raise steam you must control its force.

The Chernobyl plant was designed to raise steam equal to the power of four million horses. On the night of April 25-26 a hundred times that much got out of control. Ironically, the reactor broke loose at the moment it was being shut down. Like horsemen leading an unhitched team to pasture, Chernobyl operators had been lulled to false confidence by thirty months of near-flawless performance. The triggering event was a safety test; engineers were checking its self-generating capacity during the rundown. Could it sustain the critical coolant pumps in an emergency until auxiliary electrical power was cut in? they wanted to know.

Unit 4 had run trouble free and nonstop at virtually full load for the past year. Now it was being shut down for annual maintenance. In normal circumstances the three dozen night-shift members would have watched the rundown with quiet satisfaction. Their plant had operated almost faultlessly since it was commissioned. Once again it was likely to prove the best performer among fifteen RBMK (the graphite-moderated, boiling-water reactors in the Soviet power system). A job is a job but the crew mates on a high-tech operation invariably interact with their machine. Observe them shutting down a nuclear plant, an industrial mill, a refinery or a big jet aircraft at the end of a long, smooth run and you may hear man and machinery humming together. For this shift, moreover, it was the start of a long weekend before the May Day holiday.

They should have been attentive but relaxed. In fact the mood in the Chernobyl-4 control room was tense; the crew were distracted and restive. A higher authority had decided to run an electrical test while the turbine generator wound down. The test was being conducted by electrical engineers from a supplier firm. Dom Tech Energo people were outsiders unfamiliar with nuclear operations and unknown to the Chernobyl personnel. The objective was to determine how long the momentum of the spinning turbine would generate emergency power if the reactor was suddenly shut off. A cyclist seeing his dynamo-powered bicycle light dim out as he lost speed on an uphill climb would understand. The turbine test was yet another step in the evolution of safer nuclear operations; one more trial of equipment and operations in the endless quest by all nuclear nations to prevent loss of control. But it did not directly involve them so it was beyond the experience or interest of the control-room staff. They were aware that an outsider was calling the shots while they were anxious to close down the plant. In these circumstances the test went badly.

Valery Khodemchuk and Vladimir Shashenok had heard the test procedure outlined when they began the previous night's shift. As they understood it, there were four stages to coincide with the reactor shutdown. First, reactor power would be reduced to less than a third of its capacity. Then the emergency cooling system — the circuit to douse a runaway reactor with cold water — was to be blocked off to prevent its inadvertent use. The cooling pumps normally powered by the station's electrical supply would then be connected to one of the two turbine generators to see if it could sustain them. Finally, the reactor's steam would be cut off from that turbine to let it spin on its own momentum. ("Flywheel energy," Model T Ford drivers would have called that momentum early in the century.) In an emergency some thirty to forty seconds would be needed to switch in the standby diesel generators. Would a free-spinning turbine generate sufficient pump power during that interval to prevent the reactor from overheating? At 1:00 a.m. Friday they took steps to find out. They began the gradual shutdown of Chernobyl-4.

It took twelve hours — well into another shift — to cut the reactor power in half, to switch off one of the two turbine generators and connect pumps in the test arrangement. An hour after that they isolated the emergency core cooling system. There was no valid reason to disconnect it except that the test manager wanted things done that way. When the crunch came "the blocked-off emergency system might have been useful," a fourteen member review team told the International Atomic Energy Agency. Valery Legasov, deputy director of the Soviet's Kurchatov Institute of Atomic Energy and the man primarily responsible for finding out what went wrong at Chernobyl, was more emphatic. They had "violated the most sacred rule" by disconnecting a protective device, he said. "If at least one violation of the six committed had not been done the accident would not have happened."

As events transpired, regional authorities needed all the power they could get that Friday. So station management was told to keep Chernobyl-4 operational with one generator supplying 500 megawatts of electricity for the next nine hours. Khodemchuk and Shashenok, returning with the night crew, would have no reason to know that they were operating the reactor without emergency-coolant protection. It had been shut off in the early hours of Friday morning. "The fact the emergency system was not reset reflects the attitude of the operating staff in respect to violating normal procedures," the IAEA review team observed. "Their attitude seems to have been conditioned by overconfidence stemming from successful, trouble-free operation and an urge to conduct the test. The presumption that this was an electro-technical test with no effect on reactor safety seems to have minimized the attention given in safety terms."

Shortly after 11:00 p.m. Chernobyl management was told it could take unit 4 out of service and test preparations were resumed. The reactor at this point was at half power with 20 million litres of water pouring into its 1661 boiler tubes every hour to make 1600 megawatts worth of steam or a third that much electrical energy. This was equal to the pull of 2.1 million horses in harness. To control that activity the chief operator had two regulatory systems. With one eye on temperature, pressure and steam gauges, he kept the mix of steam and water in each of the reactor tubes within precise limits. His other eye was on the heat-making, atom-splitting process which he controlled by moving 211 neutron-absorber rods in and out of the reactor. The deeper these rods penetrate into the reactor core the more neutrons they intercept to prevent their atom-splitting, heat-making action. Two dozen of these rods were more or less permanently positioned for stability; another two dozen were automatically controlled in response to ongoing nuclear activity within the reactor vessel. There were 115 manual control rods to be regulated by control personnel such as Vladimir Shashenok while twenty-four "scram" rods were poised to plunge the depth of the reactor for emergency shutdown. The control room chief had a half-dozen senior operators, veterans like Valery Khodemchuk, to share duties. They were assisted, guided and checked by an array of semi-automated controls, digital computer data, programmed systems, protective devices and shutdown mechanisms.

Like the operators of big engines everywhere since the dawn of the Industrial Revolution, the Chernobyl crew was also subject to operational rules. One of these ordained that their reactor was not to be operated for any sustained period below 700 megawatts or 22 per cent of its heat-energy capacity. There are good reasons for this. For one thing the RBMK reactor tends to "poison"out like a car choking on a too-lean mixture at stalling speed. For another thing, at full power Chernobyl-4 converted 3200 megawatts of steam to a thousand megawatts of electricity to meet regional demand. That much power would light a lot of homes and turn a multitude of farm and factory motors. It was not to be readily curtailed nor inadvertently tripped off.

More pertinent, a nuclear reactor responds like a giant airliner. At low speed it becomes unstable and may suddenly fall out of control. The RBMK design gives this instability another dimension. Nuclear engineers call it a "positive void coefficient" which means that if too much cooling water turns to steam it leaves a perilous vapour-filled void in the reactor's pressure tubes, those fuel channels where the water flows over the finger-thick rods of uranium fuel. The water's prime purpose is to transfer the heat from the nuclear reaction in the fuel channels to the steam system. But the hot water also captures a large percentage of neutrons before they can trigger a chain reaction. Once the water vaporizes to steam it no longer has this moderating effect. The RBMK reactor is designed to heat the water in the pressurized fuel channels from 270 to 285 degrees Celsius. Within that temperature range about 15 percent of the water vaporizes to steam; the remaining water is adequate to keep the atom-splitting, heat-making process under control. In effect the steam-making heat is proportional to neutron multiplication. More steam means less water leaving a void through which more neutrons pass unrestrained to split more atoms and make more steam ad infinitum. With trillions of atoms splitting each second, the machine can accelerate at incredible speed. It did.

The turbine test was to be conducted while their reactor was between 1000 and 700 megawatts of output. As power reduction resumed the control room staff had a common thought. Watching the digital numbers spin lower they anticipated the end of a year-long record run. It seemed that nothing would mar Chernobyl-4's record performance now. In fact, the first misstep to disaster occurred a half-hour into Saturday morning. In throttling back this giant steam engine, the chief operator let the pressure drop drastically. The throttle slipped its holding notches, so to speak, and the power level plummeted. In a quarter-hour the reactor's output fell from nearly 1000 megawatts to thirty. It was as if the crew chief had more than a million horses in harness when he dropped the reins and just 40,000 when he picked them up again fifteen minutes later. In trying to recover power he put the Chernobyl reactor badly out of balance. When he picked up horsepower again it was like Ben Hur trying to drive his chariot on one wheel.

By 1:00 a.m. Saturday Chernobyl-4 had been brought back to a 200-megawatt level. This was less than a third of the minimum permissible for sustained operation. Yet to get even to this level meant withdrawing an excessive number of manual control rods. The chief operator was now in the position of the balloonist who throws too many ballast bags overboard, buying altitude in mid-flight at the cost of later control. As the IAEA review team observed, the reactor was being operated at a dangerous level with little room to manouvre and an inherent tendency to zoom out of control. He was at the point "where small power changes lead to large steam volume and hence void changes that make power and feedwater control very difficult," the review team said. "The combination of too many control rods withdrawn from the core and operation at this low power level violated a number of procedures. It also created the conditions which both accelerated the reactor's response to plant perturbations and reduced the effectiveness of the protection system."

Still the chief operator persisted. All four coolant pumps were now put into operation as the test demanded. Yet at this power, the reactor could convert only a fraction of the normal water supply to steam. Feedwater flooded the system without making more steam; it stressed pumps and vibrated pipes. Water rose and steam pressure fell in the steam drums, both beyond tolerable levels. In turn, this imbalance caused more control rods to be withdrawn, further reducing the response margin. His radius for reaction was diminishing.

Challenged, pressured, impelled by the sheer force of desperation, the crew chief made a fourth move beyond authority, beyond reason. A protective switch would shut off the reactor if the water level and steam pressure dropped beyond limits. Aware that this safeguard would be tripped at any moment and abort the turbine test, he disconnected the protective device. It was 1:19 a.m. A half-minute later the feedwater was pouring into the separator three times as fast as the reactor could make steam. Attempting to compensate, the automatic control rods withdrew as far as they could go. Now almost all the remaining manual rods were withdrawn as well. The balloonist had virtually exhausted his ballast control. There were no reins left on the horsepower. Still the steam pressure fell. Two seconds before 1:20 a.m., control room records show that the steam supply to the turbine bypass was shut off. Still steam pressure dropped. Abruptly the chief operator cut the feedwater flow. Two minutes later he had the water-steam mix in relative balance. The automatic control rods had returned to the reactor interior. But the manual rods had not.

At 1:22:30 a.m., confident that he could proceed with the turbine test, the chief operator called for a computer printout. Infallibly it mapped the position of all 211 neutron-absorbing rods and measured the neutron flow from each of the 1661 reactor channels. Under normal conditions not less than thirty of the manually-operated control rods must be left in the reactor core to sop up excessive neutron production. In exceptional circumstances, with express permission of station management, reactor operatio could be continued with a minium of fifteen rods kept in reserve. But as Academician Legasov told the Vienna post-mortem conference, "Not even General Secretary Gorbachev could authorize the removal of more rods than that." The 1:22:30 a.m. power map showed six to eight control rods left for reaction. The chief operator — or the test manager — decided to proceed anyway.

The final misstep defied all logic. The test was to determine whether the momentum of a free-spinning turbine generator would power emergency pumps *after* the nuclear plant shut off. Indeed, the reactor was equipped with a safety trip, comparable to a safety valve on a conventional boiler, that automatically triggered a shutdown the moment steam was blocked from getting to the turbine. The test program called for the reactor to trip off the moment the turbine trial began. But at 1:23:04 a.m. that Saturday — just as steam power was cut off from the turbine generator to start the test — they closed off the emergency stop valve so the reactor would keep running in case the turbine test had to be repeated.

As the stop valve was closed, steam no longer flowed to the turbine generator. So pressure built in the reactor. As the generator slowed so did the four main cooling pumps that were now powered by it. "The effect on feedwater flow, steam pressure and main coolant flow perturbed the system and introduced rapid void formation in a large part of the core," the IAEA review group concluded. "This led to a rapid increase in reactor power with which emergency shutdown arrangements could not cope."

Enrico Fermi's first experimental nuclear assembly at Chicago had a single absorber rod to soak up excess neutrons if things went wrong. It was suspended by a rope and Fermi reputedly handed a colleague an axe before they began. "If it gets away on us cut the rope and scram," he advised. The boffins have referred to the emergency shutdown control as the "scram" button ever since. At Chernobyl it would plunge twenty-four scram rods into the reactor depths within ten seconds. If thirty of the regular control rods were already providing minimal stability then the emergency rods would prove effective. But no more than eight control rods were now in position.

At 1:23:30 a.m., a quarter-minute since they had bottled up the reactor's steam supply, a power surge began. In three seconds steam production went from 268,000 to 710,000 horsepower. Six seconds after the test began a group of automatic control rods were driven out of the reactor. Eleven seconds after that two groups of automatic control rods began driving in to curb the fast-rising power. Thirty-six seconds after he had begun the test the shift foreman pressed the scram button. It was 1:23:40 a.m. and it was too late. In the following four seconds the steam generated in the runaway reactor reached a hundred times its full power rating. It was as if 428 million horses were bursting from it.

The kettle in which such awesome forces brewed was not large. Less than twelve metres in diameter, seven metres high, it was about a sixth the size of one of those million-gallon water tanks that loom on suburban horizons. Like any steam plant the Chernobyl reactor was essentially a furnace full of boiler tubes. The furnace was built of graphite blocks, 1700 tonnes of pure carbon to slow neutrons to atom-splitting speed. Some 175 tonnes of uranium fuel, stacked in finger-thick, metre-long cans was vertically suspended. Here water trapped the primal heat from disintegrating uranium atoms to become steam to drive the generator.

Like all boilers since Hero of Alexandria's day, it was built to deliver steam under pressure. But when the RBMK reactor was designed nuclear hazards, not steam explosions, were the engineers' prime concern. Their first thought was to safely confine the lethal radiation. So they wrapped the reactor core in a graphite blanket nearly a metre thick to contain the neutron flux. They enclosed it with a steel shroud and surrounded it with a metre-wide wall of water, another metre of sand and two metres of high-density concrete-mineral mix. Bursting boilers never crossed their minds. The reactor was topped by steel blocks a third of a metre thick and roofed by a 520-tonne, three-metre slab of minerals and concrete in which the vertical fuel channels were imbedded. The floor above the reactor comprised of removable blocks to admit the snout of the fuelling machine. These blocks, nearly a metre thick, were made of a dense compound of iron, barium, serpentine, concrete and stone. Exploding steam fired them upward like shrapnel.

The designers did consider the steam hazard. Beneath each Chernobyl plant they built a two-level, compartmental pool in which to douse excessive steam. The pressure-relief system would carry surplus steam twenty metres below ground to deliver it through 1200 nozzles into two metres of water. The system was designed to cope with 15 per cent over-pressure. That meant it could handle the equivalent of some 640,000 horses out of harness. What the engineers forgot in dealing with steam-age dangers was the incredible power packed in uranium atoms. Gram for gram, nuclear fuel will deliver 16,000 times the energy of oil, 24,000 times as much as coal. While the heat-making capacity of fossil fuels has been well within the range of man's control since he first fired a boiler, the nuclear age brought a new dimension to steam plant perils. "In a nuclear plant there is no limit to how far up the power can go as long as the fuel hangs together," Ontario Hydro's chief engineer William R. Morison pointed out. "The only thing that stopped it from going to a thousand times full power at Chernobyl was the fact that the fuel disintegrated."

Valery Khodemchuk and Vladimir Shashenok were among a dozen night-shift members in the control room when the turbine test began at 1:23:04 a.m. The control room was thirty metres away from the reactor and on the same level as its base. Six metal and concrete walls isolated them from the reactor and its multi-layered containment structure. The disconcerting behaviour of the automatic control rods in the next quarter-minute may have sparked Khodemchuk and Shashenok to investigate. Voluntarily — or on instruction — they went towards the reactor hall in the half-minute before Chernobyl-4 blew up.

Skala, the computer control system assessing data from several hundred sensors throughout the reactor second by second, tracked the first evidence of disaster at 1:23:41 a.m. Like lightning promising thunder to follow, neutron activity more than doubled in the next second and a half. At that moment the pen recorder went close to vertical and vanished from the graph paper. Two seconds later the fuel temperature was paralleling the neutron path like the second track of a railway. In an instant it went from 280 to 1,700 degrees Celsius, and in another half second it was past 3,000 degrees Celsius. Steam production was commensurate with the radioactivity and the heat rise in the fuel. Steam burst the pressure tubes, stripped the fuel of its last coolant, cascaded

12

into the hot graphite, reacted with zirconium tubing and near-molten uranium. In the control room crew members were stupified by the spin of digital displays, the violent swing of instrument needles, the frenzy of monitor lights, printer-head chatter, klaxon-horn warnings, alarm bells.

At 1:23:48 a.m. a steam explosion of unimaginable energy shattered the reactor core. Its force lifted the slab top of the vault rupturing every tube of the reactor. Imperceptibly diminished, it fired the concrete and metal blocks of the fuelling hall floor like shell fragments through the building roof thirty metres above. In the control room there were audible reverberations then an awesome moment of silence. Racing toward the reactor hall in the last and worst moment of his life, Valery Khodemchuk heard the ripping, rending, wrenching, screeching, scraping, tearing sounds of a vast machine breaking apart.

Now air poured through the shattered roof and the opened top of the vault. Within the core, steam reacted with zirconium to produce that first explosive in nature's arsenal, hydrogen. Near-molten fuel fragments shattered nearly incandescent graphite, torching chunks of it, exploding the hydrogen. The second blast followed the first by three seconds. For Vladimir Shashenok it was not as terrifying as the first explosion. The first had showered them with fiery debris, buried his crew mate almost at his feet, shattered steam pipes, burned and scalded him.

Fast losing consciousness, the control technician could discern rescuers running towards him. "There, Valery's there," he told them.

2

Fire, Steam and Flameless Fury

"Everyone realized what was in store for them."

— MAJOR LEONID TELYETNIKOV

WHERE THERE IS STEAM THERE IS FIRE. But you tend to forget that at a nuclear power plant because the fire is supposed to be flameless. "Suddenly I heard a powerful discharge of steam," said a firefighter standing in the Chernobyl fire-hall 700 metres from the stricken reactor. "We attached no significance to it since steam discharges happen repeatedly. Then there was an explosion and I rushed to the window. The explosion was followed instantly by others. You could see a black fireball rising above the machine-room roof of No. 4."

Flames were the last thing they expected. "You could clearly see something that wasn't quite a glow and wasn't quite luminescence," recalled another occupant of the station fire-hall. "But there was nothing that could burn over there except for the reactor's snout. We decided that the luminescence was coming from the reactor itself."

Lieutenant Vladimir Pavlovich Pravik, the duty officer, automatically logged the time. It was 1:27 a.m. The other unit commander Viktor Nikolayevich Kibenok and their twenty-five men were already pulling on fire-fighting clothes when Pravik sounded the siren. The monitor board told him the upper levels of Chernobyl-4 were aflame. But he could see that now from the fire-hall. "Priority three," he told the phone dispatcher. That meant lines to the Pripyat and Chernobyl municipal fire-halls, four and a dozen kilometres away. It established a direct connection with the provincial headquarters for fire-fighting services in Kiev and initiated communication with the Ukraine Republic

14

authorities and with Moscow. Nuclear experts would be consulted at the Kurchatov Institute within an hour.

Within minutes the deputy director of the Kiev provincial fire-fighting command, Lieutenant-Colonel Ivan Kotsyura was en route to the power station. Minutes later the Ukraine's major-general of police, Gennady Vasilyevich Berdov, the man in charge of emergency services, followed. Long black limousines, the ubiquitous carriers of officialdom, sped Kotsyura and Berdov one hundred kilometres to the Chernobyl station within ninety minutes of Pravik's alarm. By 5:00 a.m. the general had established a temporary centre for his emergency forces at police headquarters. He would subsequently move his command post to a bunker under a building close to the stricken reactor. The growing numbers of civil-defense people, dosimeter teams, medical personnel, decontamination crews, police and army officers, Communist party organizers, Pripyat and regional officials operated from a two-storey building in town. An emergency district headquarters set up on the first weekend in the town of Chernobyl, sixteen kilometres from the nuclear station, was too far from the action for top Soviets such as deputy prime minister Boris Shcherbina.

Off duty at his Pripyat home six kilometres away when the call came, fire chief Major Leonid Telyatnikov arrived at the scene in shirt sleeves. As Pravik and Kibenok deployed their crews someone helped the chief into his bunker coat. Like the protective coats worn by his men, it was designed to keep them dry and safe from fiery bits of debris but not much else. Emergency crews at airports and oil refineries wear fire-resistant clothing that lets them get close to intense heat. Respirators protect them from dense smoke and fumes. But as the major was aware there was no clothing available to protect them from the flameless fury emitted by a breached nuclear furnace.

"Everyone realized what was in store for them. No one showed slackness," the fire chief told interviewers from his Moscow hospital bed a fortnight later. *Izvestia* echoed his words a few days later in citing the first six firefighters to die of the radiation exposure they sustained in the early morning hours of April 26. "The first twenty-eight firemen on the scene knew quite well what they were getting into. They knew what sort of facility they were trying to save. If it were not for their selfless work it would hardly be possible today to define the [evacuated] zone by its present boundaries," said the paper.

Explosive sounds were still echoing through the reactor control rooms when the firemen arrived. The dials, gauges, meters and counters for Chernobyl-4 were now mostly silent. On three other control boards they still reported normal activity, however. Throughout the long turbine structure with its endless corridors and maze of compartmentalized components some 170 operators, maintenance crew, technicians and tradesmen had to continue to tend those giant steam engines. There would be futile attempts to cool Chernobyl-4 with emergency water supply. It poured from 1661 ruptured channels before it could reach the core. Soon the contaminated water was threatening to overflow into Chernobyl-3. The three other plants were still needed to electrify Soviet homes, farms and factories. In due course they would be shut down, but reluctantly. Meanwhile, everyone tended their post. It was not business as usual but it was the business they were in. Periodic reports over the public address system would update them on the firemens' progress. They felt far from secure in their sheltered work areas. But there was an unanimity in their unspoken prayer. Thank god they were not the firemen up there on the blazing roof of the turbine hall, they told themselves.

About a dozen of Chernobyl-4's night-shift members, including Valery Khodemchuk and Vladimir Shashenok, had been in exposed areas when the reactor top shattered. Well aware that radioactivity likely accompanied the steam and fiery debris, the survivors threw off their contaminated shoes and clothing and raced for the airlock exit from which they could escape without breaking the isolation barriers between zones of the reactor building. Within forty minutes twenty-nine victims of radiation sickness — operational crew, firemen and other emergency workers — were helped from the scene by medical personnel who had rushed from their first-aid post. By 6:00 a.m. 108 people had been hospitalized.

The roof of the fuelling hall above the reactor had been shattered. Most of the north wall and some of the south wall (on the turbine side) of the reactor building had been destroyed. The metres-deep shielding on the sides of the reactor remained intact but a thousand tonnes of slab roof and shielding above it had been tipped open. The leak-tight compartments protecting steam drums, pumps and other equipment were unbreached but fires were rampant everywhere. "Flames were raging on five levels of the reactor building," Major Telyatnikov said. What alarmed him most was that the fire had already swept through the top of the reactor structure seventy-one metres above ground then down onto the turbine hall roof forty metres below.

The Chernobyl reactors were built in pairs; Units 1 and 2, separated by auxiliary facilities and common services, occupy the easterly 440 metres of the multiple-reactor building. Units 3 and 4 are closer together along 360 metres of the reactor structure but extending at a right-angle from it. Each reactor powers a pair of turbine generators and the eight generating halls form one continuous structure parallel and adjacent to the multi-reactor building. Exhaust stacks for each pair of reactors, service vents, crane booms and power pylons break the long roof line of the multi-reactor structure. But the turbine-building roof forms one unbroken expanse 800 metres long and about sixty-five metres wide. It is covered with bitumin, a commonplace roofing material and this was already alight where the initial explosions had spilled flaming debris onto it. The pitch-covered roof was a burning wick to torch all four nuclear plants. It was from this roof that Telyatnikov and his station squad decided the reactor fire must be fought.

"The reactor had been opened with a mortal blow. There was a lava of burning bitumin, heavy and nauseous smoke," the chief said. "Electricity was cut off and a frightful dose of radioactivity showed on the Geiger-counter dials." In due course he would discover more than thirty separate fires had been ignited by the molten debris ejected from the ruptured reactor. His first concern was that long, tarry roof thirty-three metres above the ground. They had neither aerial ladders nor hydraulic lifters that would reach it. The only access was by iron ladders running vertically up the building side. The forty-five-year-old major went up the hundred rungs with practised ease; Pravik and Kibenok followed. They were half his age but they kept a respectful, token number of rungs below him. A dozen firemen were at their heels.

"Brown's Ferry," Major Telyatnikov might have muttered as he climbed the building side. At an American nuclear station with that curious name there had been a bad fire in 1975. The flame from a single candle held by some fool electrician in a service duct had ignited cable insulation. Like a sputtering fuse it carried the fire throughout the plant. Such a service channel carried electrical cable the full length of the Chernobyl reactor structure. Below there were tanks of diesel oil to fuel the stand-by generators, flammable wall coatings and unimaginable hazards. The turbine-hall roof was their first concern. Beyond that, the fire chief realized the prospects could be appalling.

"What had happened was never supposed to have happened, not even in theory and the firemen were the first to bear the brunt of the accident," Soviet authorities told the International Atomic Energy Agency's post-mortem meeting four months later. Because a nuclear reactor cannot explode from atomic fission like a bomb the prospect of a ruptured reactor vault had never been seriously dealt with. Engineers everywhere had considered the possiblity of a meltdown but that was one-directional and primarily threatened the water table below. The prospects of a runaway reactor emitting a cloud of radioactivity is a real hazard and various safeguards are built into nuclear stations to cope with it. The prime one is to keep people indoors untouched by fallout. What nuclear engineers had not seriously considered, however, was the shattering result of a steam explosion. The steam age was two centuries old; everyone had forgotten its explosive nature.

When steam power burst the Chernobyl reactor vault it spewed fragments from the incandescent core, detonated one natural element, ignited a second and left a third burning in its own unseen fire. Ninety-two elements — building stones of the universe — were spawned one from another in the first genetic moments of creation. Hydrogen was the first and the lightest of the elements, uranium the heaviest. Hydrogen burns explosively and with spectacular brilliance. Burning hydrogen atop the Chernobyl reactor highlighted the firemen fighting it. Their silhouettes were the heroic shapes that statues are made of. Uranium packs as much heat energy in the complex fissures of its compound atoms yet releases it reluctantly. It burns flamelessly in an inexorable way that must frustrate firefighters. Graphite, the activating blanket to make uranium generate great heat, is simply refined carbon, an element that has fuelled man's fires as charcoal, coal or coke since the dawn of civilization. It can sustain a smoldering fire for weeks.

The initial steam explosion that showered adjacent rooftops with incandescent debris breached the reactor vault to let oxygen in. While the steam hit the hot graphite and uranium to cause further explosions it reacted with the zirconium fuel canisters to release hydrogen. The incoming oxygen fed the graphite fire. The outgoing hydrogen burst into flame. Hydrogen, the primal substance that fuels the sun's fire, spelled disaster for airships and fed the fiery end of Nazi Germany's prototype nuclear reactor at Leipzig in 1942, destroyed the space shuttle *Challenger* and Chernobyl-4. Hydrogen fed flames that licked a dust-proofing plastic paint from the walls of the reactor hall and rose to tongue oxygen from the air thirty metres above the building. Moments after the initial steam explosion, the thunderclap of ignited hydrogen wrapped all the breaking sounds into one soul-wrenching noise, jagged as broken concrete at its edges.

The dozen firefighters followed Telyatnikov, Pravik and Kibenok to the roof. They went through flame and smoke and fiery bits of airborne flotsam. They smelled the acrid, scorched and almond-bitter fumes guessing what might have caused them. They had never fought a fire here before and they had no conception what went on in the reactor except that it brewed steam to make electricity. "Radiation" had been briefly mentioned at drills and as quickly dropped from discussion. Like references to anti-aircraft fire at World War II aircrew briefings there was not much to say on the subject except that it was lethal and was to be expected in their line of work. This was the job they were paid to do. No one had demanded that they be firemen.

Their boots sank in a mire of melted roofing tar. Their hoses bucked and sometimes pulled them prone into the hot pitch. The awesome tongues of flame grew shorter as they tamed them with high-pressure water jets. Then a capricious wind would spit the blue-orange fire back at them. The fire chief and his lieutenants were aware of two dimensions to their roof-top environment. One was the "frightful dose of radioactivity" registered by their dosimeters. The other was time. Every minute in that lethal radiation might slice years from their lives.

By 2:10 a.m. the fire atop Unit 3 was confined. So was the one above Unit 4 ten minutes later. By 3:35 a.m., two hours since they had mounted the ladders to purgatory, the turbine-hall roof on which they stood ankles deep in melting, smoky tar was safe. Twenty minutes after that they had the blaze out on the Unit 4 roof. "We stayed until the fire was put out. Then we went below where the first-aid vehicles picked us up. We were in bad shape," one noted in a hospital-bedside diary.

The firefighters at lower levels were not immune from dangerous radiation, of course. "Water came right up to No. 3 unit. It had to be pumped out and that meant power had to be supplied. No one but us could do that so we stayed although we knew the radiation level was very high. Even the dosimeter operator couldn't say exactly how high it was. His instrument was reading higher than the scale," a fireman recounted. Pripyat and Chernobyl brigades had been battling in the No. 4 turbine hall for hours to prevent fire spreading to the adjacent reactor building. By 5:00 a.m. more than thirty fires had been extinguished. By then seventeen firemen had been hospitalized. Soviet nuclear medical specialists could estimate the exposure they had experienced — and their chance of survival — by how quickly they vomited (the first symptoms of radiation sickness) and how soon their skin blistered from the unseen, unfelt, flameless fire.

Major Telyatnikov survived. Two months later he was pictured in a Moscow hospital grounds embracing his wife, Larisa. Their foreheads were touching, soul-telling smiles wreathed their faces. The major did not remove his peak cap. When he answered the alarm that April night he had a thick shock of hair. Now he was bald. Lieutenants Viktor Nikolayevich Kibenok and Vladimir Pavlovich Pravik, Sergeants Nikolai

Vashchuk, Vasily Ignatenko, Nikolai Titenok and Vladimir Tishchuru of his detachment were already dead. That fall the major and his two late lieutenants were named heroes of the Soviet Union. Said *Izvestia*: "The specific nature of the fire-fighting service is such that it is not easy to keep the reserves up to strength." But it said, "the best specialists are here now, many of them from other atomic-power stations. Over four hundred firemen have already worked in the zone around Chernobyl. They are now resting and others have taken their place." What engaged these crews from some fifty fire brigades in the critical days that followed was a flameless fire of two elements. Enriched uranium fuel, its atoms triggered to self-destruction in the runaway reactor, continued to give off awesome heat and radioactivity. The graphite burned incandescent. Like coals on a Dantesque barbeque, it roasted fuel fragments, wafting their lethal radiation high and far from the nuclear station.

The visible fires were extinguished by 5:00 a.m. but provincial fire chief Lieutenant-Colonel Kotsyura and the Ukraine's emergency services director General Berdov were under no illusions that the accident had been contained. They had been meeting with local authorities and station engineers for nearly three hours now. Minute by minute the news was more alarming. The first priority was to marshal manpower. Firefighters were summoned from as far distant as Kiev, police from surrounding areas. Policemen from nearby Polesskoye arrived by 4:00 a.m. Others from the adjacent districts of Chernobyl and Ivankov arrived soon after.

By daylight check points and barriers had been established to control all traffic in or out of the power station and to or from Pripyat. This is a universal action by civil-defense people to check the rush of people to an accident scene. But at Chernobyl it had another vital impact. It curbed the spread of radioactive contamination by people and vehicles from the outset — before anyone had established the extent of the radiation hazard. Yet a few hundred metres from the smoking and damaged reactor structure or from the town's police headquarters it was deceptively calm. In Pripyat early risers went about their affairs that Saturday morning oblivious to the fact it was their last day there.

As Major Telyatnikov watched his firemen roll up their hoses radiation sickness had not yet overtaken them. As he handed over control to another chief he had every reason to think that the fire at Chernobyl-4 was out. He had fought the reactor fire with twenty-eight men. Within hours he and sixteen of his firefighters would be hospitalized; half that number would be dead within four weeks. The shadow of disaster had not yet taken full shape but it was now growing apparent to about a dozen people who had been in constant three-way phone conversation since 2:00 a.m. At the Chernobyl administration building the station management conferred over computer print-outs, flow sheets, control-room data and monitor readings. Chernobyl-4 had ceased to breed neutrons at the explosive moment of 1:23:45 a.m. Yet within the reactor, temperature and radiation levels were continuing to rise rapidly. At the Kurchatov Institute of Atomic Energy in Moscow, first deputy director Valery Legasov and fellow experts assessed the information and found it disconcerting. At Pripyat police headquarters, Colonel Kotsyura and General Berdov watched the station data and Moscow's observations spell out an increasingly critical situation. It would take a few hours yet before definite conclusions could be reached.

Canadians faced a 10 per cent meltdown of the NRX reactor at Chalk River in 1952, the Brits battled a smoldering graphite fire at Windscale in 1957 and the Americans accidently vented radioactive gas from the damaged core of the Three Mile Island plant in 1979. But in none of these accidents was the reactor vault ripped open to roast fuel fragments on graphite coals like a gigantic brazier wafting infernal fumes to the sky. That was the situation confronting the accident response team at Chernobyl. It was unprecedented; there were no case histories, no applicable engineering guides, no textbook answers.

By midday General Berdov had established emergency headquarters. Here three men would take prime responsibility for containing the runaway reactor, curbing the fallout, evacuating the population and decontaminating an area of 7,500 square kilometres. As deputy minister of internal affairs for the Ukraine Republic, General Berdov was in command of its police, fire, transport and supply services. He brought to the post the prestige and experience of an eminent military career. With the arrival of Boris Shcherbina, vice-chairman of the USSR Council of Ministers, Berdov was given carte blanche to call on whatever armed forces personnel and resources were needed. The deputy prime minister had been named by Gorbachev to lead a commission to Chernobyl within hours of the accident. The commission embraced "heads of ministries and departments, prominent scientists and specialists," said *Pravda*. Their job was "to eliminate the consequences of the accident" and Shcherbina brought all the authority necessary to do it. While the Soviet vice-chairman provided the political will he left to Valery Legasov the final word on all technical decisions.

By the time the Kurchatov Institute's deputy director arrived at the Pripyat command post Colonel Kotsyura had more than fifty fire brigades assembled at the Chernobyl station but little guidance on how to deploy them. The news that Major Telyatnikov and several of his men had to be transferred by air-ambulance to Moscow for specialist treatment that afternoon was unnerving. Given the special hazards of the reactor site, Kotsyura was not going to put firemen at risk without good reason. Once the evident fires caused by molten fuel and incandescent graphite fragments had been extinguished station engineers directed his attention to cooling the fire-prone reactor itself.

When emergency feedwater pumps were connected to the primary cooling circuit, it became evident that fuel channels, header pipes and cooling lines had been ruptured. As the firefighters pumped water into the cooling system clouds of steam and white smoke poured from the reactor. Two things were obvious. The cooling circuit was useless and the reactor core was intensely hot. Water spraying onto incandescent graphite would likely produce more hydrogen and possibly further explosions, Colonel Kotsyura was advised. Meanwhile radioactively contaminated water was flooding out of Chernobyl-4 in the direction of the other reactors and a plume of intense radioactivity was continuing to pour skyward. The fire marshal was also reminded that while pure graphite was difficult to ignite it was equally hard to extinguish. It might remain incandescent at 1650 degrees Celsius for days or weeks, he was told.

But if the decay heat — the hot energy of disintegrating atoms — in the shattered nuclear fuel and burning graphite reinforced each other there was worse to come. The spectre of a meltdown rose in the smoke from the Chernobyl ruins. Beneath the reactor building there was a vast two-level, compartmentalized tank partially filled with water. This "suppression pool" served to take any sudden surge of excess steam and safely dissipate its pressure. While a meltdown of the reactor might not burn through to China it would likely drop the molten core in the pool water. That could be as catastrophic as the initial explosion, the experts said.

A French journalist, Michel Tatu, did a thoroughly objective and comprehensive analysis of Soviet press accounts in the weeks following the disaster. "Reports were sent to Moscow in the first hour. Kurchatov Institute experts were sent to Chernobyl Saturday morning. They were followed a few hours later by a goverment commission under deputy prime minister Boris Shcherbina. A crisis centre was established at Pripyat under General Berdov and the army was mobilized as quickly," Tatu wrote in Paris *LeMonde*. "Why under these conditions did they wait till the following day, Sunday at 2:00 p.m. before proceeding with the first evacuation?" he asked. Why did they wait four days before warning the world of the fallout from Chernobyl? critics in a dozen countries wanted to know.

Valery Legasov is a deliberate, forthright nuclear scientist of international repute. He was the dominant figure in examining the accident, its causes, its impact and implications. His own research had been on high-temperature reactors quite different to the RBMK design so he was free of proprietary bias concerning the Chernobyl plant. Nor did he have any responsibility for the Chernobyl station or the electricity-generation system in which it operated. At the IAEA post-mortem in Vienna, Legasov gave a day-long exposition of what happened, how and why it occurred. He answered scores of questions thoughtfully, weighing his words carefully, without evasion. More than two hundred journalists from the media world-wide covered his comments and not one of them questioned his integrity or credibility. Legasov dealt with the initial indecisiveness in Moscow and with the Soviet delay in letting the world know about it. In fact, he commented on these key questions several times.

Chernobyl management had advised authorities in Moscow "a few minutes after the fire began" that emergency conditions existed, he said. A technical team headed by Arman Abagyan, chairman of the Soviet Institute for Atomic Power Stations left immediately for Chernobyl. However, station officials had subsequently "somewhat distorted" their initial message by "informing us that they could control the already *inexistent* reactor." Considering that the nuclear plant had been ripped asunder talk of "control" was ridiculous. "They did not adequately understand the situation," Legasov said sarcastically. Abagyan's team certainly did understand and summoned the Kurchatov Institute's expertise. Legasov was commissioned by the Soviet government to head the technical team on the scene. The decision to evacuate the city was made an hour after he arrived in Pripyat.

"If Chernobyl told Moscow about it on Saturday, April 26 why hadn't Moscow told Stockholm by Monday, April 28?" the correspondent for *Nature* asked Legasov at Vienna.

"The plant staff as a matter of standard procedure informed Moscow only that there had been radiation, fire and a technically dangerous accident. That was the information instantly received in Moscow. Then the accident began to be clarified; that is, the scale of the accident, the scale of the danger," he replied. "I imagine that the appropriate government organizations made their decisions in conformity with the dynamic developments. The dynamics of the situation were very complex. The situation was changing literally every hour. In Moscow we try to give out reliable and accurate information although sometimes this leads to a loss of time."

That answer was less than gratifying to neighbouring countries which had discovered the fallout from Chernobyl for themselves. It was, however, the most credible and valid answer then or since. A scientist could only deal with that part of the reply which lay within his field. Soviet officialdom and bureacracy were notably silent until Mikhail Gorbachev made his forthright pronouncement a fortnight after the event. The Soviet leader did no more than Legasov to explain the initial silence but he addressed the nuclear accident with realism and candor. The realism came naturally to a pragmatic Russian. Candor was something new at the Politburo. "For the first time we have actually encountered the terrible force that is nuclear energy gone out of control," the general secretary told a national TV audience. "As specialists report, the reactor underwent a sudden power surge. A significant escape of steam and the subsequent reaction led to the formation of hydrogen, its explosion, the destruction of the reactor and an associated radioactive emission."

"The seriousness of the situation was obvious. It had to be evaluated urgently and competently," Gorbachev continued. "As soon as we received reliable primary information it was made known to the Soviet people and was sent through diplomatic channels to the governments of foreign countries. On the basis of this information, practical work to overcome the accident and limit its serious consequences got under way. Much depended on a correct scientific evaluation of what was happening because without this it would have been impossible to apply effective measures to cope with the accident and its aftermath." The key words were the "reliable primary information" and "correct scientific evaluation" on which they had waited. The Soviet chief did not apologize for the days of silence but implicit in his lengthy statement on Chernobyl was word that such tardy communication to the USSR's neighbours would not occur again during his regime.

In fact, Chernobyl took the Soviets completely by surprise. They had not anticipated a serious nuclear accident, let alone a disaster of its complexity, scale and consequence. Interviewed by *Pravda* a month after the accident, Academician Legasov elaborated on earlier statements. When had he found out about the accident himself? "The information arrived immediately. However it contained much that was contradictory and strange. Believe me, it was impossible to understand immediately exactly what had happened or to estimate its scale," he replied. "We were dealing with this kind of accident for the first time and so it was necessary to carefully ascertain all of the circumstances and special factors of what had happened. I won't hide the fact that at first I had not thought that the scale of the accident was as great as it actually was. It was only on driving toward Pripyat [Saturday evening] and seeing the glow that I began to guess the nature of what had happened. When I saw the fire glimmering I started to understand. To assess what was going on from Moscow was impossible." Even for those on site the graphite fire glow would have been unseen from ground level in daylight.

The scientist said that General Secretary Gorbachev's TV address, "described the situation in Pripyat precisely. It's difficult for me to add anything. As a specialist and a participant in the events I can confirm that the scale of the accident, its nature and the development of events seemed improbable, nearly impossible." In short, Soviet experts were overwhelmed by the incredible accident that had exploded the Chernobyl reactor like a burst boiler. Bared by dawn's light, the wreckage of the upper structure defied belief. Station management, firefighters, police, emergency and civil-defense authorities, nuclear scientists and engineers, local, regional and national officials could only begin to grasp the scale of destruction as the day wore on. They had scarcely digested that reality when signs of a graphite fire in the ruptured bowels of the reactor core became evident.

3

Evacuation

"Our patriotic upbringing reveals itself during these kinds of situations. We are good at evacuations. We've had a lot of practice at them."

— TAMARA DUBROTSKAYA, CHERNOBYL EVACUEE,
MAY 9, 1986

"IN THE FIRST STAGES AT MISSISSAUGA we relied on block leaders. On every street there is a man or woman who cuts ice with their neighbours. We convinced them and they persuaded others that it made sense to get out for a while," Jim Erskine recalled.

The big-fisted, soft-spoken retired Ontario Provincial Police commissioner was a cerebral cop. He was talking about the evacuation of a quarter-million people without injury, without an ugly incident when a train wreck threatened them with exploding tank cars and deadly chlorine gas. Later, without prodding, Canadian Pacific Railway paid out $9.6 million to compensate evacuated families, yet more than 30,000 household heads filed no claims. They had not "sustained any significant money loss" or else they felt it was "morally wrong to take money." Common sense, cooperation and goodwill — the Canadian approach. Others do it differently.

Within twenty-four kilometres of the badly damaged Three Mile Island nuclear plant there were a half-million people living in sixty-three municipalities and they were given almost as many versions of what had happened. When radioactive gas was inadvertently released two days after the TMI accident, Pennsylvania Governor Dick Thornburgh advised pregnant women and children to evacuate communities within

26

an eight-kilometre radius. Nearly a third of the whole population left voluntarily. On average they stayed away five days. Years later they were still suing the power utility for billions of dollars in damages.

"I was at home asleep when the gas came. I woke up coughing, my eyes burning," said a young social worker, one of Bhopal, India's 700,000 population. "I went outside and saw hundreds running in the streets. The children were crying and old men were being carried. I saw dozens of people fall down." They did not hear the factory siren until two hours after toxic gas began to leak out. It killed some 2,500 residents and injured another 200,000. There was no evacuation. A week later a best-selling San Francisco author-lawyer filed a $15-billion lawsuit on behalf of two Bhopal survivors.

The Pripyat population was marshalled with authoritarian care, concern and discipline. "The evacuation was announced at 2:00 p.m. At 1:50 p.m. one of our staff members appeared at each building entrance, made the rounds of all the apartments and warned people. He repeated the report that had been broadcast on the radio shortly before," Major-General A.I. Borovik, General Berdov's political counterpart, explained. "To avoid commotion and panic no assembly points were set up and the desired result was achieved. In two hours practically the entire population of Pripyat, about 40,000, were evacuated." A week later 95,000 others were moved out of the surrounding rural area. There is no evidence that any of the people removed from the thirty-kilometre radius around Chernobyl suffered any radiation injury. Within a year the Soviet government had spent about $1.5 billion and built 12,000 new homes elsewhere to resettle them.

The nature of the threat, time and weather, logistics and local geography all had impact on how people fared in the wake of Mississauga, TMI, Bhopal and Chernobyl. But the interaction of the people and authority was of equal importance. When those twenty-one tank cars derailed from a CPR train as it passed through the city of Mississauga, Ontario on a Saturday midnight in 1979, several cars burned, three exploded to fire balls and one containing chlorine began to leak. Like nuclear fuel which bears the stigma of wartime use, chlorine carries the scent of battlefield death. For the children and grandchildren of Canadian casualties of chlorine-filled shells at Ypres in World War I, news of the gas can be as chilling as nuclear fallout. Yet chlorine is common cargo. In the US about 150 trains hauling chlorine tankers are involved in accidents annually. Two tankers will release their gas content in such mishaps each year and Americans can expect about ten people to be killed annually by the chlorine.

At three parts per million the gas will irritate eyes; higher levels will successively cause coughing, vomiting and tissue damage. About 900 parts per million in air may prove fatal. Ontario authorities impose an occupational limit of one part per million. At Mississauga one-hundredth part of that level triggered evacuation. The level was exceeded in some evacuated areas but authorities based their decision on fears that the chlorine level would be 600 times worse than it was. Windspeed and direction were more benign than might have been expected. The decision-making "think tank" dominated by Ontario Attorney General Roy McMurtry thought it prudent to order 218,000 people, including patients of three hospitals, out of town. They were evacuated in a dozen stages within twenty-three hours after the train's fiery demise.

Ninety-seven per cent of Mississauga's 75,000 households moved out in their own cars or with neighbours. Still Mississauga Transit had the first of fifty buses on hand within seventy-five minutes of the train crash. By 2:15 a.m. the local emergency coordinator for the Canadian Red Cross, Margaret Leslie had an evacuation centre set up in a major shopping plaza. It would be vacated for other centres as the risk area widened. But only 5 per cent of evacuees used such centres and half of them stayed only a day before moving in with friends or relatives. Most of the evacuees were away from home for nearly a week. Police quarantined the empty city with barriers at key points and said there was virtually no theft. But by Tuesday they were being badgered at the road blocks by 25 per cent of the evacuees impatient to return home.

There was no panic in Mississauga but neither was there panic-making talk of nuclear radiation. There was no hassling among politicians; McMurtry handled the feisty local mayor Hazel McCallion with Irish charm. But the decade of infighting by provincial and local politicians that has obscured Ontario Hydro's on-site protection and off-site response to a nuclear emergency has sowed seeds of chaos. If Canadian leaders concerned with our nuke town populations learned anything from Chernobyl they will quit squabbling and get their plans together.

It was early on a Wednesday morning in March 1979 when a pump failed in General Public Utilities' second generating plant on Three Mile Island, Pennsylvania. The reactor automatically shut down without damage but subsequent human and mechanical failures wrecked the cooling system. Still the operators appeared to have the plant under control a day and a half later. At 8:30 Friday morning, however, an accidental release of radioactive gas produced an alarming plume. For a brief period before the wind dispersed it, this radioactivity over the TMI site rose a thousand times above the permissible level. Just across the Susquehanna River it measured 1300 times the normal background. That was when the state governor said pregnant women and young children should leave. By then they had been given various reports by the multitude of local governments. Civil defence officials offered radiation readings but no advice. GPU's subsidiaries which shared the plant's output left it to their senior partner, Metropolitan Edison to keep people posted. The utility was "less than able to do so," as one journalist put it. Then from Friday morning until the following Tuesday afternoon five of the American Nuclear Regulatory commissioners argued about what they should advise Governor Thornburgh, the US president, the public and the press. The NRC deliberations were televised and they filled 800 pages of transcript. By then 144,000 Pennsylvanians had left town. The TMI exodus — voluntary, unstructured and unassisted — exemplified life in the land of the brave and the homes of the free.

Within twenty-four kilometres of the TMI plant one in three families moved out in fear of a perceived radiation hazard which did not materialize despite high short-term radioactivity in a localized area. Within eight kilometres of the Mississauga rail crash everyone was evacuated as chlorine moved low and slowly on an uncertain wind. It was not nearly as bad as expected nor as it appeared to be. Yet it was a lethal threat. At Bhopal people died in their beds, unwarned and unassisted. At Chernobyl the radiation peril was real, serious and imminent; the evacuation was timely and warranted.

Three factors unique to the Soviet Union materially helped mitigate the Chernobyl disaster. For one thing the large-scale migrations of the Stalin era and the displacements of World War II conditioned the people to evacuation. The Soviet society is highly structured, quickly organized and readily directed to concerted action. "Our patriotic upbringing reveals itself during these kinds of situations. We are good at evacuations. We've had a lot of practice at them," said farm-wife Tamara Dubrotskaya. "We've been evacuated before," eighty-year-old Marina Ilchenko told foreign journalists. "I took two or three little blankets and pillows. We had just built a new home. We had to leave our dog." Thirdly, civil defense is taken seriously in the Soviet Union. The response to Chernobyl was a unified one by military and civilian forces who stand alert to the awesome chance of nuclear war. Army, government, science and Communist party leaders put their resources into one integrated effort as they would if the Bombs fell. That might be a madly unrealistic response but it was rehearsed at Chernobyl.

"In view of the extraordinary and dangerous nature of what happened at Chernobyl, the Politburo took into its own hands the entire organization of the work to overcome the accident as quickly as possible and to limit its consequences," Gorbachev told the Soviet people. "All work is being conducted around the clock. The whole country's scientific, technical and economic potential has been put into action. Ministries and departments, scientists and specialists, Soviet Army and Internal Affairs Ministry units are operating in the accident area. An enormous share of the work has been taken on by the party, Soviet and economic agencies of the Ukraine and Byelorussia. The Chernobyl station's operational personnel are working selflessly and courageously." That was not entirely true. Some shadows showed up in the light of Gorbachev's *glasnost* lamp. "Many station employees were offered the chance to evacuate and quite a number took immediate advantage of this, but most refused to evacuate and continued to work here," Chernobyl's new, outspoken director Erik Nikolayevich Pozdyshev said a half-year later.

The Soviet response to Chernobyl was immediate. Pripyat was not evacuated for a day and a half but plans to anticipate that possibility were underway less than a hour after Vladimir Pravik advised Kiev that a class three emergency existed. At 2:15 that Saturday morning Pripyat municipal and police officials, still wiping sleep from their eyes, shuffled chairs around a conference table. They dealt first with a ubiquitous reaction to disaster that social scientists call "convergence behaviour." As far back as 1957 the American Academy of Sciences noted that "the mass movement of people, messages and supplies toward a disaster-struck area is a virtually universal phenomenon that complicates control efforts and substantially retards organized relief." At Chernobyl it would have magnified two perils. The first defense against radioactive fallout is to remain indoors and the best response to radioactive contamination is to prevent its spread by people and vehicles. "Entry to the city is to be closed to all vehicles not involved in dealing with the accident or assisting the victims," the Pripyat city fathers declared. Chernobyl station management decided the same thing.

It was an hour's fast drive from Kiev to the accident scene, Major-General Gennady Vasilyevich Berdov reminded himself as he dressed with the measured haste of a man who expects to be up front just as long as necessary. As the Ukraine's top man for law, order, protection and rescue, he would coordinate all emergency services at the accident site for the next eight days. Municipal officials had been meeting for an hour or so when he walked into the Pripyat conference room. His "journal of combat operations" at Chernobyl began with that meeting.

The general would duly recall that dawn when the glow from the ruptured Chernobyl reactor was still evident and the silhouettes of Pripyat's early risers were taking to the streets. Soon the city was alive with normal Saturday traffic. The word "radiation" would not appear in the log for some hours. "Neither General Berdov nor the hundreds of people who responded to the disaster alarm knew about the radiation or, frankly, thought about it at the time," said *Tass*. "Neither these people nor the prominent scientists who arrived a few hours later could have known about the cause or consequences of the accident then. It would take time to get to the bottom of what had happened." In fact, they got answers in a relatively short time.

When they did learn of the radioactive dimension, Soviet leaders were notably unintimidated. General Berdov operated from police headquarters for a few hours. Then he took over a two-storey Communist party building in Pripyat which was soon "full of crates of protective clothing and humming like a beehive with phones ringing non-stop and two-way radios barking," according to a Novosti Press Agency correspondent. But this was too far from the accident scene. Within days the crisis management team was operating from a "forward control post" located in an underground bunker just 600 metres from Unit 4.

Said *LeMonde*'s Michel Tatu: "Two nuclear academicians Eugene Velikhov and Valery Legasov distinguished themselves from the first day on. The entire scientific section of the government took great risks. Velikhov, for example, flew over the reactor more than forty times during May, many times daily in the initial period. The regime had three of eight USSR vice-chairmen on the spot: Silayev, Bataline and Shcherbina. Many high ranks of Ukrainian authority, of the Ministry of the Interior and the military including Air Force General Antrochkin have had to be hospitalized for a period of time after the hot days of early May."

The Novosti correspondent seeking out Boris Shcherbina at the district civil-defense headquarters in the town of Chernobyl soon after the accident found he had gone to Pripyat to be where the action was. "At that time it was still unclear whether the people would have to be evacuated but Communist party members who had been called in were already drawing up emergency evacuation plans and working to ensure there would be no panic," said the reporter. A week later Shcherbina admitted from first-hand knowledge that, "in the immediate proximity of the site of the accident maximum radiation levels are now ten to fifteen milliroentgens per hour." In most parts of the world one would not get that much radiation exposure in a month. Later that summer

Shcherbina had a medical checkup and in July he was hospitalized for radiation sickness according to a press report. But the deputy prime minister headed the Soviet delegation to an IAEA meeting in September. The Chernobyl station would resume power generation that fall. "Mankind has moved too far into the nuclear age to go back," he said.

By 4:00 a.m. Saturday additional police had been summoned from the districts of Chernobyl, Polesskoye and Ivankov. Checkpoints were established, roads closed and the reactor area was cordoned off. Radiation patrols fanned out calling back enigmatic numbers to the crisis centre but beyond the Chernobyl-4 building, itself, there was no evidence of fallout in the early-morning hours. Nonetheless before daylight municipal and Ukraine officials were charting the movement — if necessary — of 40,000 people from within the ten-kilometre radius that embraced the town and three small villages. Pripyat, itself, was divided into five housing wards. An evacuation team jointly headed by Pripyat and Berdov's officials, were assigned to each ward. For the next eighteen hours Pripyat precinct supervisors directed the preparation of evacuation rolls. Staff were assigned according to the number of apartment buildings in each section of the city and the number of suites per building. Elsewhere in the Soviet bureaucracy other municipal, republic and party officials compiled temporary or host accommodation, family by family. Buses were allocated and evacuation routes were charted. By daylight Soviet transport authorities were calling off-duty bus and truck drivers to stand by for weekend service. At one Kiev garage eighty drivers were told of the fire at the Chernobyl station. Radiation hazards were mentioned. Did anyone wish to bow out? "Not one person declined," said *Pravda*.

Curiously enough, the Pripyat population was not told — publicly at least — to remain indoors on Saturday. Normal weekend routines might have kept a substantial number off the streets in the proximity of the Chernobyl nuclear station. By the time radiation levels began to rise significantly most people were in bed. Those who were lured by spring weather to visit the countryside that Saturday were turned back by roadblocks. For experts like Valery Legasov who could anticipate the progressive increase in radioactive fallout a few hours later, the city must have presented a bizarre scene. Explosions and fire had raged in the night. Yet for those who could see the power station from their highrise apartments there was little evidence of disaster in the morning light. A regional official was startled by the normalcy. "There were even weddings in the Chernobyl area that Saturday," he said.

By noon radioactivity in Kurchatova Street, on the edge of Pripyat closest to the wrecked power plant, was about one hundred milli-roentgens per hour. It would have to be 250 times as high before Soviet civil defense authorities would declare even a "mild alert," 750 times higher before evacuation was mandatory. On the other hand, if you stood in Kurchatova Street for an hour that noon you would have gotten as much radiation as you would standing on an average North American street for a year. By Saturday night radiation levels were rising at an alarming rate. An hour and a half into Sunday morning — twenty-four hours since the reactor had gone out of control — the reading at one Pripyat location was half a roentgen per hour. That was still only a fiftieth of the amount that would trigger a "mild" alert. But authorities had long since decided on evacuation. Up to now benign winds had carried the radioactive plume around Pripyat. They were not going to wait on a wind shift to take action.

Leonid A. Ilyin is vice-president of the USSR Academy of Medical Sciences and a past chairman of the Soviet Commission for Radiation Safety. While Legasov headed the technical team, Ilyin lead a formida-ble army of medical specialists, physicians, nurses, technicians and paramedics onto the Chernobyl scene. "I am responsible for the health of our people," he said, and at the Vienna post-mortem he made it clear the evacuation decision had been made by the Politburo commission based on the expert opinions of Valery Legasov and himself. What crite-ria triggered the evacuation? "I'd like to remind you that radiation con-ditions in that city were relatively calm during most of Sunday since the radioactive plume by-passed Pripyat. But then there was a really sub-stantial change in the meteorological situation. With the continuing release of radioactive material from the damaged reactor the situation deteriorated," he said. "The basic reason for deciding to evacuate was the constantly increasing gamma rate in the open areas."

"I hope all of you have a clear picture of the situation in that city during the night of the twenty-sixth," Professor Ilyin told journalists. "It was necessary to most urgently organize and bring to Pripyat an enormous number of vehicles. In the shortest possible time 1,100 buses drove up along routes which had been carefully worked out be-forehand. What you saw were the 40,000 citizens of this town organized and allowed to take all the essential things they could. There was an-other complex problem and that was to determine where these people were to be taken because the radioactivity was continuing and they had to forecast where the truly safe regions would be."

The order to marshal 1,100 buses and 300 motor trucks in the yards of the Kiev transit authority was made at 8:00 Saturday night. Ukraine deputy transport minister, Mikhail Reva, issued instructions just hours after undergoing surgery at a Kiev hospital. Throughout the night the cavalcade of vehicles travelled the 112-kilometre route to Pripyat. The evacuation began at 2:00 p.m. Sunday. It took two hours and forty-five minutes to empty the city. The column of buses spanned twenty kilometres of highway. "Order was maintained primarily by the population itself and by Young Communist League volunteer police," said *Pravda*. When the buses left the ten-kilometre zone they were checked to ensure they were not contaminated. They would be scrupulously checked again for radioactivity before resuming service on Kiev streets.

The role of the Komsomolskaya, Young Communist League members, was mindful of Boy Scouts, cadets, church group youngsters and youthful first-aid teams at flood or disaster scenes across Canada in those uncomplicated times before insurance men and litigation lawyers ruled out voluntary help by those too young to sign a legal waiver. The Soviet youngsters turned out early Saturday morning. "Almost no one had to be persuaded. The Young Communists were collected at their apartment houses; others were picked up at their work places. As if it was wartime many grabbed their membership cards and showed up at the district party committee office. 'Give us our orders, we're ready,' " said *Komsomolskaya Pravda*.

"They were sent to schools, playgrounds and stores. Panic couldn't be allowed to break out. People still didn't know what had happened so the league members explained the situation clearly and in detail. Some people understood at once. Others obviously underestimated the danger. Still others tried to blow it up to unbelievable dimensions. The young fellows extinguished the spreading flame of rumours which could have proven more terrible than the fire at power unit No. 4. They told the truth and the alarming truth was more readily believed than any falsely optimistic assurances."

The Young Communists distributed potassium-iodide pills (an iodine supplement) to schools, kindergartens and day-care centres. When the evacuation began they played a further role in augmenting the emergency forces. They checked apartments to make sure no one had been left behind. They manned patrols along with auxiliary police to keep all abandoned homes and stores under surveillance. Later General Berdov's ministry installed a comprehensive electronic monitoring system that kept tabs on buildings in the evacuated city. Particularly in the first few days the league youngsters were exposed to abnormal radiation levels when they assisted the police to control traffic and in other outdoor duties. Soviet medical authorities seem to have kept close watch on everyone in proximity to Chernobyl and — except for emergency crews and power-station personnel on site in the first critical hours — no one appears to have suffered over-exposure to radiation. "There are many people still working on the site," Leonid Ilyin reminded the media two weeks after the accident. "These are workers, engineers, physicists, chemists, servicemen and medics. All those working in the nuclear-plant area have been equipped with individual protection and we are maintaining a rigid control to prevent anyone still in Pripyat from getting an overdose of radiation."

Still *Komsomolskaya Pravda* wondered if the young league members had been aware of the radiation hazard. "Anelia Perkovskaya, secretary of the Pripyat Young Communist League committee, looked at us in surprise or reproach. 'Everyone was told everything,' she said. 'After all they don't just live anywhere. They live in a city of atomic-power workers. They weren't just thinking of their own Pripyat. What about Kiev and Gomel? What of the threat to them?' She was assigned to the most remote borough," said the youth publication. "She scurried up and down stairs of high-rise apartment buildings, warning residents and gently hurrying them. She found two or three quite old people living alone. They slowly made their way downstairs. Anelia ran her legs off. Some parents brought children out in shorts and light shirts, even letting them play in the streets. With firm persistence Anelia herded the children into the entranceway. She gave a sigh of relief when they were seated in the buses." A Red version of Anne of Green Gables or Mary Poppins, Anelia seemed bigger than life in *Komsomolskaya Pravda*'s account. But the youth paper duly reported that she had been hospitalized for hypertension and fatigue. "Overwork and tension took their toll but everything will be all right. In a couple of weeks we'll release her," the head of a Kiev hospital's cardiology department told the paper.

Such is life in the authoritative state. The leaders — all party members — reflect paragon perfection and they patronize the masses. But the system worked in Pripyat. Ukraine authorities dispatched a pair of major-generals of police. General Berdov, as deputy minister of internal affairs, directed the actual emergency operations while General Borovik, as head of the political department in the same ministry, marshalled Communist party personnel to organize the evacuation and resettlement of 135,000 people. Borovik epitomized his no-nonsense approach in a sentence. "To avoid commotion and panic no assembly points were set out and the desired result was achieved," he said.

More of an intellectual cop akin to Ontario's former provincial police commissioner, Jim Erskine, or to the affable, authoritarian and manipulating attorney general, Roy McMurtry, who took charge at Mississauga, Berdov applied a little textbook psychology. When a delegation of frightened Pripyat residents turned up at his crisis centre he greeted them eminently garbed with a chest full of military decorations. "Although it was difficult for them to do, these people recognized the reality of the danger. A great deal depended on the actions of our personnel and their calm, confident behaviour," he explained. "After all the people were alarmed and disturbed. Therefore, particular restraint, tact, goodwill and readiness to help them were required of us." That said, General Berdov left the conditioning of the troops to his political colleague. As *Tass* phrased it, "In this tense, critical situation active political-education work was constantly conducted with staff members of the ministry. Temporary party organizations and groups were set up in the detachments and meetings were held under General Borovik's direction. Political work was done according to a clear-cut plan that encompassed the most important questions in these emergency conditions, including admission to the party."

Just two old ladies appear to have fallen between Anelia and the generals. A month after Chernobyl, Anastasia Semenyaka of 10 Heroes of Stalingrad Street and Maria Karpenok of 27 Kurchatov Street were discovered when they left their apartments where they had successfully hidden during the mass evacuation. Mrs. Semenyaka was eighty-five and Mrs. Karpenok seventy-four. They should have known better.

Good or bad by Western standards, the centralized party-led Soviet system reacted to the Chernobyl disaster with decisive leadership, party discipline and national will. Within two days they evacuated the Pripyat area population to communities in Ivankov and Polesskoye Districts well clear of the accident's impact. By midnight Sunday half of the evacuees had been bused to a dozen Polesskoye villages. As each bus entered the district, a regional representative boarded it and directed the driver to an assigned village. Throughout the day regional radio stations had told residents of the Pripyat evacuation while Polesskoye District party members canvassed householders door to door for accommodation. "Local residents were ready and waiting," a Ukraine newspaper reported. "Despite the midnight hour they had come to the party committee offices, the point of arrival. 'Where are the victims?' they kept asking." For most of the 23,000 evacuees in Polesskoye communities, their stay was temporary. Within three weeks those who had worked at the Chernobyl power station were sent with their families to new jobs at other nuclear stations operating or under construction in the Ukraine.

Pripyat's 10,000 school-age and kindergarten children found their term ended about two or three weeks ahead of schedule. After thorough medical examination they were dispatched to youth camps in the south of the USSR. Here they were soon joined by the children of collective farms and rural communities who had been evacuated about a week later. "As a precaution several thousand children were hospitalized and there was a good reason for that," Professor Ilyin told us at the IAEA meeting in Vienna. "Like a number of older people they had to be calmed down; they had to be reassured. They were calmed down and after careful dosimetry and clinical examinations, they were released from hospital. All of the children were taken to various sanatoriums, infirmaries and rest homes where particular attention was paid to them because these small people had naturally in their own minds suffered much negative emotion during the evacuation, in being taken to new homes and so forth. So all of these children were kept under close observation and starting on September first they went home to their parents and to take up their school work."

Beyond ten-kilometres of the wrecked reactor but within the thirty-kilometre radius there were sixty-two rural communities. None of these initially sustained serious fallout, although by mid-week Orevichi on the edge of this zone was recording about twenty millirems — the equivalent of about ten weeks of normal background radiation — each hour. As Ukraine authorities assessed dosimetry readings, analyzed blood samples of district residents and plotted the course of the radioactive plume over the first week, it was evident that the population of this area would soon be at risk. In that week some farm people working outdoors within a dozen kilometres of the Chernobyl nuclear station would have sustained as much as seventy-five rems of radiation. That is six times the radioactivity the average Canadian gets from all sources in a lifetime. More pertinent, it is the level at which Soviet authorities consider evacuation necessary. On May 2, the Ukraine premier, Alexander Lyashko, made that decision. He ordered 95,000 farm and rural people evacuated. They took 34,000 head of cattle, farm equipment and essential household goods with them.

"The people who are moving aren't just coming with knapsacks. They've got livestock and poultry. Who would leave even a dog behind?" Gregory Revenko, the Kiev Province party chief observed. Reminiscent of the mass displacement of Ukrainian farm people in the wake of World War II armies, the Chernobyl-district evacuation tested the

Soviet district leaders' understanding as much as their grip on logistics. Kiev Communists saw it as an economic challenge as well. "The provincial party organization sees as its primary task to provide every kind of effective assistance to the Shcherbina commission, to prevent panic and, of course, to continue to work toward fulfilment of national economic plans," Revenko said. "No one has relieved us of those tasks. Agricultural produce is continuing to arrive in Kiev without interruption. The produce is checked for radioactivity so there need be no worries about what is being sold in the stores. The province's factories continue to produce goods. Life goes on."

The second evacuation was no mere rerun of the movement of the Pripyat population. It created its own challenges. These farm people were being told to abandon goods and produce in the face of an invisible enemy. As one Chernobyl-area party leader explained, "The specific nature of a rural area must be considered. It is painful to part with your goods and chattels, especially the chickens and the vegetable garden you planted in the spring. More than one granny begged, 'Just leave me here. I've spent my whole life on this land.'" On the one hand, evacuee Maria Bakun told a reporter: "I'm not worried about radiation. I just took off the dress that I was wearing, threw it away and had a shower." On the other hand the occupants of one rural area — a thousand people, 3,700 head of cattle and four hundred chickens — arrived in Karlova, a village of about five hundred households. This was an exceptional pairing up but they were accommodated. Generally collective farm residents were dispatched to other collective farms further south in the Ukraine.

No problem was apparently beyond the comrades' control. Ten days after the evacuation of 135,000 people the deputy minister of communications in the Ukraine claimed, "You can calmly send a telegram or a letter to an old address and it will find the evacuated people to whom you addressed it." The Maidanovka state farm received 1,140 dairy cows of which five hundred came from private farms where they had never been milked by machine. "Thank goodness our retired dairymaids came to the rescue," sighed the farm director. Polesskoye District party members kept a big-brotherly eye on both the evacuees and their host communities. "Report about shortcomings," they demanded. "And there were shortcomings," a Ukraine newspaper declared. "Sometimes controllers at highway checkpoints went too far. 'Don't go there! Don't do that!' They were corrected. Some evacuees smelled of alcohol. 'No drinking allowed,' they were warned. 'The village assemblies have banned it.'"

Ann Kirilchuk, bookkeeper, mother of two and wife of the Chervonna Polessye collective farm chairman, described her family's reception at the Fasovaya collective farm. "We were treated like family by the Fasovaya chairman's people. The day following our relocation my two children went to school and I went to work." Other evacuees would find it harder to slip into post-Chernobyl life. Evacuated to Moscow, Viktor Kibenok's widow read the *Komsomolskaya Pravda* account of her husband's heroic role on the morning of April 26. She preferred to think of two mornings earlier when she had told him she was pregnant.

Yalta is on the Soviet Union's riviera. Here the USSR rewards its elite and their kin for leadership. Here at a Communist youth camp in May ten-year-old Misha Telyatnikov shyly offered a photograph of his father while his twelve-year-old brother Oleg explained their dad's line of work. Another of the 60,000 children removed from the thirty-kilometre zone around Chernobyl, ten-year-old Oleg Khodemchuk remained quiet. He knew his father worked at the same power station but he had not heard from him since the night of the fire. No one had yet told Oleg that Valery Ivanovich Khodemchuk was dead.

4

Air Drop

"A typical nuclear runaway accident may start and be over in less than a second. . . . It may disrupt the structure sufficiently so that radioactive poisons escape or it may lead to . . . a chemical explosion of considerable violence."

— ROGERS MCCULLAGH, MARK MILLS AND EDWARD TELLER,
GENEVA, AUGUST 1955

LIKE COALS IN A BRAZIER OF HELL, graphite in the ruptured Chernobyl reactor burned incandescently. Nuclear fuel fragments roasted, broke into smaller bits, became gaseous and rose a kilometre high on the hot updraft. Steam and light grey smoke issued through much of Saturday. Still the fire in the reactor core was, itself, flameless. Its glow was not evident until dusk. Valery Legasov saw it as he approached Pripyat and knew why he was there. "It was only on seeing the glow that I began to guess the nature of what had happened," he said. In his mind's eye he could see the contaminable, radioactive plume rising from the shattered structure.

Three American scientists had anticipated this. At the United Nations' first international Conference on the Peaceful Uses of Atomic Energy thirty-one years earlier Edward Teller, a father of the H-Bomb and two research associates, pointed out that "a typical nuclear runaway accident may start and be over in less than a second. . . . Another feature is that it does not seem to be very violent. Nevertheless, it does appear possible to have an accident fast enough that portions of the machine may be propelled with velocities of a few metres per sec-

40

ond. This does not resemble an atomic bomb or any ordinary chemical explosion; rather it is similar to events that might occur in an automobile accident." They emphasized that "a nuclear runaway, in itself, does not represent a serious hazard to off-site people. However, a nuclear runaway may disrupt the structure sufficiently so that radioactive poisons escape or it may lead to [heat-making] chemical reactions between components of the reactor core and a chemical explosion of considerable violence."

All of that occurred at Chernobyl. Steam initially shattered the reactor's containment and this was immediately followed by a hydrogen explosion, the production of other burnable gases, their ignition to flame and the ejection of fiery fuel fragments to light some thirty fires around the building. These were extinguished in the early morning hours. But the incendiary forces burst in the bowels of the nuclear furnace to torch 2,500 tonnes of graphite. In the days ahead 10 per cent of it burned implacably as coal in hell. Oxygen fed the combustion and the oxygen-graphite mix added a further dimension. The interaction of these two elements is exothermic, that is heat-making in itself. It raised the temperture of the already burning graphite so it burned more intensely. The process was not only self sustaining it became progressively worse.

In the first moments of the accident the fuel was heated to about ten times its normal operating temperature. Heat and the initial explosive forces shattered many of the finger-thick fuel rods to release radiation. Over the next half hour or so the fuel gave off heat to the graphite. As the uranium fuel cooled slightly it emitted a little less radioactivity. Then as the graphite burned hotter it roasted more volatile fission products from the fuel. All told Chernobyl-4 would pour 4 to 5 per cent of its radioactive inventory skyward and a quarter of that would escape the reactor in the first day. For days to come the burning graphite would sustain the fire, the roasting of fuel and the emission of radioactive poisons. In the first twenty-four hours the fuel temperature dropped by 40 per cent and the radioactive emission rate fell off by two-thirds. But on Sunday it was still creating more nuclear contamination than any accident had ever done before.

The extent of the damage was incredible. Said Legasov: "We were dealing with this kind of accident for the first time. As a specialist and participant in the events I can confirm that the scale of the accident, its nature and the development of events seemed improbable, nearly impossible." The first word was confusing. "Information arrived immediately but it contained much that was contradictory and strange. It was impossible to assess what was going on from Moscow." On the scene by nightfall "it was necessary to carefully ascertain all the circumstances and the exceptional characteristics of what happened." The first reactions had been to douse the graphite fire with water. "An attempt was made to reduce the reactor vault temperature and keep the graphite from igniting by using the emergency, auxiliary feed pumps to supply water to the core. This attempt proved ineffective," said the official Soviet report. Water leaked from a hundred broken pipes to form a frightening new wave of steam and chemical reactions with the incandescent graphite.

The emergency response team was left with two options. They could smother the fire and radiation with something other than water or they could let the runaway reactor burn itself out. It was obvious to Valery Legasov and his expert team that to delay their response would leave major city populations — at least within parts of the Ukraine and Byelorussia — at risk of dangerous fallout. They opted to isolate the reactor under a dry blanket of sand, lead and minerals. By Monday morning Soviet Air Force helicopters were attacking the smoldering reactor as an enemy target.

The air force operation was one facet of an integrated national response which General Secretary Gorbachev initiated within hours of the accident. He had immediately dispatched a government commission under deputy prime minister Boris Shcherbina to establish on-site authority for whatever actions were required. At the Politburo, another deputy Nikolai Ryzhkov headed a second group primarily to marshal resources with authoritative clout. Within eighteen hours of the accident the most knowledgeable nuclear experts in the USSR, including Academicians of Science Valery Legasov and Yevgeny Velikhov, were at the Chernobyl station. "The dynamics of the whole situation were very complex. The situation was changing literally every hour," Legasov explained. In these circumstances temperature and radiation measurements within the reactor were of critical importance. The first calculations were to evaluate the state of the fuel in the reactor vault; that would determine the nature, severity and extent of the fallout. It would help answer an even more immediate question: How was the fuel standing up?

Their worst fear was not of a meltdown *per se* but one that would concentrate the nuclear fuel to the density of a bomb. The chances of this were slim but the consequences would be appalling. The official Soviet report dealt succinctly with that peril. "The potential danger that some melted fuel would concentrate, creating conditions in which a critical mass might be reached and a spontaneous chain reaction occur, made it necessary to take appropriate precautions." Neither the Soviet experts, nor the IAEA's own fourteen member INSAG (International Nuclear Safety Advisory Group) team said what "appropriate" measures were taken to prrevent such a happening. It would be as hard to prevent as to contemplate. But the thought of it undoubtedly added to the urgency with which they prepared to monitor the infernal forces now out of control.

Like an aircraft's accident-proof "black box," the control room's Skala computer program tracked the reactor's parameters. But to monitor the turbine-generator test, Chernobyl-4 operators had changed some of the input requirements normally recorded. Soviet engineers would in due course backtrack by computer modelling to determine the actual changes that preceded the accident. However, most of the sensors that fed temperature, pressure, radioactivity, fuel composition and chemical content to both computer monitors and to the array of control-room instruments had been destroyed either by explosion or by fire. To replace them meant penetrating unimaginable heat and radiation levels. Moreover, the intensely high radioactivity during the first day effectively zapped Soviet, Swedish and American-made electronic thermometers. Legasov's technical team were obliged to devise alternative devices. Sensors were inserted within the vault by drilling holes through the metres-thick containment wall. The radiation that poured from these small openings was so intense the detector units had to be positioned and sealed off within minutes by technicians working by remote control from a shielded position.

The first post-accident measurements were noted by the dosimeter operators who virtually followed on the firefighters' heels. Beginning on Saturday the Soviet meteorological network was alerted to augment its normal reporting system with hourly air, ground and water sampling of radioactivity as far afield as the Berezinsky National Park, 120 kilometres northeast of Minsk. Airborne radiation patrols were intensified. By Tuesday the accident response team was materially aided by video pictures taken at crater-top level from an air force helicopter and from a heavily shielded truck that drove as close to the structure as possible. These showed the burning graphite glowing through the cracks and crevices of the shattered reactor. Airborne gamma surveys were begun on Tuesday as well. By mid-May Soviet Army chemical unit technicians had developed a moon-walker vehicle to collect air, soil and grass samples for plutonium detection over a wide area.

Reviewing events with a journalist's cold eye, Michel Tatu told Paris

LeMonde readers that, "Things were organized progressively but on the first day the whole thing started with very dramatic improvisation." Quoting the Soviet Army newspaper *Red Star*, Tatu described how Major-General of Aviation Nikolai Timofeyevich Antoshkin's helicopters poured some five thousand tonnes of sand, clay, lead and minerals on the reactor, most of it in the five days following the accident. "The work started during the night of April 26-27, only a few hours after the initial fire was put out. The general, himself, perched on the roof of a Pripyat hotel and looking constantly at the destroyed side of reactor No. 4, guided the first aircraft into the target," said Tatu quoting *Red Star*.

Whether an air force general would first test the helicopter sandbagging of a burning reactor after dark — and by improvised phone line from a hotel roof top five kilometres away — is questionable. Something may have been lost in translation here. But certainly by Monday morning, April 28, Antoshkin's fliers were laying a barrage of sandbags on the shattered roof of Chernobyl-4 under very dicey conditions. No one yet knew just how lethal the radioactivity might be immediately above the fractured reactor roof but the general was not going to have his pilots stick around to find out. He was mindful that in peace or war the odds on survival are in inverse proportion to the time spent over a deadly target. The target was a 600-square-metre area of shattered masonry, steel, brick and fire-scarred debris. The debris tumbled into the crater where the reactor had once been securely roofed. The lip of the crater was fifty metres above ground and it was flanked by undamaged building structures rising another twenty-three metres above that. The two 150-metre chimney stacks on the long building were ideal to navigate by but they were menacing obstructions. Power lines were yet another distraction.

"The first flights were the most difficult," the general observed. "Picture a crater of very limited dimensions to which one must fly by the shortest possible route, then try to drop a bag of sand in a precise spot, all in a matter of seconds." The first sortie was done by military pilot first class, Aleksander Ivanovich Serebryakov. "What he did in the air over Chernobyl can only be called an aerial slalom," said the general. "There were the three other power units and those chimney stacks sticking up. While the bombing was going on we were mindful of the people maintaining necessary conditions in the shut-down reactors below. Somehow loads of up to ten tonnes had to be dropped from less than an altitude of 200 metres and the target couldn't be missed."

On the first day the Serebryakev crew dropped thirty tonnes of sand, lead, dolomite and boron carbide. By Friday a thousand tonnes of sand had been laid to smother the fire and trap the radioactive particles. Some 2400 tonnes of bagged lead shot was dropped. It readily melted where it fell into the crevices of the debris. Then it solidified again to provide a radiation shield. Dolomite is calcium-magnesium carbonate commonly used as building stone in Europe. About 800 tonnes of dolomite chips were dropped at Chernobyl to dissipate the heat from the burning graphite. Some forty tonnes of boron carbide was deposited to poison out any further nuclear reaction. The chances of Chernobyl-4 going critical again were infinitesimally small but they were not taking them.

"We stayed suspended hovering over the crater, opened the helicopter door, then looking in the opening and judging with the naked eye we would let go with the bag," a helicopter flyer told *Red Star*. "It was not the sun's rays coming out of the mouth of the reactor and everyone was well aware of it," said the army paper. The integrated response promised by Gorbachev was evident in the way Soviet authorities met the logistics involved in putting 5,040 tonnes of materials in more than 100,000 sandbags, in equipping the helicopters with special hooks to target-drop the bags and in shielding the crews from the high-radiation field they flew through.

Sand is a universal barrier to trouble. By Sunday morning hundreds of soldiers and Communist Youth were filling sandbags. *Red Star* claimed that General Antochkin had a Kiev district factory open its machine shop on Saturday night to produce release hooks which, based on his World War II experience, allowed the helicopter pilots to drop four sandbags at a time on the reactor target with some accuracy. To minimize crew exposure the aircraft cabins were shielded, the fliers wore respirators and they flew in and out very quickly. No one suffered a radiation injury but they certainly courted danger. Using a collective-farm grain field twelve kilometres from the Chernobyl station as a base, most crews did four flights daily for the first five days. Each night they would return to the farm to scrub down, replace clothing and undergo medical examination. The helicopters were decontaminated at the same time.

Captain Alexander Volkov had flown the big Soviet MI-3 helicopters over water, desert and mountain country. Here it was flat and open, safe enough if it was not for that 150-metre stack alongside the reactor target. One wondered if its rigid anchoring and support cables had been shaken loose by the explosion. A veteran of the Afghanistan campaign, Volkov might have pondered the relative peril of invisible radiation versus flak from unseen guns. "Respirators on," he told his navigator

Lieutenant Viktor Krokhmalev and flight engineer Vasily Daysyuk. Now they were hovering just above the crater. What they saw was tumbled masonry and brick, torn metal structures and the felled 400-tonne fuelling machine prone as a giant robot victim of Star Wars. What they didn't see they measured with scintillation counters. The detectors recorded trillions of atomic disintegrations rising every second from the nuclear furnace. Recording this radioactivity was as important a part of their mission as the sandbagging. It fed the network of data on which precautionary measures, evacuation plans and the mending of diplomatic fences across Europe would be based.

The helicopter banked sharply away from the reactor building. It flew over the silent streets of the Chernobyl Atomic Power Station, over the empty Pripyat apartment blocks from which clothes-line garments waved vainly. It skirted the Pripyat River where army troops were building an embankment and it flew across a boatless stretch of the Kiev reservoir. A five-minute flight brought them back to their grain-field landing patch. Volkov pulled open a lead-coated window to let in air and light. He proded the navigator with a pocket dosimeter, a pen-sized radiation counter. "Now let's look the instrument in the face. What dose did we get this time?" he wondered.

"Normal," Krokhmalev assured him without looking.

"Well, till the next flight then," Volkov responded. That was the kind of business they were in.

Back in their make-shift mess, Captain Yuri Prokofyev told the Volkov crew: "Today the radiation has fallen off by nearly 75 per cent. That's in just three days." He had got a hold of overly optimistic data and they told him so. "Well, we'll chase the genie back into his bottle yet," Prokofyev assured them.

Chernobyl was the business of other Red Army forces, as well — veterans of skirmishes on the lukewarm side of the Cold War. Soviet troops protecting the Pripyat River embankment from contaminated runoff water did what soldiers have done since the Spartans entrenched themselves at Thermopylae 2,500 years earlier. They dug doggedly. Chernobyl also tested nuclear-age forces under battle conditions. Army transport wheeled in lead-shielded vehicles to carry reactor crews the last few hundred metres through lifeless streets. Engineers used robot-controlled bulldozers to clear debris from the wrecked reactor's flanks. Soviet contamination fighters, another nuclear-age innovation, made an appearance at Chernobyl. Wide-eyed, *LeMonde*'s Michel Tatu wrote of "This famous body of chemical troops who particularly worry the Western world." Equipped to detect, monitor and measure any level of radioactivity anywhere, they were trained to "brush and refurbish" the vehicles they encountered along the road within the sanitized thirty-kilometre zone. At Pripyat the decontamination brigade used telescoping washing equipment to scrub down the exterior of multi-storey buildings. Where it was impractical to wash away the contamination they sealed it off with various compounds. "For every poison we have a counter poison," they claimed. One might consider this little taste of nuclear devastation and wonder if they were over confident.

The Soviet leader put the nuclear station disaster in perspective in a mid-May television address. "The accident at Chernobyl showed again what an abyss will open if nuclear war befalls mankind. For inherent in the stockpiled nuclear arsenals are thousands upon thousands of disasters far more horrible than Chernobyl," Mikhail Gorbachev reminded the world. In the wake of Chernobyl he had a four-fold message. (1) The nuclear genie was an awesome creature when unrestrained. "For the first time we have actually encountered the terrible force that is nuclear energy gone out of control," he said. But nuclear war would be unimaginably worse. (2) "This has strengthened still more our conviction. . . for the complete elimination of nuclear weapons, the ending of nuclear explosions and the creation of an all-embracing system of international security." (3) The genie could not be stuffed back in a bottle. "More than 370 nuclear reactors now function in different countries. This is a reality; the future of the world economy can hardly be imagined without the development of nuclear power." (4) It was time for comprehensive global collaboration through the IAEA "to create an international regime for safe development of nuclear power. . . a system of prompt warning and information in the event of an accident, specifically when this is accompanied by the escape of radioactivity. . . [and] an international mechanism, both bilateral and multilateral, for the speediest rendering of mutual assistance."

Throughout the summer, culminating in their technological *tour de force* at the IAEA post-mortem meeting, Soviet scientists reminded the world of another relevant truth. The USSR was no longer a nation of barefoot peasants emerging from pre-industrial barbarism. They admitted that they had suffered fools in the control room at the Chernobyl station that morning of April 26, but they quickly applied state-of-the-art technology to contain and clean up the damage. At the Vienna meeting they laid out their expertise without reserve and they welcomed advice from the other IAEA members. The Soviet Union was not about to plead technological poverty, however. Initially they ignored worldwide offers of nuclear expertise apparently because of embarrassment.

By the time Gorbachev invited collaboration in his May 14 address, the Shcherbina commission had demonstrated that Soviet science and technology could cope with Chernobyl on their own.

One incident was indicative. When they decided to spray sodium silicate — the "water-glass" that our great-grandmothers used to preserve eggs — to seal off contaminated surfaces, Vice-Chairman Ivan Silayev discovered that a Swedish supplier was asking twenty-six dollars a kilogram for the stuff. By mid-May Soviet industry was producing thirty tonnes of sodium silicate daily for the Chernobyl decontamination work, presumably at a much lower cost. By this time the Politburo was putting development work to the practical test. "The experimental activity of the scientists and the discoveries they have made in regard to the atomic-power station are significant," Silayev said. "With the expanded scale of emergency work, the swiftest possible decontamination is needed." One method was to pour liquid glass, impervious to rain, on roof surfaces. Another was to drop a barrage of sacks filled with liquid, synthetic rubber. The sacks broke on impact and the rubber spread and hardened into a radioactive dust cover.

The Soviet chemical industry offered a new composite film that sealed off contaminant particles so they could not get into soil and water. Academician Boris Gidaspov, chairman of the Soviet commission on radiation safety and director of the State Institute for Applied Chemistry, noted the scale of the operation. "Having tested this decontaminating film in an emergency situation, we are now laying it down on an area of 200,000 to 300,000 square metres per day." A number of General Androchkin's helicopters had been quickly fitted with agricultural-spray equipment to apply the film at this rate. Others were equipped with parachute static lines to permit the precise placement of bags of lead pellets where cracks in the rubble atop the reactor still let radiation escape. Yet other aircraft were equipped to monitor radiation levels by radar, gamma-ray detection and air sampling.

The orderly shutdown of Chernobyl units 1, 2 and 3, their controlled cooling, the herculean efforts to keep them free of contamination and the early return of two of them to service, was an exercise of Politburo will. The Soviet leaders had dispatched Shcherbina to Chernobyl to see that it was done. He was determined to show ill-wishers that the Soviet Union could take such disaster in stride, quickly recover and that the Politburo had no intention of curbing nuclear-power generation. When the IAEA met again at Vienna in September — this time for the politicians to remasticate the scientific and technical information provided a month earlier — the deputy prime minister announced: "We have entered the final stage of the Chernobyl cleanup." Unit 1 would be back in operation within weeks he said and it was. The safekeeping of the three Chernobyl units, the entombment of the fourth, and the decontamination of the station site within months of the accident spelled out, not just Politburo determination, but the will of the Soviet people.

Their unified response to Chernobyl and to a hostile world was evident in the first days of the accident aftermath. To man each operational shift in the post-accident period meant housing people safely off site and getting them in and out of the reactor building without undue radiation exposure. It also meant having a sufficient pool of qualified personnel so no one would be exposed to barely tolerable radiation limits for more than a short period of time. Several hundred reactor operators and maintenance people were housed at two Young Pioneer campsites beyond the thirty-kilometre exclusion zone. They were bussed daily to the Chernobyl station gates where they transferred to lead-shielded army personnel carriers which sped them to the reactor building. Soviet journalists trying valiantly to meet Politburo demands for heroic treatment of Chernobyl workers choked a bit in citing one of the young Communist campsites. It was not easy to report that the defenders of Chernobyl were temporarily quartered at The Fairy Tale Young Pioneer Camp.

"We're working on the three operational generating units with a reduced staff," night-shift superintendent Gennady Dik told a Ukraine reporter. "One third are young people. We travel by bus then transfer to special vehicles. We're ensuring the viability of the three reactors that are being cooled down. They need cold water constantly and we're assuring the operation of the pumping equipment around the clock." How bad was the radiation? "It's constantly changing for the better. At least we're able to work there," the shift boss said. Had he encountered any "scaremongers?" No, but concern was natural in these circumstances.

"How are people acting?" the reporter wanted to know.

"Skillfully, with uncommon efficiency," he was told.

Those exposed to high radiation levels prevalent that first week were ordered on sick leave as a matter of occupational health policy in the Soviet Union. At Forest Glades Sanatorium category-five welder Valery Pechorin was asked what he had been doing. "Generally speaking, the usual sort of work at the station — but admittedly in an unusual situation. We've sealed up doors to eliminate drafts and taken apart damaged electrical circuits. There's plenty of housekeeping work to be done as well." For example? "We were given an assignment to close up a window between the damaged reactor and the third unit. Because of the radiation this had to be done in no more than twelve minutes. That was the amount of time the dosimeter operators had set for a safe stay in the work zone. The shift superintendant, the foreman and the other fellows helped us speed it up. We did it in ten minutes. Then, of course, the doctor examined us. Everything was normal. Now we'll rest and when we go back we'll get a specific assignment just before we reenter the station zone."

Gennady Dik and Valery Pechorin were among a dozen Chernobyl superintendants, foremen and tradesmen cited as Soviet heroes in the fortnight following the accident. Not all of them survived those early hours of Saturday, April 26. Vladimir Lyskin and Nikolai Oleshchuk recounted how a fellow foreman in the Chernobyl electrical shop, Sasha Lelechenko sustained fatal burns and radiation. "I was called right away. 'Get people up,' I was told. Out of seventeen on my shift seven were at home. Enroute I realized how serious it must be if ambulances were going to the station," Oleshchuk recalls.

"Graphite had fallen out and was lying on the floor. Background radiation was high. But we forgot about that because there were transformers to be repaired. Then the cable ducts began to catch fire," said Lyskin, picking up the story. "Lelechenko was thinking about peoples' safety. Everyone but himself. The hydrogen valves had to be closed and he wouldn't let anyone else do it." The two survivors were talking to newsmen a few minutes after learning of Lelechenko's death. "Aleksei Grigoryevich Lelechenko really liked working with young people. He was a real leader. He made very sure none of his men received dangerous doses. He literally drove them out of the shop, but stayed to do what had to be done himself," Vladimir Lyskin explained. "Later when he was barely able to stand he noticed the state that Nikolai and I were in, probably from the looks on our faces. Suddenly he began to tell jokes."

Reminded of his own participation, the electrical shop foreman tried to explain how it was. "It's an unusual sensation. You don't feel anything. You're neither cold nor hot. But then we got the transformer going and the mood lightened. We had managed to get the power on again." Lyskin was uncomfortable in the first-person narrative. He couldn't hide his emotions. "Those who were at the station that day didn't leave. Everyone is ready for more work and the first in line are those who experienced that first terrible night. I'm so much in love with this city, with the station, with this job that I can't imagine my life in the future without it."

He shifted uneasily. "People who work in atomic energy are devoted to it," the foreman said.

5

In a Crisis, Ad Lib

"The structure tumbles, the white-hot reactor falls into the water and radioactive vapour breaks out to contaminate the area to an even worse degree."

— YEVGENY VELIKHOV, *IZVESTIA*, MAY 12, 1986

"The accident caught us unprepared. We had to ad lib."

— VALERY LEGASOV, NOVOSTI PRESS AGENCY,
NOVEMBER 25, 1986

VICE-PRESIDENT OF THE SOVIET ACADEMY OF SCIENCES and reputedly a good friend of Mikhail Gorbachev, Yevgeny Pavolich Velikhov arrived on the Chernobyl scene three days after the accident with no special authority but considerable clout. In the following month it was Velikhov who kept the Soviet public posted on how the runaway reactor was subdued. Deputy director of the Soviet's premier nuclear establishment, the Kurchatov Institute, and an academician himself, Valery Legasov went to the site with deputy premier Boris Shcherbina within hours of the explosion and he was soon in evident control of the recovery program. Legasov's subsequent day-long presentation to 380 international experts attending the IAEA post-mortem in Vienna has been described by *Nucleonics Week* European editor Anne MacLachlan as a *"tour de force."*

Velikhov and Legasov had equal status on the Shcherbina commission along with Academician Boris V. Gidaspov who headed the State

Institute for Chemical Engineering, Environment Minister Yuri Izrael, the vice-president of the USSR Academy of Medicine Leonid A. Ilyin, radiation health expert Yuri Grigoryev and Minister for Machine Building Ivan S. Silayev. In the first critical days Velikhov and Legasov had equally competent but different ideas on what should be done. "We saw the danger in a less apocalyptic and more practical light than did most of the Western press," Velikhov told *Izvestia* on May 12. Still his own concerns had been of epic-making proportions. What he feared most was Legasov's decision to douse the graphite fire and cap the radioactivity with five thousand tonnes of sand, clay, lead and other materials. "We were afraid the structure would not resist the heat and weight and we worried most about the giant slab foundation." Beneath that slab floor was the two-level, steam-suppression pool. Velikhov conjured a grim scenario of what might have happened. As he visualized it, "The structure tumbles, the white-hot reactor falls into the water and radioactive vapour breaks out to contaminate the area to an even worse degree."

Legasov shared Velikhov's fear of a *rasplavleniye*, a smelting of the reactor core which is the Soviet version of the China Syndrome where a fiery ball melts down through the earth. "There was the greatest apprehension of the molten fuel burning through the plant floor and still continuing to spew radioactive fragments into the atmosphere," Legasov confirmed. But a greater fear prompted his decision to airdrop a protective cover. "To wait for the natural burnout of the graphite moderator would be to invite more trouble in the form of spreading radioactive contamination, for it was impossible to guess how long the radioactive volcano would be active." Those who weigh the relative risks in a crisis situation, make a judgment and shoulder the consequences, don't warrant second-guessing; in any case, he was proven right. But Legasov volunteered the rationale for their action a half-year later. "The Chernobyl accident caught us unprepared. We had to ad lib our strategy and perform operations unheard of in international [nuclear engineering] practice," he told the Novosti Press Agency. "The chosen strategy was adequate, effective and a justifiable risk."

A cataclysm did not occur but by Friday, six days after the accident, the reactor began to grow hotter and more radioactive again. Initially the blanket of sand, lead and dolomite chips did what it was expected to do. It curbed the graphite fire and it checked the column of radioactive particles issuing from the reactor vault. However, it also stopped the natural cooling process. When the hot air had risen unchecked cold air was drawn into the nuclear furnace. In the first twenty-four hours —

before General Androchkin's helicopters began their assault — the fuel temperature dropped from about 725 to 325 degrees Celsius and the radiation release rate fell from half a million curies per hour to a third that much. Most of the sandbag blanket was laid in five days, Tuesday through Saturday. During that time the rate of radioactive emission dropped sharply while the temperature of the fuel remained almost constant. Soviet engineers subsequently calculated that some twelve million curies were likely emitted on Saturday, April 26, four million on Sunday. By midweek two million curies a day were escaping.

Decay heat continued to pour from nuclear fuel that was still very reactive and the graphite still smoldered nearly incandescent. But now the capped reactor again became an oven in which the heat accumulated. A week after the reactor runaway the temperature and radiation release rate were both rising rapidly again. Now, despite the air-dropped blanket, radioactivity doubled and on Friday the fuel temperature rose about 40 per cent. By Sunday night the nuclear fuel had become almost as hot again, around 1,600 degrees Celsius, as it had been when it initially caught fire. On Monday, May 5, some eight million curies of fission products were discharged, two-thirds as much as had escaped on the first day of the accident.

Beneath this volcanic structure weighted beyond engineers' expectations the two compartmentalized suppression pools had been designed to receive any sudden discharge of excess steam and dissipate its pressure in water three metres deep. Velikhov could visualize the reactor core dropping like a molten meteorite into these pools. How much water remained in them? "Would we manage to keep the core intact or would it go down through the earth? No one in the world had ever been in such a difficult position," he told *Pravda*. To resolve it Legasov and Velikhov now agreed on two immediate steps. Thousands of tonnes of nitrogen were pumped into the reactor vault to cool the core and the suppression pools were drained. That last operation was "a genuine act of valour," said Velikhov.

Kiev provincial fire marshal Colonel Ivan Kotsvura had nearly a hundred fire pumpers working to drain the pools when a new problem was encountered. A substantial amount of water could not be pumped out until two drainage valves at the base of the lower pool were opened manually. The passageway to the lower pool was pitch-black, partially flooded and highly radioactive. The trio who volunteered to release the valves down there were survivors. They had escaped the explosion that rocked Chernobyl-4 ten days earlier. Boris Baranov was a shift superintendent and Valery Bespalov a senior engineer in the turbine shop.

Alexi Ananenko, a senior mechanic, knew where the valves were located. He would open one of them and direct Bespalov to the other. Baranov would stand by in case they got into trouble.

"We planned it all out beforehand so as not to lose time in the radioactive area," Ananenko recalled. "We looked something between cosmonauts and deep-sea divers in wet suits and respirators and we carried flashlights and radiation monitors. We were told clearly what the radiation situation was above and beneath the water. Where it was possible we went through on the double to save time. Then my flashlight beam picked up the pipe that led to the valves and we followed it." From that point the journey seemed endless. The water got deeper and the pipe more difficult to see. At the end he could just keep his head above water as he groped for the valve. "Finally I felt it with my fingers. I tried to turn it; suddenly I could feel it give. I'm sure my heart actually missed a beat. Then I showed Valery where the other valve must be. It gave way as well." After that events seemed to collapse one on another. Like a war veteran recounting the exact moment when he knew the battle was won, the twenty-seven-year-old mechanic compressed the story to a dozen words. "We heard the water flowing and then our buddies were hugging us," he said.

Nitrogen, the inert gas that makes up 80 per cent of the atmosphere, cools under pressure and makes a powerful refrigerant. It had a dramatically fast impact in the reactor vault. Above about 350 degrees Celsius, the nuclear fuel had been vaporizing and pouring like invisible smoke through every crevice. Only a few degrees blow that temperature the fission products stabilized and became inactive. While nitrogen cooled the core Antochkin's pilots sealed the last cracks and holes in the sand, lead and mineral blanket. In the early morning hours of May 6, ten days after the reactor core erupted, the radioactive emission virtually stopped. Eight million curies had escaped the reactor on Monday, May 5; just over *one per cent* of that was emitted the following day.

"The escape of radioactive gases and volatile substances was connected with high temperatures in the reactor zone. Now that the temperature has fallen sharply the escape of radioactivity has virtually stopped," Environment Minister Yury Izrael announced on May 11. On the station site, where radiation had been ten to fifteen millroentgens per hour shortly after the accident, it was now less than a fifth of that. The Chernobyl station in proximity to the reactor was still untenable for more than an hour or so at a time but work to decontaminate buildings and roadways was already underway by the army's special teams using state-of-the-art equipment. A day earlier Academician Velikhov had given *Izvestia* much the same message as Izrael though in more dramatic terms. "Up to today a catastrophe was theoretically possible. A large amount of fuel and graphite was in an incandescent state. This is no longer true but the specialists face a very difficult task."

"The reactor has lost its criticality; it is no longer emitting radioactivity. Now intensive work is under way to reduce the radiation and ultimately to eliminate it completely," said Legasov in mid-May. The immediate task was to tunnel under Chernobyl-4 and reinforce the reactor foundation with a massive air-conditioned concrete slab floor. This was first to meet the fears Velikhov still harboured of a meltdown into the water table below but the Soviet experts could now afford to think longer term. The Shcherbina commission's mandate was twofold. They were to eliminate Chernobyl's dangers, then to rehabilitate the station. The return of the first three Chernobyl reactors to service became a priority the moment the wrecked fourth unit could be safely isolated. Units 1, 2 and 3 had been secured by operational crews and firefighters at great personal risk. The 3,000 megawatts of power they generated would electrify a Canadian city of 2.5 million people. More relevent, it would meet the needs of Chernigov and Kiev within a hundred kilometres.

Velikhov had the same message. "The nuclear-power industry is indispensable but we have to make it safe," he said. In tapping energy sources there was no free lunch. "Take good old coal. It's far from safe to mine and burn and it is expensive to transport. Take the problems it poses in Western Europe. Denmark protests against Swedish nuclear stations but buys the electricity they produce. Almost in revenge the Danish coal industry contaminates Swedish forests with acid rain." Velikhov was referring to the Swedes' two-decades-old Barseback nuclear plants at Malmo, thirty-five kilometres from the Danish coast. He might have been talking about Prince Edward Island and Nova Scotia which rely on New Brunswick Power for electricity while decrying the perils of the Point Lepreau nuclear station. Or he might have been mindful of Ontario and New York State utilities which have long traded electricity, coal, acid rain and the philosophical export of nuclear-debate issues.

"Our country attaches priority to the construction of nuclear-power plants. Unless we use nuclear energy to a considerable degree we cannot master the next stage of our technological development," Legasov said. Returning Chernobyl's three undamaged reactors and building two new ones was entirely dependent on entombing Chernobyl-4 in a shroud that allowed no further contamination of the station environment. Legasov continued: "The sarcophagus to entomb the wrecked reactor forever took almost seven months to build. This complicated engineering structure shows what technology can do when pushed. At the same time it is a grim reminder of what can happen when technology goes wrong as a result of irresponsible attitudes, poor discipline and violation of operating procedures for a sophisticated technological system."

Confronted by an accident of unprecedented consequence, Soviet engineers were inventive. "The specialists are calling what is now to be done a sarcophagus. We must not oversimplify things," said Ivan Silayev, the machine-building minister. "Some people will think the reactor is to be hidden in concrete, completely shut up and that's all. In fact it will be a very complex engineering structure to fully control the internal heat and remove any excess." Academician Ivan Yemelyanov described the encasement as "a concrete refrigerator." The Soviet deputy chairman responsible for technical supply, Lev Voronin, elaborated: "Keep in mind that the tomb is a crucial structure. It's not just a canopy meant to cover the damaged part of the station but a rather complex design. After all it will be necessary to carry out constant monitoring inside the tomb, primarily of temperature." For how long? Another deputy chairman of the Soviet Council of Ministers, Yuri P. Batalin answered that. "Unlike conventional burial this means creating a structure that will be under constant monitoring for many years and will automatically control the natural processes taking place inside the reactor," he said.

Thus the entombment of Chernobyl-4 had apparently gone around Gorbachev's cabinet table. But they declined to get on the time-scale treadmill where anti-nuclear activists run Western-world politicians so ragged. In their comprehensive report to the Soviet government passed along for IAEA discussion at Vienna, Valery Legasov and his colleagues studiously avoided any predictions or estimates of just how long the radiation from the wrecked reactor would be cause for concern. "Long-term entombment of the fourth unit should ensure a normal radiation situation in the surrounding area and in the atmosphere and preclude the escape of radioactivity into the environment," they said without mentioning years.

The IAEA's fourteen-member INSAG group read this with some skepticism. "The long-term entombment of Unit 4 will, of course, be a major technical innovation of great interest to nuclear-safety experts," they said. They did not question either the concept nor design of the pyramid-scale sarcophagus. But they wondered out loud about its longevity. "Plant lifetime — the duration of a nuclear-power plant's exposure to extreme events — is generally taken as about fifty years." How long did the Soviets expect the encasement to last? If the answer was much more than fifty years did they provide for updating the structure a half-century hence? Would its containment value hold up in relation to the decaying radiation within? The Soviet authorities did not definitively answer such questions, though Legasov said towards the year end that the underlying slab structure could accommodate laboratory facilities to monitor radiation and temperature, the concentration of nuclear-fission products, rate of radioactive decay, physical changes and the seismic stability of the structure for years to come.

The scope and timing of the entombment project was impressive. The combined structure that houses Chernobyl power units 3 and 4 approximates the Great Pyramid of Cheops in size. Soviet engineers were about to encase half of this structure in radiation-proof concrete, equip it for long-term ventilation and build an air-conditioned slab floor below the reactor vault, beneath the two-level suppression pool, under the existing foundation. To first cool and isolate the base of the reactor vault with nitrogen and to move construction crews and supplies to the subterranean work place required a man-sized tunnel 136 metres long. It was underway in late May and completed in about two weeks. "Subway builders, Donetsk miners and servicemen are working shoulder to shoulder here in difficult conditions," said vice-chairman Silayev, noting that combat conditions were a lot different from those on paper.

Said *Nature*: "Operations around the damaged reactor have been organized in typical Soviet style with planned targets and campaigns to beat them. The miners drilling under the reactor have a target of five reinforcement rings to be installed per shift, a rate twice that in normal mining operations." The science magazine had been covering the international scene since 1870 and tried not to sound impressed. In fact, the pace of the work was set by caution, not zeal. Every minute in the hot, humid and radioactive environment beneath Chernobyl-4 was one too many. The temperature where they tunnelled "did not exceed" forty-five degrees Celsius. Radioactivity measured three to four roentgens per hour — nearly a year's safe exposure under normal working conditions. The tunnellers were kept under close and constant medical surveillance. Blasting posed another concern. Said *Pravda* with judicious understatement: "Precaution was necessary because the tunnel openings had to be made with minimum blasts as unwarranted shaking in the area of the reactor was undesirable."

Leningrad subway builders began with a pit "steep as the side of an ocean vessel" alongside Chernobyl-3. From this pit, 388 Donetsk coal miners began to tunnel in solid sandstone. "Shaft drivers from the Donetsk Basin, the Donetsk Provincial and Moscow Basin Mine Construction Combines are spearheading the attack to eliminate the accident consequences as quickly as possible. Specialists from the Ukraine Institute of Coal Mining Geology are working on lowering the groundwater level. The best people and most up-to-date equipment have been assembled. Over four-hundred people in all are participating in round-the-clock combat against radiation and water," a *Trud* correspondent reported. They worked in brigades that comprised of tunnellers, machine operators, electricians and bulldozer drivers. There were eight three-hour shifts daily and their "tour of duty" lasted fifteen days.

"We were given a very tight schedule for reaching the damaged reactor and putting a cooling slab under it," the Donetsk construction combine director told *Trud* on May 21. "But I see that we'll be able to get it done several days early. They began by doing forty centimetres and one ring of tubing an hour. Today the shaft drivers are handling sixty centimetres of rock in that time. The teams replace each other at the rock face, at the tunnel entrance or in the pit. Those in here today are closing the pit with polyethylene film leaving only enough opening to take out the dirt and bring in necessary building materials. The cabs of the excavators, the cranes and the bulldozers are lined with lead sheets. The air intake will soon be covered with filtering material and fitted with a fan to send fresh air to the rock face. The tunnel is extending farther and farther from the pit and we can't get along without ventilation." The tunnel was 1.8 metres in diameter, the height of a man, but the miners were accustomed to such close working quarters said *Pravda*. What took conditioning was their location. They were not far below a ruptured reactor vault which just days earlier had been incandescent hot and leaking more radioactivity than any nuclear plant had ever done before.

The tunnel was equipped with high-voltage power lines, piping to supply refrigerating nitrogen, a conduit to carry fast-forming cement under pressure, conventional mine-style rail cars to remove more than a thousand cubic metres of excavated material while supplying men, tools and materials to the construction area. Where the tunnel took them the underground brigades cautiously carved out, formed up and back-filled to build a gigantic slab-shaped reinforced-concrete cooler. Sixty days after the Chernobyl disaster the crucial subterranean construction work was completed. The slab structure served four purposes.

It formed a water, heat and radiation-proof barrier between the reactor building and the water table. It contained a unique heat-exchanger built into it for long-term cooling of the reactor core above. It reinforced the suppression pool compartments to isolate contaminated runoff water and it formed a base for the cement coffin that would entomb Chernobyl-4. Initially conceived as "double insurance against the extremely low risk" of a *rasplavleniye*, the vast slab structure had become the engineered basement for a sarcophagus. Perhaps it, too, might centuries hence become a tourist wonder like the Great Pyramid of Cheops.

Before the sarcophagus structure could be built, of course, the site had to be sufficiently decontaminated to allow construction crews to work three or four-hour shifts without undue exposure. Late in May vice-chairman Voronin promised, "In the near future two concrete walls would be brought in on powerful trailers to enable us to expand the work front behind this biological protection." Meanwhile *Trud* reported that "work directly with pieces of Unit 4 is only permitted by robot equipment and machinery that is, itself, reliably protected against radiation by lead sheets and thick armour." Throughout the summer decontamination proceeded in three stages. Adjacent to Unit 4 a surface layer of soil was peeled back like sod and removed for burial. This was done by robot-controlled, earth-moving equipment. Then the area was paved both to provide a waterproof surface and to facilitate the movement of self-propelled cranes and other construction machinery. Beyond the immediate area of Chernobyl-4 the Red Army's decontamination teams applied their "counter-poisons." One was a polyethylene spray that "on hardening gripped the dust and other radioactive refuse so tightly that the film formed can be easily rolled up like a carpet and carried off to a burial site."

In the first hours of the Chernobyl disaster as firemen fought to quell some thirty blazes, the ventilation system continued to operate carrying radioactive contamination from the wrecked reactor vault through the common turbine hall to the surfaces of equipment and walls of the other units. Radioactive dust churned on the hot drafts. Molten graphite and fuel fragments burned through the turbine-hall roof. Three weeks later gamma radiation in compartments of the first and second Chernobyl units ranged between ten and a hundred milliroentgens per hour, that is 800 to 8,000 times the normal background. In the turbine hall it was two to six times worse. Plastic, steel, concrete and other wall surfaces differed in the degree to which they retained radioactive dirt or released it to washing agents. The contamination fighters had a special approach in each case. High-pressure water from fire hydrants, automated washing equipment, steam ejection, sand-blasting, decontaminant sprays, plastic-polymer covers, scrub brushes and elbow grease were all employed. By late summer the gamma radiation had been reduced to a tenth or fifteenth of its initial level to meet international occupational health standards.

To get Units 1 and 2 going again meant isolating them from the high radiation levels emitted at the other end of the reactor complex. The two reactor wings — Units 1 and 2 at one end, Units 3 and 4 at the other — shared a long, common turbine hall. Step one was to isolate the first wing with a heavy metal shielding wall across the turbine hall 200 metres from Chernobyl-4. Step two was to separate Units 3 and 4, an operation akin to parting Siamese twins after one has died. A massive concrete wall blocked off one from the other but the ultimate engineered encasement structure around Unit 4 would utilize the common 150-metre chimney as part of its complex ventilation system. The third step was to build metre-thick protective walls around the perimeter of Unit 4. These walls, seventeen to seventy-one metres in height, would later form the sides of the tomb. The large pile of radioactive debris spewed out at the northwest corner of the reactor building, the ruptured reactor top, the fire and explosion-ravaged roofs, were all to be enclosed within massive concrete terraces. The perimeter of the entombed reactor site was 800 metres.

The INSAG team tallied up the weights of these metre-thick walls and terraces and found them disconcerting. "The effect of this new load on the foundation or leakage into the ground water through the foundation slab were not discussed," they said unhappily. On the other hand they were impressed that Soviet engineers had planned a very durable structure. Tests showed that the concrete they had developed with a calcium-hydrate binder for the entombment would withstand temperatures above 2000 degrees Celsius, almost double the heat at which most concrete will melt.

In October Valery Legasov told participants at the World Energy Congress that he and his colleagues had been able to personally examine rooms and facilities of the ruined reactor earlier that month. "Very close by operational people were restarting Unit 1 in a normal radiation environment," he said. The second unit was soon to follow. By mid-December the concrete shroud completely enwrapped Chernobyl-4. Eight months since the world's worst nuclear accident the Shcherbina commission reported that, "The destroyed reactor has ceased to be a source of radioactive contamination."

6

Jolly Little Beggars

"Ions are such jolly little beggars, you can almost see them."

—— ERNEST RUTHERFORD, MONTREAL, 1903

ONE MORNING IN 1903, AT THE DAWN of the atomic age, Ernest Rutherford struck a concept in his mind's eye. He was thinking of ions, atoms stripped of their electron controls to dance free and bedevil mankind. "Ions are such jolly little beggars, you can almost see them," he told a fellow professor at McGill. He was anticipating a century in which the little gremlins would srtike images on the bile-green screens of fluoroscopes, television and radar sets, computers and electronic games. He did not foresee their darker bellwether role, little demons sounding the tocsin of Bomb tests and runaway reactors.

Midway through the nineteenth century German glass-blower Hans Geissler fashioned a novel piece of laboratory equipment. It was a misshapen bulb that gave off a weird green light. Subsequent investigators tracked its glow to the "cata" or downside of an electrical circuit and concluded that this cathode tube was emitting electrically charged particles at light-like speed. In November 1895 Wilhelm Konrad Roentgen found that cathode rays did more than make the glass glow green. They triggered an unseen beam of energy from a metal target to fog well-packaged photo film as if it had been exposed to daylight. Within weeks physicians as far afield as Montreal's Royal Victoria Hospital were using these unseen X-rays — X for the unknown — to probe for bullets in flesh, to examine broken bones. Within a year Henri Becquerel in Paris found similar penetrating rays coming from uranium ore. Across the channel at Cambridge, Joseph John Thomson studied the electrified wake that X-rays and uranium rays left in the air to mark their passage.

On the boundary of a new realm where measurements verged on obscurity and numbers ran close to the infinite, Becquerel and Thomson sensed that keener, young minds and ingenious measuring devices were needed. That summer Becquerel sent Marie Sklodowska Curie in quest of uranium's rays. She duly identified them as gamma radiation, atomic emissions so energetic they penetrated two inches of lead or a foot of concrete. Tracking them Marie and Pierre Curie discovered radium. Thomson set Rutherford on the electrified track that X-rays left behind them. The young scientist soon concluded that X-rays and gamma rays knocked electrons off the surface of atoms to put them out of electrical balance. In their wake such invisible radiation left a trail of dancing electron-short atoms, "ions" Rutherford called them, using the Greek for "to go." He was thinking of their migration to a battery post or electrical terminal. Or perhaps he had read of the young god Ion, son of Apollo, who was almost poisoned by his mother. In any case, the ion was a forerunner of forces on the move and they frequently spelled trouble.

Rutherford built modern atomic theory on his concept of ion behaviour. With a graduate student, Hans Geiger, he developed a radiation counter based on the jolly little travellers. Radioactive rays electrified atoms into an ionized path that formed a circuit from one end of the counter to the other. You could hook the circuit to a meter, dial or beeper and record radiation intensity. At McGill he also used a gold-leaf electroscope which waved an arm to signal electrified air. This duly evolved in miniature to a finger-sized dosimeter that measures radiation dosage. He found, as well, that alpha rays — helium atoms stripped electron-free — would ping scintillating light from a zinc-sulphide screen. That was another way to detect and measure radiation. About 1920 Vladimir Zworkin in the Soviet Union and Phil Farnsworth in the States applied this scintillation to develop a TV screen. As George Orwell predicted it took another half-century to subdue the masses so they would squat trance-like in front of it. Meanwhile the boffins found that the most effective radiation detector was based on the original discovery that the invisible rays fogged photo film. So nuclear workers everywhere wear film badges to record the radiation they receive.

Roentgen, Becquerel and Madame Curie gave their names to units of measurement in this strange business. A roentgen is equivalent to about one two-hundred thousandth of a horsepower of potential energy. A becquerel counts one atomic disintegration per second with its attendant burst of radiation. A curie is equal to the frenzy of 2.2 trillion self-destructing atoms every minute. The rays from those disintegrating atoms electrify air to buzz a Geiger counter, make a scintillometer ping, fog film. They also penetrate clothing, skin, flesh and bone to electrocute human cells or warp their growth. Beam enough atomic radiation at body organs and the cells will degenerate to cancerous growth. Beam more and you may kill the cancer.

Ions, the jolly little messengers, report these energetic happenings meticulously. But since August 6, 1945 they have been weighted with semantic ballast. Words dim reality. At best, words prompt pictures in the mind. In the wake of the Bomb the word "Hiroshima" triggered the picture of a violent thundercloud roaring upward till stratospheric winds rounded its top to a mushroom shape. Such word images fade quickly. Details disappear; shapes are blurred. The picture becomes an abstraction. Just days after the man-made apocalypse the Hiroshima cloud dimmed in our collective psyche. It lost its convulsive motion, the awesome darkness within its stem. Its furious outreach was capped. In awe, fear and incomprehension we repressed the reality of the Bomb. All we retained in conciousness was the vague mushroom shape. In guilt, we reduced that to a mere symbolic configuration. Nuclear warfare was reduced to a pictograph. Then in the early 1950s the Bomb tests began and the tocsin of frenzied ions gave sound to repressed images.

The Americans exploded eight nuclear weapons, two in anger, and the Soviets tested just one in the 1945-1949 period. But in the 1950s there were 188 Bomb tests by the States, seventy-one in the USSR and twenty-one by the British. Within weeks of these detonations the radioactive iodine content of the Bombs had spanned the earth, fallen in rain, gone to milk. The strontium and caesium atoms formed in the Bomb bursts of the fifties seeped into growing bones of an entire generation. The Test-Ban Treaty of 1963 stopped most — not all — atmospheric weapon testing but by then the fallout was providing about one eighth of the radiation exposure the average person experienced from all sources in any year. It was enough to warrant constant watching. Canada, like most developed countries, established an environmental, radiation-monitoring program in 1959. When Chernobyl triggered ion alarms, Canada Health and Welfare alerted airport weather personnel at twenty-eight locations from Vancouver to St. John's from Resolute south to Windsor, Ontario, to check air filters and rain gauges for the tell-tale bellwethers. So did authorities around the globe. The pings, beeps and scintillations of trillions on trillions of frenzied ions were again a reminder of nuclear fury.

Zinaida Fyodoroyna Kordyk collected the air filters herself that Saturday morning. As head of Chernobyl's weather office she had a staff of six to take air and rain samples, analyze soil moisture and observe cloud movement eight times daily. But on April 26 she was called from sleep before dawn to see to the readings herself. The toneless voice of authority awakened her. It came from the Ukrainian Hydro-meteorological Centre at Kiev and the weatherwoman acknowledged it without making conversation. She saved her questions until she had hung up and was hurriedly dressing. What was so vital as to demand her personal attention to a routine chore before daybreak? And why the special concern about air sampling? Perhaps there was a radiation leak at the Chernobyl atomic power station. Perhaps someone in Kiev, or perhaps Moscow, was just being officious. The weather office is about two kilometres south of the town of Chernobyl. As she cycled there Zinaida Kordyk may have recited the Russian version of a universal ditty: "Bigger fish have bigger fish upon their backs to bite them. And bigger fish have bigger fish and so *ad infinitum*."

The one-storey Chernobyl meteorological building is near the junction of the Uzh and Pripyat rivers, twenty kilometres downstream from the Chernobyl nuclear station. The Uzh and the Pripyat are among a half-dozen rivers tapped to fill the Kiyevskoye reservoir, a man-made lake of 700 square kilometres that drains a watershed 140 times larger. The great Dnieper flows in and out of the reservoir and on the south it is joined by the Desna River. As she collected the air, water and soil samples from outdoor cabinets, Zinaida Kordyk was aware that she stood at the hub of a giant waterwheel which supplied the capital city of Kiev. More than that, to contaminate this water system would be to pollute the heart of the Ukraine.

A heavy fog had settled in through the night; the surface wind was light and variable. Back in the weather office she found that a stronger wind was blowing from eleven to fourteen kilometres per hour at 1500 metres and that it was moving northerly towards Finland. With its global connections, the teletype printer told her, "The weather in Europe is dominated by a strong high-pressure area over the western parts of the Soviet Union and a low-pressure area that reaches from Iceland to northwestern Europe." As the day advanced she was advised that a new low-pressure centre had formed in Scandinavia and moved west to the Norwegian Sea. That made room for the very warm air mass that was presently fogging in the Ukraine. It would move quickly north in the afternoon. STUK, the Finnish Centre for Radiation and Nuclear Safety, would duly report that, "Upper wind velocities varying between thirty and sixty kilometres per hour meant that the emission plumes moved easily in a good twenty-four hours from the accident area to Finland."

Like her counterparts at STUK in Finland and Sweden's SSI, like meteorologists everywhere have done routinely or on demand since Bomb tests began, Zinaida Kordyk collected a glass-fibre air filter from an outdoor case. Back at the Chernobyl weather lab she inserted the sheet, identical to a furnace filter though smaller, in a scintillation counter. That device counted the nuclear sparks twinkling from excited atoms. Casually she watched the scintillometer's digital read out spinning numbers. But the instrument was apparently misbehaving this morning. In seconds it had piled up a ridiculous count. Unaccustomed to doing this chore herself, Zinaida checked the settings and did a recount. Then she summoned a lab technician. He confirmed the reading. Anyone outdoors twenty kilometres south of Chernobyl Atomic Power Station that morning was getting as much radiation in an hour as they would normally get in four months.

"Thirty-six milliroentgens an hour!" Zinaida was incredulous. When no one in Kiev disputed the reading she was more confused than ever. John Runnalls remembers similar incredulity at Chalk River the day of the NRX meltdown. No one readily accepts disastrous news. Brian Finlay recalls the health physicist at Windscale who thought the monitors were faulty the day a graphite fire set sirens screeching. Like all weather people, Zinaida Fyodoroyna Kordyk knew what the laboratory apparatus was measuring, how it worked and that she was not mistaken. After years of conditioning that nothing ever went wrong it was difficult to believe indisputably bad news. But the weatherwoman was professionally trained. When she was certain of her data she passed it along to the Ukraine weather service headquarters. After all more than 130 years of technology assured its validity.

Zinaida was the first of thousands of meteorologists, radiologists, engineers, bureaucrats, politicians and journalists worldwide who would be confounded by the roentgens, becquerels and curies of errant energy that poured from the Chernobyl-4 reactor that week. Radioactive particles rose on the hot updraft of a furious, then smoldering, graphite fire. The fragments fixed on water droplets to form cloud, a plume that moved on upper winds. In its wake this irradiating plume left ionized air. Trillions times trillions of jolly little beggar ions bedevilled an innocent world.

Equally confounding were the myriad of bureaucratic corridors through which the news of these Chernobyl radiations were processed. The Chernobyl weatherwoman was just one of several throughout the Ukraine reporting to the republic's weather service centre in Kiev. As the Soviet response to the nuclear accident intensified several offices in Moscow were fed by national sources of nuclear information. The Soviet ministries for hydrometeorology and environmental protection, for health, for agro-industrial activity and the Soviet Atomic Energy Commission each had their own teams monitoring air, water and soil samples in the path of the Chernobyl plume. So did the USSR Academy of Science. At the nuclear power station itself, in Pripyat and throughout a thirty-kilometre zone around Chernobyl yet others were tracking the jolly little radiation bell-ringers. Before dawn that Saturday morning General Berdov ensured that firemen, police, civil-defense teams and Red Army patrols were all equipped with dosimeters, those pen-sized detectors that Rutherford had suggested some eighty years earlier.

"Immediately after the accident measures were taken to implement continuous, effective monitoring of radiation conditions both at the Chernobyl nuclear-plant site and in the neighbouring populated areas," said the Soviet report issued at Vienna. "As the radiation conditions developed the scale and volume of dosimetric monitoring increased significantly. In the end more than seven thousand subdivisions of radiation laboratories, epidemiological centres and many groups of radiation-safety experts of scientific and laymen establishments throughout the USSR were mobilized to carry out the monitoring." Much of this effort was concentrated in the thirty-kilometre zone and on the 135,000 evacuees. They were checked two or three times if that was necessary to reassure them that they had not been harmed. The 203 radiation-sickness patients were examined, tested and measured by techniques and instruments at the forefront of nuclear medicine.

Much of the radiation monitoring was used to map out station decontamination strategy. In the month following the accident there was increasing application of monitoring services to the peril apparent to Zinaida Kordyk that first morning. About 12 per cent of the radioactive fallout was on the station site itself where it could be cleaned up with relative certainty. About 38 per cent was carried well beyond the Chernobyl district. But half of the fallout was within a twenty-kilometre radius — the hub of the waterwheel that serves the heart of the Ukraine, Kiev in particular. In all about 3 per cent of the Chernobyl reactor's nuclear inventory fell out on Byelorussia and the Ukraine.

"The initial radioactive plume from the reactor by-passed Pripyat," Leonid Ilyin told us at Vienna. "Then a really substantial change took place in the meterorological situation that caused the constant increase in the gamma dose rate one would receive in the open air." That prompted their decision to evacuate the town early Sunday afternoon. "Then we had another complex problem to determine where these people were to be taken. The radioactivity was continuing to come from the damaged reactor and it was necessary to ensure that we found truly safe regions and forecast where they would be." Ontario emergency planner Furrukh B. Ali heard Ilyin's report at the IAEA meeting with mixed feelings. "The Russians told us they would not consider evacuation if radiation levels were below twenty-five rems; that it was not mandatory to evacuate below seventy-five rems. In Ontario we would probably get people out of the area of a nuclear station with much less exposure not only because of different triggering levels but because we would take action much sooner based on computer models of anticipated radiation." The provincial emergency response organization has the computer facilities to correlate wind speed and direction with projected fallout. Moreover, Ontario Hydro has installed wind speed and direction instruments alongside radiation monitors in the control rooms at their nuclear stations.

Ali was less confident of the political process to implement emergency planning at home. Nearly twenty years since regional governments in proximity to Chalk River and Pickering nuclear reactors began to develop their own off-site emergency arrangements and months after Chernobyl, Furrukh Ali said, "We do have very elaborate plans for all of our nuclear stations. But there is a considerable amount to be done in transforming those plans into preparedness on the ground. We're quite satisfied with Ontario's plans. Now it is a question of putting them into terms of preparations."

The Soviets did not appear to have any site-specific emergency plan for Chernobyl. They relied on Ukrainian emergency services under General Berdov, on the armed forces decontamination teams, and on the team under Boris Shcherbina's direction. A remarkable aspect of their response was the ability of the nuclear experts to collate the numerous streams of information. Initially there must have been near chaos. Eventually the information from the thousands of monitoring sources was channelled to the twenty-three-member expert team under Valery Legasov's *de facto* direction. The nuclear research branch of the Ukraine Academy of Sciences played a key role. They established a "monitoring complex" in close contact with the republic's ministries for health, geology, natural resources, water use, housing and municipal services, and with the USSR meteorology and environment ministry. The Academy helped Ukraine authorities test milk and dairy products initially then they focussed on the water supply, particularly in Kiev.

Kiev city officials, themselves monitored soil, water, air and foodstuffs from the first word of the Chernobyl disaster. Within hours all four dairies serving the city population were equipped with radiation monitors, the first step "in a chain of manifold checks on dairy products enroute from farms to shop counters." That, said Kiev's chief sanitary inspector Vladimir Shestakov was "preceded by control over the quality of every litre of milk even before it went to the dairy."

As public concern mounted about fallout on water reservoirs Shestakov not only stepped up monitoring activity but made sure the population was aware of it. A fleet of minibuses, each boldly marked "Radiological Laboratory," sampled the water of the Desna and Dnieper rivers at ten-minute intervals in all districts of the city. The immediate danger was rain. If it fell on the Chernobyl Atomic Power Station it would almost certainly wash the radioactive fallout from the reactor, roadway and ground surfaces into the Pripyat River. The first move was to seed rain clouds milking their contents a safe distance away from Chernobyl. This was done effectively until the Pripyat was dyked. By May 4 Red Army soldiers were building an embankment for 7.5 kilometres along the river in proximity to the station site. Later dykes were extended for twenty kilometres along the Pripyat and one of its tributaries.

Rain didn't fall and the dykes did isolate the Kiev reservoir from contaminated runoff. With the collaboration of Kiev provincial and city resources, crews drilled three hundred deep wells within a week to supply the Kiev population with drinking water if rain polluted their source upstream.

In the end it was dust not water that threatened to spread the radioactive fallout from Chernobyl. A fortnight after the accident Ukrainian deputy health minister Anatoly Kasyanenko warned that weather conditions had "somewhat elevated the background radiation in Kiev and nearby localities." It was "hundreds of times below the level threatening to health" still officials were taking every precaution. "The residual background radiation is maintained primarily by dust. A moist atmosphere helps the dust to settle," Kasyanenko explained. Kiev streets were being heavily watered and he advised people to wet-mop their apartments, frequently dust clothing, keep their shoes clean.

"It is desirable to limit outings to the woods, to garden and orchard plots and to the beach. Children should not play in the sand. People should wear head coverings." Five days after the accident the radiation level in Kiev had peaked at about one millirem per hour. That was about a hundred times normal background but it dropped off quickly. In the first fortnight a Kiev resident — remaining outdoors — might have acquired about the same amount of radiation he would normally get in a year or about one-sixtieth the amount that would warrant evacuation.

Mindful of the demon images that tumbled down alongside the jolly electrifying ions, Kasyanenko kept his voice down and his tone homey. His boss, Health Minister Anatoly Romanenko took much the same approach. He weighed reality against human behaviour and put sound advice in calm terms. There was no profit in citing radiation numbers but it would have been recklessly dishonest not to advise prudence. "There is no direct threat to health of residents of Kiev or Kiev Province," he said on May 7. "The weather conditions right after the accident at Chernobyl ruled out the spread of radioactive substances toward the city. The work done at the station substantially reduced the escape of radiation to the environment. However, in the past few days with changes in wind direction and strength, a certain rise in the level of the radiation background has been observed in Kiev and in some districts of the province. This radiation level is not dangerous to health and is not an obstacle to regular work."

That said, Romanenko dealt with irrationality. "The unsupervised consumption of various so-called self-treatment preparations may harm one's health," he said. So would smoking. "One should sharply limit smoking or better yet stop it altogether. It is not just a harmful habit that weakens the body but dust particles are drawn in along with the tobacco smoke. Moreover, the opinion that alcohol possesses benefical properties these days has no basis whatsoever." A *Tass* correspondent pursued the booze issue. "We have heard serious discussion that round-the-clock trade in vodka has been opened in Kiev, that its price has been drastically lowered and how all the drivers working in Chernobyl are given special-issue Cabernet since the wine and vodka people are again saying this is very effective against radiation," he told Police General A.J. Ivashchenko.

"In Kiev and other cities of the province all alcoholic beverages are sold in conformity with the same rules that prevail everywhere and at the same prices. Of course all the cock-and-bull stories about alcohol's supposed beneficial effect against radiation are a patent fabrication," the police general advised.

"Normal tranquil life is proceeding in the Ukraine capital and in the adjacent areas. All enterprises are in operation," declared *Tass* on May 7. "Of course there is some anxiety, too, especially anxiety of parents for their children. Summer vacation is approaching. Lines have appeared at railroad and Aeroflot ticket offices. Dozens of extra long-distance suburban trains and Aeroflot flights are now being scheduled. Children from the evacuated area will be the first to be sent to Young Pioneer camps, sanatoriums and vacation homes." Said the health minister: " Those who make even the slightest complaints relating to general indisposition or a stressful situation are hospitalized and given a detailed examination. If necessary they are sent to specialized institutions although those have been isolated cases. The great majority of those hospitalized are people who have been truly in stressful situations such as the accident itself, the emergency evacuation or anxiety for relatives and friends."

In the wake of Chernobyl, Soviet press and officials spoke with a calm, candid and concerted voice. There was the unanimity of the centralized state where the mass of the population expects leadership and direction. But Western observers could not miss — unless they were venally disposed — the deep concern that the leaders felt for the mental and physical well-being of the people throughout the parts of the USSR that were touched by the actual and psychological fallout from Chernobyl. *Komsomolskaya Pravda* columnist Pyotr Polozhevets caught scraps of conversation on Kiev streets in those early days of May. "Do you know the level today? It's twelve hundredths!" "Twelve hundredths!" These exchanges would begin in surprise, fright or alarm but Polozhevets always knew where they were headed. "How does that compare with natural background radiation? What's the level per hour? Per month? Per year? What is it for an entire lifetime? Insignificantly small doses were received but some people refused to believe this."

The columnist tracked down popular rumours. "We know some physicists who set dosimeters on the balcony and registered three roentgens in two days. It's terrible!" Polozhevets phoned the physicists concerned. "What dosimeters? What roentgens? We have just returned to Kiev from a business trip," he was told. There are Canadian papers who could use a columnist like Polozhevets even on days when demons don't fall with the rain.

7

Fallout on Europe

"Nuclear power is to many an unkown quantity which inspires fear. So is the Soviet Union. . . . Even without Chernobyl the Soviet Union was facing an image problem."

— *LONDON TIMES,* MAY 1986

MODERN HISTORY HAS CONDITIONED THE FINNS TO sleep lightly. Like Canadians they lie on the restless shoulder of a superpower. Yet unlike Canada Finland was a latecomer to the nuclear age. Its first nuclear station was built at Loviisa in 1977 and it now operates a pair of Soviet-built plants both there and at Olkiluoto. There are other differences. Canadians witnessed the first Bomb test at Alamogordo, New Mexico in mid-July 1945 and were forewarned. The Finns, like other Scandinavians, did not sniff the air until atmospheric fragments brought hot news of nuclear-weapon testing a few years later.

Finland's Ministry of the Interior and its armed forces jointly maintain 270 radiation-monitoring stations. Under normal conditions loudspeakers amplify the desultory chatter of Geiger counters recording background radiation. When higher radiation levels are encountered pulse meters at twenty of these stations translate the number of atomic disintegrations every second into meaningful exposure from a human health point of view. The Finnish Meteorological Institute has its own network of ten stations where more sophisticated detectors can read the tell-tale particulates to get a fair idea of their origin. The state meteorologists were on strike that last week of April but events would hasten their return.

STUK for Sateilyturvakeskus, the Finnish Centre for Radiation and Nuclear Safety, maintains continuous sampling in proximity to Loviisa and Olkiluoto stations. When necessary it dispatches radiation patrols equipped with both disintegration counters and portable devices that identify the fingerprints of gamma rays, so to speak. There is a station at Nurmijarvi in the south and a mobile unit at Helsinki specially equipped to sample atmospheric dust. Rain gauges at both nuclear stations and at eighteen weather stations collect samples that are normally analyzed monthly. In the wake of Chernobyl this was done daily. Under normal conditions milk is sampled weekly up to six miles distance from Loviisa and Olkiluoto stations and at four more distant points. After Chernobyl, dairy farms throughout the southern half of Finland were subjected to control of every shipment while throughout the northern part of the country milk was sampled daily. Grain is usually sampled seasonally within a dozen miles of the nuclear stations; beef raised within twice that distance is checked twice yearly. The radioactivity in fruits and vegetables is generally monitored by taking a composite sample from several farms in each area every season. Chernobyl put such checks on a daily basis.

The Swedes began building nuclear-power plants in 1972 and today they have a dozen at four multi-unit stations. Back in 1957 they established twenty-five radiation-detection units to monitor the fallout from atmospheric nuclear-weapon testing. As Bomb-test fallout diminished these stations tracked the variations in natural background radiation. Then Sweden's own nuclear-power program relied on the monitoring service. "Now they have proved very useful to follow the gamma radiation levels after a severe nuclear accident," a Stockhom spokesman for SSI, the National Institute for Radiation Protection, told the clamoring world in May 1986. SSI stations were augmented by FOA, the Swedish National Defense Research Institute with its own nuclear detection laboratory, by the labs at each nuclear station and those at Swedish universities, by FOA sampling teams who were leap-frogged across the country in air force helicopters and by FOA's own high-altitude detection facilities.

The explosions and fire lofted a column of radioactive air and gases a kilometre above Chernobyl-4. In the first twenty-four hours that plume contained about twelve million curies of radioactive elements — about one per cent of the reactor's atomic energy. With low winds and fog prevalent that Saturday morning STUK experts figured the radioactive cloud must have "risen as a tight plume on the warm exhaust air." It did, moving northwesterly at between five to ten metres per second (eleven to twenty-two miles per hour). Most of the fuel fragments, radioactive dust and pulverized debris was heavy enough to drop out within the proximity of the reactor but the cloud contained sufficient jolly little ions to ring alarm bells in Scandinavia thirty hours later. On Sunday four million more curies of radioactivity was emitted. Some of that followed the same northerly path but much of it was carried almost due west into Poland two days later. The air-dropped blanket of sand and minerals cut the radiation by half in midweek. But on Friday the blanketed reactor heated up again and the emissions doubled. By Sunday the flow rate had doubled again and on Monday, May 5 some eight million curies were discharged. The plume that formed in midweek took two paths. One fallout route arced east, south and southwesterly through the Ukraine towards Romania; the other moved directly southwest into Romania.

The Legasov team calculated that about 4 per cent of the actual nuclear fuel in Chernobyl-4 was fragmented and thrown clear of the ruptured reactor. A small part of that fell on the station site to bedevil the firefighters in those first awful hours but most of the fuel was carried throughout the thirty-kilometre zone that would be evacuated on the second day. One microscopic bit of the reactor fuel landed on top of a boxcar headed for Finland. It was duly detected and removed by the vigilant Finns.

About noon Sunday, April 27, while Soviet authorities prepared to evacuate Pripyat, the first cloud ionized by Chernobyl radioactivity crossed the Gulf of Finland to drop its charged particles on a STUK monitoring post a thousand kilometres to the north. Those first droppings were perhaps three to six times the level of the normal background radiation. "They told the experts very little," STUK director Antti Vuorinen said. But by evening heavy rain washed a small sample of fallout from the Chernobyl plume onto filters at Kajanni radiation monitoring station in central Finland, 500 kilometres further north. It measured about one ten-thousandth of a roentgen per hour or about ten times the background radiation. It was not consequential but to experts manning radiological outposts every deviation from normal begs an explanation. STUK people discussed the Kajaani reading Monday morning and attributed it to accumulated radon released by melting snow. That afternoon a report from Sweden gave the Finnish readings new meaning.

"We heard that there had been a rise in the radiation level at Sweden's Forsmark nuclear power plant and that several fission products had been measured there," a STUK official said. "Now it became clear that their observations and ours were interconnected and there was exceptionally extensive fallout at hand." Forsmark is above Stockholm, due west of Helsinki, some 550 kilometres from the Finn's Kajaani station. The radioactive plume was indeed widespread. STUK instructed operators at twenty monitoring stations equipped with pulse meters to begin sampling the air for radioactivity every hour. By the following evening all three hundred stations in the Finnish network were measuring the fallout. The Finns were concerned but not alarmed by Chernobyl. People were advised not to drink rainwater for a few days but were assured lake and river water was safe. The Finnish authorities reported no radioactive iodine in milk or green vegetables since neither cows nor produce were outdoors so early in the spring. Nor did they report contaminated reindeer as Laplanders elsewhere in Scandinavia did. The only apparent casualties were a flock of four hundred migratory birds which must have flown through the Chernobyl plume enroute to a sanctuary in western Finland.

"We don't forget those whose livelihoods have been disrupted in other countries because of the radiation. Clearly an accident in a nuclear plant is an international matter," said Seppo Lindblom, Finland's trade minister. "But to consider resorting to fossil fuels as an environmentally easy international solution would be tantamount to refusing to face the facts."

The biggest of Sweden's nuclear-power stations, Forsmark has three high-performance reactors all built in the 1980s. Like nuclear facilities everywhere, Forsmark monitors every person entering or leaving the site. You thrust your hands into glove boxes and step on a pair of foot plates. If you are uncontaminated a green light signals an okay to proceed. But if you have picked up radioactivity above the normal background then the monitor will tell the world about it with a loud and insistent siren wail. A detection wand passed around any vehicle going in or out does the same thing. Several morning shift members reporting for work that Monday triggered the monitor alarm. It was evident that they or their cars had picked up a measurable amount of contamination. The most likely source was leakage or effluent from one of the three reactors. Sure enough a quick check found fallout everywhere on the station site. Station management could not locate the source of it but deciding "to play it safe" they began to shut down the reactors and evacuate six hundred employees.

The evacuation had just begun when the SSI network operated by the Swedish National Institute for Radiation Protection reported exactly the same experience at Studsvik energy research station. Studsvik is two hundred kilometres down Sweden's east coast from Forsmark. Given the wind direction that fallout was not of Swedish origin.

FOA, the Swedish National Defence Research Institute, and Studsvik's hot-cell lab facilities are geared for coordinated testing that will shape scattered evidence into a picture as vivid as a hologram. By noon Monday they were getting radiation counts four to fifteen times the normal background. More pertinent the airborne particles contained radioactive forms of argon gas and cesium in a combination that could not have originated in a Bomb test. Sweden's meterological institute now got into the act. As a daily service it provides Swedish defence authorities with radiation data analyzed in relation to wind speed and direction. "Monday morning they indicated that the radiation source was to be found in the direction of Lithuania, White Russia and the Ukraine," SSI's Mikael Jensen and John-Christer Lindhe recalled. "Suspicion first fell on the big nuclear station at Ignalina, Lithuania because it was the closest of the Soviet's nuclear facilities."

Public health advisories, stepped-up water testing, milk control and iodide pill distribution were tangible evidence that the radiation-detection nets had caught clouds of unusually high radioactivity. Moreover, as Swedish nuclear analysts quickly determined, the radiation did not emanate from a Bomb test. "What we have are readings which give a mixed picture all over Sweden. On average the ground-level radiation is two to three times higher than normal background radiation," SSI spokesman Bengt Peterson announced. "There are indications that there has been a fairly major accident although we have no substantive information as to the nature or extent of it."

That word from Sweden's nuclear safety institute was issued in mid-afternoon Monday, about twenty-four hours after the first fallout had been recorded on instruments at Studsvik and at Finland's south coast monitoring station. The Swedish announcement spanned the world with the speed of light. The world's worst nuclear accident had begun a thousand kilometres away with an explosion at 1:23 Saturday morning. General Berdov's emergency forces had identified it as a disaster by Saturday noon and the local population were evacuated a day later just as the first fallout from Chernobyl triggered alarms in Scandinavia.

At 10:00 a.m. Monday, Denmark's Riso National Laboratory noted "a surprisingly high radioactive content" in grass routinely sampled there. A second sample an hour later confirmed there had been no mistake. Their first reaction was to check on their own facilities. By early afternoon, however, they were advised of similar readings at Sweden's Forsmark nuclear station. They examined an air filter which had been in place since April 24 and were reassured. "It did not indicate any notable health risk." The evidence suggested that a nuclear accident had occurred somewhere east of them and this was confirmed by the Soviet statement carried on Danish radio about seven o'clock Monday evening. The plume from Chernobyl had actually passed over the Riso station about Sunday noon raising the background level by about 10 per cent.

At the Studsvik lab on the Baltic, seventy-five kilometres southwest of Stockholm, the fallout was not significant on Monday, April 28. In some isolated areas north of Stockholm rainfall later in the week resulted in radiation levels of fifty to a hundred times normal. By Monday evening, however, Swedish research personnel had identified several fission products, that is elements produced under intense neutron bombardment in a nuclear reactor but not normally found in nature. The most significant of these was iodine-131 which represented perhaps 70 per cent of all the radioactivity spewed from the Chernobyl-4 reactor. Since it's half life is eight days it would be nearly half gone in a week, three-quarters depleted in a fortnight, virtually disappear in a month. On the other hand iodine-131 is water soluble which means it mixes with rain, feeds grass roots from ground water and within a day or two winds up in milk. When consumed in milk or water, iodine-131 heads for the thyroid gland which is not surprising since the thyroid's function is to supply the body with iodine. Irradiating iodine in the thyroid can cause cancer. To prevent that authorities may distribute normal — non-radioactive — iodine tablets. They did this in the region surrounding Chernobyl, in parts of West Germany, northeast Poland and Romania. It was not necessary in Finland or Sweden.

The fallout was not significant in Finland until Tuesday when it amounted to about forty times the background radiation level at Uusikaupunki on the southwest coast and twelve to fifteen times the background at two other southern locations. The radiation at these points fell off by half in the following week. By Tuesday noon SSI reported that radioactivity levels appeared to have peaked in Sweden the previous evening and were now falling off as the wind shifted from southeast to northerly. It was at this point, about sixty hours after Chernobyl-4 exploded, that the chairman of the Soviet atomic energy commission Andranin Petrosyants advised IAEA director-general Hans Blix in Vienna that, "There was an accident at the Chernobyl Nuclear Power Plant. One of the nuclear reactors has been damaged. Appropriate measures are being taken to deal with the consequences of the accident and persons affected are being taken care of. A governmental commission has been set up."

Fallout on Europe

Nucleonics Week European editor Ann MacLachlan read the Soviet announcement on the teletype in McGraw-Hill's Paris office. A day earlier the endless chatter of the printer head had spelled out the first message from the Swedish nuclear institute. Now she resumed ringing phones along her beast from Britain's watchdog station at Didcot, Oxfordshire to the NATO ramparts of Scandinavia. At Studsvik Bengt Petersson again responded. "There are areas of the country which are normal and areas where the level of radiation is ten to twelve times higher than normal," he told her. Then he gave her the analysts' findings. Air, grass and milk samples had been examined by gamma-ray spectrometry, a process that, in effect, took the fingerprints of radioactive elements. There were elements in the fallout —neptunium-239, a daughter product of plutonium, for example — that could only have come from a runaway reactor. Particles a millionth part of a metre in diameter were probed with an electron microscope. They confirmed the fearsome heat that must have been generated. "The form and composition of these particles lead to an estimate of about 2,500 degrees Celsius in at least part of the reactor core," Studsvik lab experts said. They concluded there had been a meltdown. Nobody dreamed that a steam or chemical explosion might spew out radioactive vapour, fuel fragments and gobs of incandescent graphite.

While the first word of Chernobyl fallout came from Sweden on the Monday it had been detected both in Scandinavia and in Poland a day earlier. Increased background radioactivity was first detected in the northeast part of Poland Sunday evening by SRM, the Polish radiation monitoring service. SRM operates about two hundred monitoring stations and they were immediately switched from periodic examination of the radiation filters to an emergency schedule. By Monday air, water, soil and food samples were being examined. At several SRM stations the fallout was inspected by gamma spectrometry and radiochemical methods. By Tuesday the Polish Air Force was collecting samples at up to fifteen kilometres altitude while ground-hopping helicopters were measuring the fallout on food crops and the environment. All radiation data was coordinated through Poland's central radiological protection laboratory in Warsaw.

Beta and gamma radiation measured near ground level in Poland was only about double the background on April 29 and four times the background a day later. At that rate the average Pole might have accumulated, if he remained outdoors, about twenty-five millirems in the four days following Chernobyl. That, said an IAEA report, would have been equivalent to normal exposure over eighteen days time. Still radioactive iodine quickly collected on grass, soil and water. On Tuesday the iodine-131 level in milk was fifty times normal. By Saturday it was still a dozen times above the usual content. At no time did it exceed 2 per cent of what the IAEA considers a safe level.

European authorities tend to rely on a World Health Organization recommendation not to drink water or milk that has more than 2,000 becquerels of iodine-131 per litre, which means not more than about six hundred disintegrating, irradiating iodine atoms per second in a glassful. That standard is based on what is safe for *long-term* consumption. With its eight-day half life, this one-time output of iodine-131 from Chernobyl was not going to be around very long. Nonetheless, cautious authorities took prudent measures. Most cattle in Finland and Sweden were not outdoors in May but one Finnish cow that had been on pasture did accumulate nine times the iodine-131 level that WHO thinks is safe. Finnish emergency controls quickly spotted and dumped that cow's milk. On average in the month following Chernobyl Finnish and Swedish milk contained about thirty becquerels per litre of iodine-131, or just 1.5 per cent of the WHO standard. The West German government applies the European Economic Community's yardstick that milk and water should not contain more than five hundred becquerels per litre and in some parts of West Germany iodine pills were issued to the population under eighteen years of age. Poland nominally sets a 10,000 becquerel per litre limit but after Chernobyl it applied the International Atomic Energy Agency standard for children, which is half the WHO figure and a tenth of Poland's nominal limit. Iodine pills were issued to Polish children on April 29 and some milk was dumped because it was over the thousand-becquerel level.

Romanians in the eastern part of their country were advised to drink only deep well or mineral water, to wash fruit and vegetables thoroughly, and not to leave children outdoors too long because radiation levels were "much above" normal on May 1. The government was sufficiently concerned to have deputy prime minister Elena Cesusescu head up a commission to supervise precautions. But the Romanian press agency Agerpres angrily denied a West German foreign ministry report that the country was in a state of alert with people instructed to remain indoors and await further instructions via television and radio. Such reports were "completely groundless," said Agerpres. In Yugoslavia gamma radiation was measured at ten times normal in Belgrade on May 2, three times the normal background a week later. In Zagreb, Yugoslavia, fallout from Chernobyl peaked on May 4 when it was about five times normal and it sustained this level for about a week. In East

Germany the interior minister said, "There was no danger to us and there is none now. Atmospheric radioactivity rose for a short period then dropped again to normal."

In Western Europe, there was less radioactive fallout but more heat. At the Netherland's Bilthoven weather station near Utrecht gamma radiation peaked at triple the normal background rate on May 4 and returned to normal within a week. But there was enough political fallout in the first days of May for the Dutch cabinet to delay a decision on building more nuclear-power plants. Belgium's environment minister said the radiation level remained "virtually normal." The political fallout was most evident in West Germany where the Green party had conditioned the public to anticipate a Chernobylian disaster for years. Polled two months after the Soviet accident four of every five West Germans continued to oppose any expansion of their already large nuclear-power system; seven in ten wanted the sixteen existing plants phased out; one in five wanted them stopped immediately.

Sweden's minister of environment and energy, Mrs. Birgitta Dahl, told an IAEA meeting in September that, "Our experience of unacceptable damage from air pollution, nuclear-power accidents both in the West and East and chemical-industry disasters such as Seveso and Bhopal must make us avail of efficent and environmentally sound technology. Chernobyl led to comparatively serious radioactive fallout over parts of Sweden and measures to mitigate these consequences will have to be taken for many years to come. They will cost us hundreds of millions of Swedish crowns but the most serious effects are human and social." Acting on the electorate's instructions expressed in a 1980 referendum, the Swedish Parliament had already decided to cut fossil fuel consumption to a minimum and phase out its dozen nuclear plants by the year 2010. Chernobyl certainly stiffened Swedish resolve. Most of the cost to the Swedish government will be to compensate Laplander reindeer herdsmen who reported virtually all their animals in the central part of Sweden contaminated by the Chernobyl fallout to a degree that made them unfit for human consumption. The government agreed to compensate the Laplander herdsmen and sell the slaughtered animals for feed to fur farmers.

Laplander reindeer breeding is big business offering $100,000-a-year incomes to large-scale helicopter-borne herdsmen. Three Lapp herdsmen turned up at a press conference at the Ontario legislature a half-year after Chernobyl. Under Canadian anti-nuclear and Indian brotherhood auspices they were touring Eastern Canada to decry the nuclear industry that they said had destroyed their livelihoods. Paul

Doj, a Swedish publicist who herds reindeer himself, said they had been compensated that year but there was no assurance the Swedish government would continue to do so. What did he want from the Ontario government? "Stop selling your uranium to Swedish nuclear utilities," he said. His fellow herdsmen concurred. That was on October 16. Ten days later the touring Lapps wanted to take up reindeer husbandry in the Canadian north. They were no longer worried by Canada's north-country uranium mines, mills and refineries, nuclear-power plants as big as Chernobyl's nor the thought of their herds blundering into nuclear-waste dumps in the distant future.

Among members of the European Economic Community it was good business to think of Chernobyl in catastrophic terms. Italian authorities reported that normal background radiation had about doubled in the north of the country and was perhaps 50 per cent above the usual background in Rome on May 2. They emphasized that there was no danger and two days later the prime minister's office said that radioactivity was returning to normal faster than expected. Nonetheless, the health ministry banned the sale of leafy vegetables and milk consumption by children. Italian farmers were furious; the two-week ban would cost them $130 million, they said. The Italian government made no move to compensate its farmers but it was ready to deflect their anger. Italy was the most militant of EEC member-states calling for an indefinite ban on imports of fresh foods from Eastern Europe.

"The ban represents a coordinated EEC reaction to the Chernobyl accident and spread of radioactive fallout over most of Europe. However, the restrictions seem as much intended to place political pressure on the Soviet Union to release information on the radioactivity effects as to guard against any possible health risk from contaminated food," said *Agra Europe*, a British-based weekly publication covering European farm markets. "The Shcherbina commission cordoned off an imaginary area of a thousand-kilometre radius around Chernobyl and declared that fresh foodstuffs within this zone were suspect and should for the time being be refused entry into the Community. The zone takes in large areas of the USSR, Poland, Czechoslovakia, Hungary and Bulgaria, all of Romania. Large areas of Serbia and the productive farming area in Yugoslavia also came within the thousand-kilometre zone but were not included in the restrictions until Italy exerted pressure. Austria is similarly unaffected by the ban. Neither Austria nor Yugoslavia are members of Comecon."

A *Pravda* commentator raised the same question in mid-May. "One might wonder what connection there might be between the trade war raging on both sides of the Atlantic and in Western Europe with the Chernobyl accident," he said. He explained that the Americans had been threatening to take 'punitive measures' against West European produce suppliers for a long while. With Chernobyl there was pressure to get a congressional ban on food imports from Europe "under the pretext of sharply increased radiation there." World Health Organization authorities had been quick to state that there was no need for such a ban nor for a continuance of the initial precautionary measures in European countries. Despite this, "fears continue to be assiduously built up." It was, *Pravda* said, "irradiation by anticommunism."

The Chernobyl accident, said the French television program "TF-1," "was a convenient excuse for certain politicians to impose an embargo on agricultural products." "TF-1" noted that while Italy complained that other EEC countries had stopped buying its milk after Chernobyl the Italians had barred French produce. The ban on Eastern European produce by EEC member states, said France's *L'Humanité-Dimanche*, was "openly discriminatory and dictated by purely political considerations."

The fallout from Chernobyl reached Britain on May 2 and the National Radiological Protection Board predicted that the average Briton would get about 4 per cent more background radiation in the year ahead. However, the fallout was relatively short-lived and the British Department of the Environment downgraded even that figure. The average exposure would likely be imperceptibly higher than normal, they said. Brits who drank tapwater that week or milk on May 2 would have consumed about one-tenth of one per cent of their normal radioactive intake for the year, said Sharon Kingman in *New Scientist*. Yet other British media were incensed. Said *The Economist*: "The political fallout from Chernobyl is slowly settling on Moscow. One casualty is Mikhail Gorbachev's reputation for decisiveness and openness. Distrust the Kremlin's count. The world's worst nuclear accident may have killed scores of people already. Hundreds perhaps thousands will probably die from cancer and other delayed effects well into the next century."

The venerable *Times of London* observed that, "Nuclear power is to many an unknown quantity which inspires fear. So is the Soviet Union. The combination of the two in the world's biggest nuclear disaster has consequences far beyond the vicinity of Chernobyl. Even without Chernobyl the Soviet Union was facing an image problem." In fact, when the rhetorical smoke lifted from the Cold War battlefield it was notably calm. The world's worst nuclear accident had happened and its impact had been widespread in the USSR, but certainly not catastrophic. Thirty-one people had been killed on site, none off it. There had been 203 cases of radiation sickness including twenty-nine of the fatalities; all of them involved nuclear-plant staff or firefighters. The 135,000 evacuees had been subjected to exhaustive examinations and none showed evidence of illness or injury. Theoretically and statistically some thousands of Soviet and other European mortals would die of cancer induced by the Chernobyl fallout — instead of cancer from some other pathological agent or from another fatal affliction. A thousand square kilometres of prime farm land had been immobilized, probably for some years. The Soviets put the disaster cost at two billion rubles or about $4 billion, a substantial sum but less than 5 per cent of the value of the USSR's industrial output in 1986.

The Economist was wrong about Gorbachev. Within ten hours he had directed deputy prime minister Boris Shcherbina to round up a score of the USSR's top nuclear experts and get Chernobyl under control. Within sixty hours he assured that the IAEA knew all that the Soviets did themselves. Within a week the ambassadors or charges d'affairs of Austria, Britain, France, Finland and the Netherlands had been received at the Kremlin to hear Soviet concerns and regrets. Within ten days the Soviet leader had invited the IAEA director-general to inspect the Chernobyl site himself.

At mid-month Mr. Gorbachev spoke to the Soviet people on television. The Chernobyl accident had been "extraordinary and dangerous" but he reminded the world that it now had more than 370 nuclear plants generating power and they would not go away. Then he ticked off the more hysterical claims of the mass media in the Western world. "Thousands of casualties," "common graves," "extinction of Kiev," "all of Ukraine's soil has been poisoned." It was the old cry of havoc in barbaric Russia. Did "the leaders of the capitalist powers want to use Chernobyl as a pretext to distract the world public from uncomfortable but real problems? How to end the arms race? How to rid the world of the nuclear threat?" Gorbachev asked. "We perceive this tragedy quite differently. We understand that it is yet another ringing of the bell, yet another stern warning that the nuclear era calls for new political thinking."

What is called for, Gorbachev said, is "a serious deepening of cooperation within the framework of the International Atomic Energy Agency to create international rules for safe development of nuclear-power engineering. . . a system for prompt notification in the event of accidents or malfunctions. . . an international mechanism on both a bilateral and multilateral basis to provide mutual assistance as fast as possible." He urged that the IAEA hold a "highly authoritative conference" at Vienna and he proposed that its member states increase the IAEA budget to update its staff, resources and expertise. UN agencies such as the World Health Organization and the UN Environmental Program should "become more actively involved in the safe development of peaceful nuclear activity."

The IAEA did hold a "highly authoritative conference" a dozen weeks later at which Valery Legasov and Leonid Ilyin were the star performers. Three hundred and eighty nuclear scientists and engineers and 204 journalists listened in fascination to the Soviet report on Chernobyl. They looked over a TV cameraman's shoulder as his lens swept through wrecked sections of Chernobyl-4; they saw deputy premier Boris Shcherbina, Legasov, Ilyin, and General Berdov dealing with a crisis in a bunker six hundred metres from the reactor. They were taken through a three-hundred-page report of data and diagrams which they were invited to challenge — and did. Three months after Chernobyl the 584 participants at Vienna returned to their fifty countries with an update on the USSR's state of technology, its ability to cope with disaster, its readiness for international collaboration.

"Chernobyl made it clear the IAEA had to produce the international collaboration that would guarantee that the world could reap the benefits of nuclear power in safety," said British Energy Minister Peter Walker. "Our prospects of achieving that aim have been considerably enhanced by the manner in which the Soviet Union has provided the facts to the international community. They have not covered up."

For a leader "facing an image problem even without Chernobyl," Mikhail Gorbachev had orchestrated a remarkable recovery. It was a bravura performance.

8

Nuke Towns

"Women are found here who have married seven husbands, all of whom this terrible consumption has carried off to a premature death."

— GEORGIUS AGRICOLA, *DE RE METALLICA*, 1556

"Generations of Port Hopers have worked at Eldorado and you don't play games with over five hundred jobs and the best wages in town."

— PENNY SANGER, *BLIND FAITH*, 1981

"The town council has given us a good apartment. My husband has a well-paid job. We don't even notice that we live close to a nuclear-power plant."

— GALINA SYCHYOVSKAYA, PRIPYAT RESIDENT,
FEBRUARY 1986

JOACHIMSTHAL, ON THE BOHEMIAN FACE of the Erzebirge mountain bordering Germany, was the world's first nuke town. When Georgius Agricola became the town doctor in 1527 its eight thousand miners had not yet dug through the silver ore down to the shiny black pitchblende below. Yet by the mid-1500s — centuries before Joachimsthal supplied the Curies with radium ore, Rutherford with uranium or the Czechs with a tourist-rich spa — the miners were coughing up the first symptoms of lung cancer.

"Bergsucht," they said, meaning mountain sickness. They thought it was borne along the stopes by evil, underground dwarfs. In fact it was dust borne, Agricola told them. "The dust has corrosive qualities; it eats away the lungs and implants consumption. There are Bohemian women here who have lost seven husbands to the miners' disease." He advised the women to make fine lace-net hoods that their husbands could wear as dust filters and he devised a way to ventilate the mine shafts with horse-driven bellows. Agricola's *De Re Metallica* was the first mining handbook and probably the first on industrial medicine. At Joachimsthal in succeeding centuries it fostered an ambivalent mix of serious research into radiation hazards and a tourist industry based on the radium mystique.

Joachimsthal citizens backed into nuclear industry. Pitchblende was first mined here in 1790, just a year after a Berlin druggist identified uranium in the ore. Half a century after that the Imperial and Royal Uranium Colour Factory was established to supply glassware and pottery makers with uranium-based orange, yellow and green dyes. They developed a yellowish hue for false teeth and another by-product as well. Small amounts of mine tailings were ground to powder which they spooned into little leather pouches. These found a ready market among arthritis and rheumatism sufferers taking the mineral waters at the nearby Karlsbad Spa. Beneath the pouches the skin would tingle, warm, itch and inflame to confirm the mystical powers cast from Erzebirge depths. These radioactive amulets led in due time to such American nostrums as Radiumite — "Put one or two pieces in your pocket or in a chemois bag. It keeps you well when you carry it" — and Aqua Radium — "Mixed with milk it makes it more digestive for children and invalids." An English firm made Sparklet's Radon Bulbs which the British masses could squirt into soda water to enjoy "the benefit of radium emanation normally obtained by residence at a spa."

Yet Agricola established occupational health studies in these Erzebirge towns. *De Re Metallica* in hand, Schneeberg physicians just across the mountain from Joachimsthal began a systematic review of miners' deaths about 1870. As Agricola had suspected, lung cancer was the dominant cause. When they improved underground working conditions the yearly death toll from lung cancer among local miners dropped from more than 3 per cent to less than one. That was still a fearsome annual toll but so was the mortality of all other workers in those days. In the 1920s Aug Pirchan, chief physician at Joachimsthal's Radium Institute, narrowed the search for the cause of the *Bergsucht*. Treading in Agricola's footsteps Pirchan began performing autopsies with each miner's death. Of thirteen who died in 1929, nine had lung cancer. Such data spelled out a morbid pattern. About a dozen to fifteen years after miners opened a new section of the Joachimsthal mine they began to develop the symptoms of lung cancer. In the first days after tunnelling into a new area they would have inhaled air in which the radon, accumulated to potent strength over the years, had not yet dissipated. On such findings the Czech government later established the renowned Academy of Microbiology adjacent to the mine.

A generation earlier, in 1898 the Austro-Hungarian government gave Marie and Pierre Curie one hundred kilograms of leached uranium tailings from Joachimsthal mine and the Curies bought more at cost over the next four years. From this they isolated a fraction of a gram of radium, a naturally radioactive element on which the medical profession based hopes for a cancer cure and charlatans launched an age of quackery. Said *Nature* in April 1904: "Radium is the latest addition to the therapeutic armamentarium. The romance of its discovery, the mystery of its radiations and emanation, its relation to some important scientific theories and above all the possibility of it being the long-desired cure of cancer, have fixed upon M. and Mme. Curie's discovery the attention of the world." No one likely read past that reinforcement of their hopes but the magazine continued: "Radium has to be used with great care for it is powerful for evil as well as for good."

Radon, the radiating gas emitted by radium, competed with its mother element in medical usage. It preceded radium into turn-of-the-century labs before anyone understood the radioactive effect of either. By 1901 the Curies in Paris and Ernest Rutherford with Miss Harriet Brooks in Montreal independently isolated radon. Two years later Rutherford's collaborator Frederick Soddy was touting radon in the *British Medical Journal* to treat tuberculosis. Since it lost half of its radioactivity in four days it was not hazardous to patients, he said. At about the same time a British scientist found radon in Buxton and Bath waters. Such spas have promoted tourist traffic — a very competitive business — since Roman times. Joachimsthal was just twenty kilometres away from Karlsbad, famous for its mineral-rich water since the fourteenth century. Mindful of how their canny forebears exploited uranium dust, Joachimsthalers beat others to the radon water trade; in 1906 they claimed their town was "the first radioactive spa in the world." Six years later town fathers built the Radium Palace sanatorium which drew its water direct from the Joachimsthal mine.

Radium production was established as a government monopoly in 1903. Within a year the magic element was valued at $10,000 a gram.

Eight years later it was worth fifteen times as much but the price was nominal since they sold none of it. In those early years thirteen grams was processed and loaned out for clinical and research use. A Pittsburgh undertaker Joseph M. Flannery put an end to such non-enterprising radium trade. In 1912 he established the Standard Chemical Company to process low-grade radium ore found in Colorado and Utah. It was soon going abroad at $170,000 a gram. Standard Chemical's radium output overshadowed Joachimsthal production for a decade. Then an aggressive Belgian firm, Union Miniere du Haut Katanga, ran Flannery out of business. In 1932 a rugged Canadian individualist Gilbert Adelore LaBine challenged Union Miniere and split the global radium market with it. In an abandoned seed plant of a depression-hit town on Lake Ontario, LaBine established a radium refinery. Port Hope became Canada's first nuke town.

World War II changed countries and markets. Joachimsthal, which had been Bohemian, Austro-Hungarian, Czechoslovakian and German, became a Communist nation in 1948. Radium was replaced in medical practice by new radioactive sources, more precise and potent radioisotopes brewed in Canadian reactor kettles that had been designed to make Bomb fuel. The world's first nuke town was now called Jachymov and the ancient mine went back to uranium production. Cold War demands prompted its modernization. "After extensive uranium extraction and intensive exploitation," to meet Soviet requirements, Jachymov was mined out by 1963. But no resource was abandoned in postwar Czechoslovakia. They declared Jachymov a resort area and again exploited its historic potential to draw aching and pained spa-goers to soak in and sop up radioactive hot water. In 1975 the Czechs built a 268-bed sanatorium to which they pumped the radon-rich water from the Jachymov mine.

The radon-watered spa industry spanned national boundaries, ideologies, medical knowledge and an age of enlightenment. Bad Gastein's thermal springs near Salzberg, Austria has attracted health seekers since the Middle Ages. Challenged by Joachimsthal's first radioactive spa, Bad Gastein hotelmen installed therapeutic pools and piped water of high radon content from a local mine into bedroom sinks. Then German Reichmarshal Hermann Goering heard that conscript miners were improving in health despite twelve-hour shifts in the depth of the Bad Gastein mine. Goering exploited the tourist potential with a government-built *Heilstollen*, meaning thermal tunnel. Here the ill, the neurotic and the curious could ride small electric cars down hot, radioactive mine stopes and return for radon baths and "radium cocktails."

Said *Atom* magazine, "In 1980 one million nights lodgings were spent by tourists in Bad Gastein and each day 25,000 radon baths were prescribed there by the National Health Service of the USSR." *Atom* is the house organ of the United Kingdom Atomic Energy Authority. It did not explain why the Soviets were steering their citizens into capitalist Austria instead of to Czechoslovakian spas.

While tourists irradiated themselves for pleasure, miners did it for a living. By the century's turn occupational health studies — largely centred on Joachimsthal — had notably reduced mortality among uranium miners. Coal miners enjoyed no such respite; coal mining continued to be perilous for miners and coal towns. The dust and damp caused consumption; the gas exploded. Coal poisoned the atmosphere, acidified lakes, killed those who mined it. Consider that 388 miners died in the Oaks Colliery, Yorkshire explosion in 1866; another 268 died at Ebbw Vale mine in Wales a dozen years later; 344 more at Hulton Mine, Lancashire a generation after that. Another 430 perished at Senghennhydd, Wales a year before World War I; yet another 264 Welshmen died at the Gresford Coal Mine a half-century before Chernobyl. And in 1966, half a century after Welshmen had abandoned the Aberfan coal tip, its waste slid down the mountain side to bury 116 children with twenty-eight of their elders. Those were just the coal-related catastrophes. Solitary deaths went unnoted. In 1979 the US Bureau of Mines reported that more than two million people in nineteen states were suffering damage to their health and property from about 250 fires burning out of control in abandoned coal mines and pits. That was *fifteen* times the number of Soviet residents moved out of harm's way around Chernobyl. All consequences of the Chernobyl accident, said Valery Legasov a half-year later, "will not be any larger than the damage from coal during one or two years. Carcinogenic [cancer-inducing] substances released by coal are much higher than the effects of Chernobyl."

Harnessing running water would be safer, the power people said. Instead of burning coal to make steam to spin wheels and turbine blades it was simpler to put turbine generators in the path of rushing water. But the water had to be dammed so it would rush through a millrace. The trouble was that dams burst. About 2,200 people died when the South Fork Reservoir broke above Johnstown, Pennsylvania a century ago. Nearly 1,200 perished when the Vaiont Power Dam collapsed and washed out an Italian town and six villages in 1963. Dwarfed by Alpine peaks, the Mattmark Dam seemed secure enough but it drowned ninety Swiss in 1965. Fourteen years later the Gujarat Hydro-power

Dam ruptured killing at least 1,500 people in India. Two centuries into the Industrial Revolution it was becoming apparent that energy was not free of cost. The gods had put a price on it. The toll from those four power-dam bursts was almost *double* the estimated cancer fatalities that Chernobyl fallout *may* cause among 74 million Soviet people over their normal life span.

The Gujarat disaster was overshadowed by another power-plant accident in 1979. Three Mile Island generating station, a dozen miles downstream from Pennsylvania's capital city, had a reactor run riot. Nobody died from fallout but TMI blew ill winds around the world as Chernobyl would do seven years later. The TMI accident triggered the biggest headlines and scariest TV news since World War II. TMI was on an island in the Susquehanna River within proximity to eight towns but adjacent to none of them. Was it the insidious nature of the invisible and potentially lethal rays they spewed out that made TMI and Chernobyl so much more sensational than exploding tank cars or ships? Blast waves strike with the same sudden treachery as radiation. They are as unexpected by guileless victims and as deadly. The US warship *Maine* exploded in Havana harbour killing 260 sailors and starting the Spanish-American War. A Belgian relief vessel collided with a French munitions ship during World War I to devastate Halifax and leave 1,600 dead. A cargo of nitrates blasted Texas City thirty years later claiming four hundred lives. Despite these maritime disasters, on average *twenty* times as deadly as Chernobyl, in spite of oil-tanker spills and the fearsome weaponry that lurks in submarines, few question the perils of such commerce. Gas travels on the wind as silently, invisibly and lethally as a nuclear plume. Yet what industrial chemical enterprise anywhere on earth was closed down in memory of the 2,500 fatalities and 200,000 casualties of a poison gas leak at Bhopal, India in 1984?

All nuke towns were not born equal, of course. Port Hope, begun as a trading post, weaned and starved by alternate fortunes, was reborn in the radium boom and prospered with uranium demand. Deep River, Ontario and Hanford, Washington were established in wartime secrecy to brew plutonium for the Bomb. Deep River was carved from the Ottawa Valley backwoods a prudent ten kilometres from Canada's first atomic plant at Chalk River. "The plant may entail hazards of a nature and on a scale beyond all previous experience," Canada's wartime minister-of-everything Clarence Decatur Howe warned the builders. It did. On December 12, 1952 a power surge caused about 10 per cent of the reactor fuel channels in NRX (Nuclear Reactor Experimental) to melt and a million gallons of radioactive water spilled into the basement.

The water contained ten thousand curies of radioactivity, which is quite a bit considering that one curie amounts to 2.2 trillion atomic disintegrations every minute. On the other hand, Chernobyl-4 emitted at least five times that much radiation.

It took two years to clean up the NRX mess. But because it was well contained there were no injuries and no off-site consequences. A generation later Chalk River had become a national high-tech centre while Deep River down the road remained a picture-postcard town, peaceful and prosperous. The NRX accident sent Canadian nuclear engineers back to their drawing boards to design a better, faster-acting emergency shutdown system. Robert Popple, an eight-year-old Deep River schoolboy when the NRX meltdown sounded the sirens that winter day in 1952, was one of four Ontario Hydro engineers who discussed the applicability of Canadian fast-acting "scram rods" to Chernobyl-type reactors with the Soviets in Moscow in September 1986.

"Atom for atom the energy in radioactivity is 100,000 times that in most modern high explosives," C.J. Mackenzie told the Mackenzie King government. But Dean Mackenzie and C.D. Howe looked beyond the Bomb. "Canada has a unique opportunity to become intimately associated in a project which may revolutionize the future world in the same degree as the invention of the steam engine and the discovery of electricity," they said. Half a century since Rutherford's discoveries at McGill they were pushing Canadians into twentieth-century high technology.

The Chalk River project spawned other nuke towns in Canada. Elliot Lake thrived in Ontario's hard-rock country as miners drilled for the new smokeless, non-pollutant fuel. Cluff Lake and Key Lake sites became dormitories at the top of Saskatchewan as native northerners flew in from remote villages to produce uranium, one week on and one week off. On one arm of Ontario's Golden Horseshoe, where a third of the Canadian economy turns on low-cost electric power, electricity was generated by Niagara Falls in bygone days. On the other arm, where LaBine's Eldorado made Port Hope a company town, Ontario Hydro would build a world-class nuclear-power station at Pickering and another larger one at Darlington.

Across the southwestern Ontario peninsula on Lake Huron more than five thousand construction workers found seventeen years employment building eight nuclear-power plants, two heavy-water refineries and a nuclear-steam system for industry at the Bruce nuclear power development. Breadwinners from nearly half the homes in nearby towns worked there for most of that time. When construction wound down local councillors, businessmen and residents collaborated to lure new industry into their community with the promise of cheap nuclear-fuelled, process steam. "Before the nuclear complex came to the area this was basically a tourist town with minor industries and very few opportunities to keep young people in the area for a reasonable future," the mayor of a close-by town, Ian Jamieson, reminded citizens in later years. "There has never been any deputation to council showing any concern over the nuclear program. We accept it as a safe method of producing power." On two summer days in 1984 a hundred Bruce area residents pledged $1.4 million to help finance the industrial-steam project in partnership with Ontario Hydro and one of their own, Sam Mac-Gregor. A one-time electrician at the nuclear complex, MacGregor made and sank about a million dollars into his dream of an industrial development based on cheap atomic energy.

The Bruce communities, like Deep River and Pripyat, were new nuke towns born in an enlightened high-tech era where, as young Anelia Perkovskaya put it, "Everyone was told everything and they weren't just thinking of their own Pripyat." Port Hope, like Joachimsthal, was an old nuke town that evolved with the radium mystique. In the postwar world of heightened environmental concerns, public activists, news-hungry media and opportunist politicians Port Hope had an historic problem — more than a million tonnes of accumulated refinery waste, that could not be buried. Despite repeated engineering studies commissioned by the Atomic Energy Control Board and Eldorado Nuclear over a ten-year period the relatively safe, highly visible and extremely provocative crud remained undisposable because of the NIMBY — not-in-my-backyard — reflex. The waste problem pre-dated World War II when Eldorado was still refining radium. Then the wartime supply of radium for luminous dials and uranium for nuclear weapons greatly increased the volume of low-level radioactive waste. By 1955 the company was processing yellowcake, milled uranium oxide — not ore — which meant that less than one per cent of the radium content got to Port Hope. By then they had installed modern extraction circuits to radically cut the disposal problem. But the highly publicized rediscovery of two long-neglected waste disposal grounds and many radioactively contaminated home sites put the problem up front in 1976. The AECB dealt expeditiously with the contaminated home sites but the dumps defied solution.

It was a problem of concentric circles. Frustrated by politicking all around him, Eldorado president Nicholas Ediger was at the centre. "Port Hope will have to decide what it wants to be — a retirement town or an industrial town," he expostulated in 1979 as the company struggled to get approval to build a new world-class uranium refinery. In fact, the townspeople, themselves, had made their decision. As Penny Sanger put it in *Blind Faith*: "Generations of Port Hopers have worked at Eldorado and you don't play games with over five hundred jobs and the best wages in town." But the town itself could no longer accommodate the waste and the communal regard for Eldorado stopped at the city limits. The company's Port Granby waste site, in particular, bothered the rural people around them. Allan Lawrence, the area MP was their spokesman. "I hate to join the chorus of not-in-my-backyard," he said with no visible regret, "but surely there is some fairly remote place up north which would be interested."

Hanford, Washington was another nuke town born in wartime. US Army engineers bulldozed 430,000 acres of farmland and two small villages on the Columbia River to build the Hanford project. Within a year it housed 60,000 people and became the state of Washington's fourth largest city. Few residents in 1944 realized their community contained the world's first full-scale nuclear reactor. A year later three reactors were burning uranium to extract an even more potent substance from its ash. In the last months of World War II Hanford processing plants squeezed a few pounds of plutonium from the spent uranium fuel. It was enough to make two of the three Bombs that ended the war. By 1955 eight plutonium-breeding reactors had been built on the Hanford site. "Not only are these atomic piles widely spaced for safety — several miles apart — but the separation plants are well away from each other," an US Army historian observed. The Bombmakers' caution paid off. They had just one fatality in their laboratories but none in their wartime plants.

About twenty years later, almost as an afterthought, the Americans built a nuclear power plant at Hanford that is still humming. In subsequent years US utilities built nuclear-generating stations in more than sixty communities across the country. None of these has ever had a fatality though three operators were killed at an Army reactor site in 1961. They died when an explosion shot fuel fragments from a research reactor in Idaho. There was a sudden surge of power while the trio were reassembling a control-rod mechanism on top of a reactor which was supposed to be shut down. A fortnight later the reactor was radiating 1100 millirems an hour at a hundred-feet distance. That accident might have been a preview of Chernobyl though the fallout was not serious off site.

The Windscale nuclear complex squats on a narrow seaside strip of

England's isolated Cumbrian coast. Stand on Scafell Pike, Britain's highest peak, with the poets' fabled Lake District at your back and look seaward. On a fair day you can discern the Isle of Man floating on the Irish Sea. Almost at your feet the conical cooling towers of Calder Hall's four little prototype nuclear plants still puff coolant steam. There is nothing to show that one of Windscale's two big plutonium-making reactors once erupted nor that the plutonium-extraction plant on the seashore spews 4.5 million litres of radioactive, liquid waste into the ocean every day.

For two days in 1957 graphite burned like coal in a Windscale reactor heating the uranium cartridges till they glowed red in 150 fuel channels. That fire was a prelude to Chernobyl as well. A dozen workers received more than a permissible amount of radiation though not enough to incapacitate them. No one was hurt off site but cautious north-country farmers dumped thousands of gallons of milk for which they were promptly compensated. The canny farmers were taking no chances; they didn't wait a day for the milk to be tested. Ruminating a quarter century later British radiologists calculated that "theoretically" the Windscale fire might cause 260 thyroid cancers among their countrymen over a forty-year period. If so, about thirteen of those cancers would prove fatal, they said. Conversely, a government spokesman declared that, "There is no evidence anybody in the UK has contracted or died of cancer" in consequence of the Windscale reactor fire. The dean of Canadian radiation health studies, David K. Myers has made a relevant comparison. For every year that a coal-fired station generates as much electricity as Chernobyl-4 did there will be, on average, two cancer deaths induced by the pollutants coal emits.

The continued flow of radioactive sewage from the Sellafield plant in the Windscale complex infuriated environmentalists and damaged British relations with the European community. But in the modest homes of Whitehaven, Egremont, Seascale, Gosforth, St. Bees and Bootle, Windscale meant high-tech employment for six thousand people. They remember the years of poor catches and not much else in these Cumbrian fishing ports. How worried were they about radiation around the Sellafield plant? "Not at all personally," said 55 per cent of residents queried in 1984. But 61 per cent of them did worry about the long-term effect on their children.

From their apartment windows many Pripyat residents could see the reactor building at the Chernobyl power station. The structure, nearly a kilometre long, housed four nuclear plants but displayed nothing more memorable than a pair of 150-metre ventilation stacks, gantry cranes and air-conditioner housing bridging its roof. "It resembled a ship with white superstructures on deck. Transmission lines radiated from the ship," someone said.

Mayor Vladimir Voloshko recalled bulldozers levelling the sand and forests and the dyking of water meadows to build the Chernobyl Atomic Power Station and the dormitory community of Pripyat nearby. The station is located sixteen kilometres upstream from the town of Chernobyl where the Pripyat and Dnieper rivers merge to form the vast Kiyevskoya reservoir that serves the Ukranian capital of Kiev a hundred kilometres downstream. The town of Pripyat is five kilometres north-west of the nuclear power station. Three major rivers drain into the reservoir in the Pripyat-Chernobyl area putting the station itself almost at the hub of a watershed draining 100,000 square kilometres.

"We built the town and the plant at the same time but the town moved ahead somewhat faster because the construction workers wanted to live in comfortable apartments," the mayor said. The population was young, average age twenty-six, and they embraced thirty different nationalities of the Soviet Union. As the republic's electric power minister Vitali Sklyarov observed, several Ukrainian universities and technical institutes were now training nuclear operators. "Professions and trades to service nuclear equipment are also growing in popularity. Young people come to us willingly."

As Galina Sychyovskaya told a Soviet publicist: "The town council has given us a good apartment. My husband has a well paid and interesting job. I'm a librarian by training. We don't even notice that we live close to a nuclear-power plant." Her four-year-old son went to nursery school but the younger one was at home. Day-care facilities had not kept pace with the birth rate in Pripyat. That was the only drawback as far as she could see. Mayor Voloshko candidly admitted other "teething problems." Many of the young wives couldn't find employment. "We're creating new jobs for them by developing service industries," he noted. Too many cars were also a problem. "We're out of breath from building new garage facilities and parking lots. We don't want the cars to squeeze out the people. We believe the town should be as safe and clean as the Chernobyl power plant."

"I wasn't afraid to take a job at a nuclear-power plant. There is more emotion in fear of nuclear plants than real danger," Boris Chernov, a twenty-nine-year-old turbine operator told *Soviet Life*. "I work in white overalls. The air is clean and fresh; it's carefully filtered. My work place is checked by the radiation-control service and if there is even the slightest deviation from normal, the sensors will set off an alarm on the central radiation-control panel." Safety superintendent Pyotr Bond-arenko made a similar comparison. "Robots and computers have taken over a lot of operations. Nonetheless, the occupational safety and health authority requires that all personnel strictly obey the rules and regulations. In order to hold a job here you have to know industrial-safety rules to perfection and pass an exam in them every year." Bondarenko told *Soviet Life* that, "working at the nuclear plant is safer than driving a car." So it was until some of those safety rules were ignored and the force of 428 million horses kicked apart Chernobyl-4 a dozen weeks later.

For the previous fifteen years Pripyat had been a typical nuke town. Its tree-flanked residential streets, its plentitude of kids, schools and cars, even the bored young mothers like Galina Sychyovskaya itching to be back at work, were all indicative of dormitory towns alongside nuclear facilities the world round. Other Soviet nuclear stations are much closer to major cities of the Ukraine just as Three Mile Island is to Harrisburg, Pennsylvania, France's five-unit Bugey station is to Lyon or British Nuclear's Windscale complex is amidst fifty thousand residents of a dozen Cumbrian towns. C.D. Howe ordained that Canada's first reactor would be built at least a hundred miles from Ottawa but Ontario Hydro's Pickering station is on Metropolitan Toronto's doorstep.

Three months before disaster struck Chernobyl, *Soviet Life* asked the Ukraine power minister Vitali Sklyarov a loaded question. "Nuclear plants are being built close to big cities and resort areas. How safe are they?" The minister replied with an almost universal generalization. He said that "the odds of a meltdown are one in 10,000 years. The plants are safe and protected from any breakdown with three separate safety systems. The Chernobyl station's chief engineer Nikolai Fomin was quoted as saying that, "both man and nature are completely safe. The huge reactor is housed in a concrete silo and has environmental-protection systems." Fomin was one of the first of Chernobyl's management to be fired after the accident.

Chernobyl like Ontario Hydro's nuclear stations, evolved from the same early twentieth-century dream of cheap electric power for every home, farm and factory. "The water power of Niagara should be free as air, not the sport and prey of capitalists," declared James Pliny Whitney, Conservative premier of Ontario in 1905. "Cheap power — now," demanded fifteen hundred demonstrators who marched on the provincial capital the following spring. Every farm should be illuminated at the rate of a twenty candlepower lamp for every three cows, Hydro's founder Adam Beck told farmers a half-dozen years later. "Communism is the Soviet government plus the electrification of the whole country," declared Vladimir Ilyich Lenin soon after the revolution. In the quarter century before World War II the Soviets built an industrial nation with blood, sweat and tears. They mechanized farming, built factories, applied technology, developed their power resources. The revolution was first fuelled by hydro power as they tapped the energy of fast-moving rivers in the Ukraine.

Here the Soviets began meeting the industrial demands of a nation that first had to make its own boot straps before it could pull on them. Dneprodzerzhinsk and Dnepropetrovsk iron and steel were fired and forged. Zaporozhye motor plants and machine shops were energized by the great Dneproges Dam. Upriver Smolensk, a railway town, was electrified by Dnieper River power. Where the Dneiper, now become the Dneister, flows into the Black Sea, Odessa was served by another hydroelectric station. A generation later the Soviet State Committee for the Utilization of Atomic Energy constructed nuclear-power plants at Smolensk, Chernobyl, Zaporozhyne and Odessa to complement the hydroelectric output. It was logical to string more wires on the same transmission towers. By the 1980s a fifth of the Soviet Union's electricity came from the Ukraine and a growing portion of it was being generated by nuclear units. With four thousand-megawatt generating units and two more to be built, Chernobyl was to be the largest nuclear station in the country. "Since it produced its first electricity in 1977 the station has generated more than a hundred million megawatt-hours of electric power and the misfortune at Chernobyl has made our job considerably more difficult," said Power Minister Sklyarov. "By the end of the year the station will have a significant shortfall and it will take considerable effort to cover the losses."

Certainly the efforts to put Chernobyl's undamaged reactors back into operation at the earliest possible moment were unprecedented. They involved the decontamination of units 1, 2 and 3 and the entombment of Chernobyl-4 in an air-conditioned concrete shroud almost half the size of the Great Pyramid of Cheops. Moreover this was pursued apace with the resettlement of 135,000 evacuees, including the building of eight thousand farmstead-type homes for rural families in fifty-two new villages; the retraining, staffing and accommodation of three thousand workers who now commute from Zeleny Mys, a new and temporary nuke town about fifty kilometres east of the station; the construction of new housing in Kiev and Chernigov for ten thousand members of their families; and plans for Slavutych, a more permanent dormitory city of 30,000 population, a little closer to the Chernobyl station. Incidental to these rehabilitation measures in the latter half of 1986, Soviet crews built a thirty-eight kilometre road to Zeleny Mys in two summer months, 130 radiation-filtration dams in the Chernobyl area in three months, and a 450-metre long underwater weir, one hundred metres wide and sixteen metres deep in the Dnieper at the new town of Zeleny Mys by the year end. Evacuees were provided with up to four thousand roubles compensation in addition to new housing and household requirements. In the first fortnight after the Chernobyl disaster, evacuees were supplied with no less than 16,400 sets of bedding, 62,000 roubles worth of dishes, 300 propane stoves, and 7,500 tonnes of detergents. By the year end, twenty-four settlements in the Chernobyl district had been decontaminated and could be safely reoccupied. Residents were already back in two communities when IAEA director-general Hans Blix visited them in January 1987.

"The accident caught us unprepared. The members of the commission and the experts we had to enlist had to improvise the strategy for this work and perform operations unheard of in world-wide practice," said Valery Legasov. "Our success was due to the courage of people, justifiable risk, the assistance that the country gave us, the ability of government bodies to mobilize and regroup to cope with disaster. Not a single one of our requests, whether for transport, materials or equipment, was turned down. All orders for Chernobyl were given priority."

This was done in a Communist state with centralized authority, of course. Neither the Shcherbina commission nor Legasov's experts nor the multiple Soviet state and provincial authorities had to deal with task force inquiries, environmental reviews, legislative committees or the diverse public hearings of a democratic society. During that same seven-month period of 1986 the Mulroney government of Canada announced two new and very different policies — but no new plans — for dealing with Eldorado's forty-year-old nuclear waste problem at Port Hope. Allan Lawrence, with more nuclear-industry workers within his constituency than any other MP in Canada — including those at Eldorado, Pickering and Darlington stations and two fuel-fabrication plants — insisted that the radioactive waste should be dumped in somebody else's backyard. In the time that Chernobyl was being rehabilitated Lawrence brought two successive mines ministers to town to badger Eldorado and harangue the activists.

The October week that Soviet authorities put Chernobyl-1 reactor back into operation on the safely decontaminated accident site, MP Lawrence announced that an environmental review scheduled for later that month to consider Eldorado's most recent proposals had been cancelled. Furthermore, the Canadian government was telling Eldorado to drop its fourth plan in as many years to safely dispose of the radioactive crud. This sudden and final reversal of the government's position made worthless the last of $3.6 million worth of engineering studies and options that Eldorado had been obliged to undertake at government direction under both Liberal and Conservative regimes. On November 20, in the same week that *Pravda* reported completion of a million-cubic-metre cement sarcophagus to seal all radiation within the ruined reactor, Eldorado Nuclear announced that for budgetary reasons it was firing thirty-five employees. A company official admitted that the $3.6 million of wasted effort would have kept them on staff for at least another three years.

In the week following the IAEA post-mortem at Vienna my wife and I made a pilgrimage to Joachimsthal, now renamed Jachymov, where Agricola had established the foundations for radiation medicine and occupational health practices four centuries earlier. Cedok, the Czech state agency to promote tourism, welcomed our visit. "Czechoslovakia is a world leader as regards spas and Jachymov was the first radioactive spa in the world," we were advised. Here in the world's first nuke town the sanatorium was named for Czech physicist Frantisek Behounek who studied with the Curies and brought their nuclear science back from Paris. The nine-storey sanatorium looms high on the Erzebirge, bold and mod as an IBM think-factory. It is especially recommended for those suffering "diseases of the motor apparatus, nervous disorders, vascular and metabolic disorders," the brochures say. "The principal medication is the thermal radioactive springs with a high radioactivity of 10.5 kilobecquerels per litre of the rare gas radon." The water is pumped and piped from the depths of Joachimsthal mine where the underground dwarfs were once thought to produce the *Bergsucht* mountain sickness. Now their brew is benign. One would have to drink two glasses of the mine water to match the radioactivity normally present in our bones; four glasses to exceed Canada Health and Welfare's cautious radiation limit.

A postcard pictured Jachymov Museum with its giant globular model of the atom and brilliantly lit displays of mining on these Erzebirge slopes. But Jachymov Museum is no more. The four-and-a-half-century-old building that housed it a hundred metres from the mine site now shows its age. It is boarded up, padlocked, stripped of all identity. A grilled iron gate leading to the once renowned Jachymov Microbiology Academy swings on rusted hinges and a sign directs visitors to an address in Prague. The centuries-old minehead structure rises eighteen metres above a buttressed terrace. Windows and frames have long since disappeared from the lower levels. Incongruously, windows are glassed and flanked by flower boxes around the top storey. Gypsy squatters occupy this penthouse position, we were told. A banner spanning ten feet of terrace wall far below them declares that, "Strongly united and headed by the Communist Party of Czechoslovakia, we fight for successful development of socialism."

At the edge of town a rusted version of the civic atom motif has escaped the wrecker's eye. It swings in the wind unnoted by the tour buses bringing the spa goers to the Erzebirge slopes. They will drink glasses of radon-laced water in which atoms disintegrate at the rate of about two or three per second. But that Chernobyl summer no one was mentioning atomic radiation in spa country.

9

Countdown

"Mankind will acquire a new source of energy surpassing a million times everything that has hitherto been known. . . . Human might is entering a new era."

—*IZVESTIA*, DECEMBER 31, 1939

"Canada has a unique opportunity to become intimately associated in a project which. . . may revolutionize the future world in the same degree as the invention of the steam engine and the discovery of electricity."

— C.J. MACKENZIE, OTTAWA, APRIL 10, 1944

CHERNOBYL BROUGHT NUCLEAR SCIENTISTS from fifty nations to Vienna in August 1986. Here they resumed a global dialogue begun in the pages of the Royal Society's *Philosophical Transactions* in March 1665 and extinguished by winds of war 275 years later. But the countdown to their technology had started in antiquity.

It began when a shaggy ancestor, his belly full and his juices spent, lay contemplating the stars or his fire pit. Curiosity, that quality of primates, impelled his quest. He may have noticed that the stars glowed with varying hues as fire embers do. He may have wondered whether all things in heaven and earth were made of an elemental stuff. Or were there many different elements? Our hairy forebear saw particles rise from burning wood to become transparent as smoke, invisible as smell. How did solid stuff burn to flame and heat? How minutely could they be fragmented, those bits of matter that fell back as char or grit or powdery ash?

The Greek philosopher Democritus ducked a quantitative answer. He called such particles "atoms" meaning bits too small for further division. He conjectured that all primal substances were formed of indivisible, impenetrable atoms. It was a logical idea. Man had no experience, no instruments nor reason to conceive of anything smaller. Twenty-three centuries later science penetrated to the core of uranium and radium atoms to find that they were self-destructing to even smaller bits. That discovery was inevitable when humanity paused to ponder, contemplate and think.

> *An atom is the smallest bit of matter*
> *But put it in a pile and watch it shatter*
> *If it's the smallest bit, then what words fit*
> *The littler chits an atom spits*
> *When atoms start to spatter?*

Answers were forthcoming when investigators took a scientific approach. Midway through the thirteenth century a Franciscan monk Roger Bacon fathered the rational, systematic method of inquiry that would sweep the charlatans from the church's doorstep. "Observe, try, record, speculate logically, try out your speculation, confirm or correct; communicate to other investigators," he urged. In the alchemists' smoke Bacon identified three chemicals — charcoal, sulphur and saltpetre. By systematic step-by-step effort he combined them to make gunpowder. Then he spelled out the formula in words that a twelve-year-old could understand. Following his directions in *Boy's Own Annual* or *Popular Mechanics* my generation made firecrackers to celebrate the Queen's birthday, Guy Fawkes' heresy or American independence. Regardless of the occasion the three chemicals, when mixed to Bacon's recipe, always went off with a flash, bang, smoke and smell. Prove your findings and compare notes with other researchers, said Roger Bacon.

Four centuries later his namesake but no kin, Francis Bacon advanced the concept of experimental research. When he wrote *New Atlantis*, Britain's ex-chancellor had done time in the Tower and seen his outspoken friend Walter Raleigh get the chop. So the latter Bacon used a cautious allegorical style. Still he spelled out the rules of the science game. "We have twelve who sail into foreign countries. . . who bring us the books and abstracts and patterns of experiments of all other parts. . . three to direct new experiments of a higher light more penetrating into nature. . . . We have furnaces that keep great diversity of heats, fierce and quick. . . engine houses where are prepared. . . ordnance and instruments of war and engines of all kinds. . . some degrees of flying in the air. . . and boats going under water," he said.

Europeans got the message. Within forty years of Bacon's *New Atlantis,* France's Academy of Sciences, the Royal Society of London and Italy's Natural Science Academy were founded; Robert Boyle and Issac Newton established the physical sciences — physics and chemistry — on which Britain based its Industrial Revolution and the Royal Society's *Philosophical Transactions* became an international forum. Its first issue reflected the range of discovery: "An account of the improvement of optic glasses at Rome. Of observations made in England of a spot in one of the belts of Jupiter. . . . Experimental history of cold together with some thermometrical discourses and experiments. . . .Of a peculiar lead ore in Germany very useful for assays . . . . Of a Hungarian bolus . . . . Of new American whale fishing about the Bermudas. . . . A narrative concerning the success of pendulum watches at sea for the longitudes and the grant of a patent thereupon. A catalogue of philosophical [meaning scientific] books published by Monsieur de Fermat, counsellor of Toulouse, lately dead."

Pacing each other through the pages of such learned journals in a hundred months at the beginning of the twentieth century, half a dozen scientists at Cambridge, Paris and Montreal probed to the atom's core. Their findings were inevitable when investigators followed the Bacons' injunctions. The science of chemistry took two hundred years to develop from Francis Bacon's primer to Henry Cavendish's laboratory evidence that the scientific method worked. The chemical atom took another sixty years to evolve from John Dalton's whole-number concept to Dimitri Mendelyeev's exquisite proof that atomic weights would predict the precise properties of a chemical substance. In the century between Dalton and Rutherford's research there were at least 125 significant discoveries that clarified atomic behaviour. Dalton saw atoms as orderly building blocks. Michael Faraday thought of them as blobs of electricity. To James Joule they were minute electrical furnaces. William Prout conjectured that atoms were bits of hydrogen. A man named R. Angus Smith said, "The atom is not necessarily indivisable." William Crookes, Oliver Lodge and J.J. Thomson confirmed Smith's hunch by knocking electrons off the atom.

The first threshold was crossed in those electric years of 1895-1898 when Roentgen identified X-rays, the Curies discovered radium, Thomson and Rutherford tracked ions to the atom's core. Then some inspired leaps of learning breached the dark uncharted voids like lightning across space. Rutherford and Frederick Soddy founded the new alchemy in 1901-1902. Rutherford and Otto Hahn conceived of the nuclear atom as a microscopic solar system in 1905-1906. The strands of learning begun in antiquity, fed from the bobbin of science for seven hundred years were spun into unbreakable thread at the century's turn. Now this thread was about to give a new warp to the human fabric. Rutherford's Cambridge team used the primal cores of hydrogen atoms as projectiles to smash other atoms.

"ATOM IS DISRUPTED BUT WORLD GOES ON," said the *Toronto Globe* on a May day in 1932. "It is a discovery of great importance," said Rutherford but he cooled the media's hyperbolic reaction. "Up to the present it has not yielded anything of immediate commercial value. But the experimenters are not searching for a new source of power or rare or costly elements. They are bound up with the urge and fascination of a search into one of the deepest secrets of nature," he said. Primate curiosity.

Other primitive instincts moved other men. Trapped in worldwide economic chaos, national leaders were suspicious and fearful, angry and aggressive. One of Rutherford's Cambridge team was Pyotr L. Kapitza. In 1934 when he returned to Moscow to accept honorary membership in the Soviet Academy of Sciences he was not allowed to resume a research program with Rutherford in Britain. The Soviet Embassy in London explained that their country, "could no longer dispense with Kapitza's services in view of the danger from Hitler." Neither the Soviets nor anyone else had begun to consider nuclear science in military terms in 1934. Kapitza was called home because Stalin was repatriating all possible Soviet talent from abroad. In fact five Soviet research establishments had been tracking the development of nuclear science since the 1920s. These were the Radium Institute and Technical Physics Institute in Leningrad; the Lebedev Institute and Institute for Physical Problems in Moscow; another establishment in Kharkov. The Soviets needed the scientific leadership Kapitza could provide.

Cambridge's Cavendish laboratory under Rutherford's aegis indirectly contributed another leader to Soviet nuclear science at this time. Igor Vasilevich Kurchatov, a thirty-year-old physicist at Leningrad's Technical Physics Institute, had been involved in other research fields for a decade when the stream of discovery from the Cavendish lab caught his attention. Kurchatov's brother-in-law, K.D. Sinelnikov, had just returned to the USSR from Cambridge and his enthusiastic reports confirmed all that was being written in the scientific press. Kurchatov switched to nuclear research in 1933. By 1935 his research team at the

Leningrad Institute identified a new phenomenon, atoms of the same weight which decayed in different ways. Three years later Kurchatov was in charge of nuclear physics at Leningrad and enroute to helping the Soviet Union became a postwar superpower.

Kurchatov and his Leningrad colleagues were swept up in a feverish global quest for atomic mastery that surged forward in the mid-Depression years. Perhaps the atom held the key to economic recovery. In Stockholm with his wife Irene to receive the Nobel Prize for their discovery of artificial radioactivity that autumn, Frederic Joliot-Curie observed: "Scientists who can construct and demolish elements at will may also be capable of causing nuclear transformations of an explosive character. . . . If such transformation in matter can be brought about, in all probability vast quantities of useful energy will be released." What the atom-smashers needed now was a heavier hammer. James Chadwick, one of Rutherford's Cambridge proteges, provided it with his timely neutron discovery. In Paris the Joliot-Curie team used these neutrons to bombard such elements as aluminum. In Rome, Enrico Fermi used them to destabilize nearly fifty different elements.

The next logical step was to fire neutron bullets into the dense depths of uranium and thorium atoms which contain more than 140 neutrons at their core. When he shattered the nucleus of these heavy elements Fermi found their atomic parts reforming into atoms of quite different elemental substances. The Joliot-Curies did similar experiments with equally startling results. At the Kaiser Wilhelm Institute in Berlin, Otto Hahn and his Viennese associate Lise Meitner began an exhaustive analysis of these fission fragments which became new and different elements. Somehow their experimental results failed to conform to the known laws of chemistry.

1936 was a pivotal year. In Britain Edward VIII succeeded his father then abdicated the throne for a Boston divorcée. France had two premiers in the first six months, stood transfixed as German troops reclaimed the Rhineland and nervously signed a naval convention with Britain and the US. Frenchmen watched Nazi forces begin building the Siegfried Line with the fatalistic, fear-filled eyes of snake-threatened prey. Mussolini won his little war with the Abyssinians. With Hitler he declared the Rome-Berlin axis. Acclaimed by 99 per cent of the German electorate, the Fuhrer launched his four-year plan. Trotsky was exiled to Mexico. Franco began the Spanish Civil War in July and was self-proclaimed chief of state by October. Germany and Japan signed their Anti-Comintern Pact and Chiang Kai-shek declared war on the Japanese. That autumn Jesse Owens, a black man, won four Olympic gold medals at Berlin. Allowing that to happen in his showcase stadium was Adolf Hitler's last concession to miscegenate humanity.

The athletes went home, leaves fell from the linden trees, the "Jews forbidden" signs reappeared. At the Kaiser Wilhelm Institute Otto Hahn and Lise Meitner increased the tempo of their atomic pursuit. The Nazis had not yet discovered the Viennese scientist's Jewish roots. For the next two years Hahn and Meitner set the pace of nuclear research. Their reports appeared every few weeks in *Naturwissemschaften* or *Zeitschrift fur Physik* which the Joliot-Curies read in Paris while reporting their own work in the French Academy's *Compte rendu*. All of them, Rutherford's boffins at Cambridge, Fermi in Rome, Nils Bohr at Copenhagen, the Joliot-Curies in Paris and the Hahn-Meitner team in Berlin, used the weekly science publication *Nature* for more immediate communication.

Midway through 1938 Meitner's name vanished from the science journals. When it reappeared a few months later to co-author a letter to *Nature* with her nephew Otto R. Frisch, the last threshold to nuclear energy had been crossed. Frisch worked with Bohr in Denmark; his aunt had taken sanctuary in Sweden. Tramping through the snow on skiis near Goteborg that Christmas week of 1938 Otto Frisch and Lise Meitner worked out the fundamental mechanism of atomic disintegration. "It seems possible that the uranium nucleus has only small stability of form and may, after neutron capture, divide itself into two nuclei of roughly equal size," they advised *Nature* readers in February 1939. "These two nuclei will repel each other and should gain a total kinetic energy of about 200 million electron volts."

The Frisch-Meitner letter to *Nature* was written on January 16, 1939. Ten days later Nils Bohr attended a conference on theoretical physics in Washington. Enrico Fermi, who had left Rome to collect his Nobel Prize in Stockholm and quit fascist Italy, was with Bohr. They described the classic Frisch-Meitner nuclear fission concept at a physicists' conference in Washington. The day Bohr and Fermi addressed that conference Frederic Joliot-Curie, Hans Halban and Lew Kowarski tested the Frisch-Meitner concept in their College de France laboratory. Using radium as a source of neutrons, and a block of beryllium to moderate the neutron speed, they split uranium atoms, at will, again and again and again.

In mid-March the Frenchmen took the world a step closer to nuclear power. "Neutron bombardment of uranium and thorium leads to an explosion of the nucleus and a considerable amount of energy is liberated in the process," they told *Nature* readers. A month later they produced a sub-critical chain reaction, one just short of being self sustaining. They were at the door to the nuclear age. Primate curiousity born on the edge of ancestral firepits was about to tap primal energy at will. An American science writer calculated that, "The input of only five million electron-volts of energy can release from the atom's heart 200 million electron-volts of energy, forty times the amount shot into it by a neutron."

Physicists as far afield as Tokyo tested the French team's findings. At the Leningrad Institute Igor Kurchatov watched graduate students fire neutrons into uranium atoms and concluded that a chain reaction was probable. He calculated that for each neutron that struck its atomic target from two to four more neutrons were emitted. In Moscow physics professor Igor Tamm told his students, "It means a bomb can be built that will destroy a city out to a radius of maybe ten kilometres." He was paraphrasing what Nils Bohr had told fellow scientists at a Washington conference a few weeks earlier. "Dr. Nils Bohr of Copenhagen, a colleague of Dr. Albert Einstein, declared that bombardment of a small amount of pure uranium isotope 235 with slow neutron particles would start a chain reaction or atomic explosion sufficiently great to blow up a laboratory and the surrounding country for miles," Associated Press had reported. "Many physicists declared, however, that it would be difficult if not impossible to separate isotope 235 which is only one per cent of the uranium element."

It was difficult but not impossible. Uranium-235 would fuel the Bomb dropped on Hiroshima. It took five years to produce a few pounds of it. Perhaps half of the $2.6 billion Manhattan District project was involved in separating U-235 from the other 99 per cent of the natural uranium. The material used for the Nagasaki Bomb was plutonium, an element extracted from spent uranium-reactor fuel. Uranium-235 and plutonium remained the two weapon materials. To produce either required a billion-dollar plant and a very high level of nuclear technology. American and British demand for plutonium was the incentive to build Canada's NRX and NRU reactors. Canada got the technology to build nuclear-power plants; they got Bomb material.

Canada became a junior partner in the wartime nuclear-development program because C.D. Howe and Dean Mackenzie played our trump card, the Eldorado uranium mine and refinery, with finesse. Yet Canadians were no barefoot water-boys when atomic science matured to nuclear technology. A few expansive people in high places had kept us apace with developments. They tended to be engineers or old soldiers or both. Momentarily between wars back in 1935 Canada's chief of the general staff, Major-General Andrew G.L. McNaughton had reflected on Canadian military deficiencies and been hustled into the presidency of the National Research Council. He used the science agency to lever Canada's prostrate industry into the technological age. He encouraged industrial use of radium for radiography, the X-raying of dense materials. Then NRC engineers worked with Eldorado to improve refinery processes. This was the first government involvement with the nuclear industry.

Chalmers Jack Mackenzie took over at the NRC when McNaughton went to war. He was a Maritimer who had gone west before fighting in World War I. He brought an innovative and nationalistic approach to Ottawa. In World War II he provided a trans-Atlantic bridge to link Allied scientists and engineers. Like his boss C.D. Howe, Dean Mackenzie had no colonial reflexes. He was perhaps the only man on earth who could have worked in close collaboration with the American Bombmaker, General Leslie Richard Groves, and Churchill's minister for the Bomb, Sir John Anderson, without ever raising his voice or letting them raise theirs.

When Frederic Joliot-Curie, Hans Halban and Lew Kowarski reported in the *Nature* issue of April 22, 1939 with demonstrable evidence that they were close to triggering a chain reaction — one that would create vastly more energy than they put into it — it electrified the scientific community from London to Leningrad. Mindful of fearful Londoners beneath the German zeppelins' lethal loads twenty years before, George Thomson at the Imperial College and William Bragg at the Cavendish Lab visualized the atom's explosive power fuelling a super-bomb. As a May 10 British cabinet document tersely reported, Thomson and Bragg now believed, "It might be possible to disintegrate a mass of uranium of sufficient size and, if so, it would be a source of heat and power almost inconceivably greater than anything yet known. There was also a chance, though a good deal less probable, that it might have an explosive quality very much greater than any known explosive."

In Berlin, German Army nuclear expert Kurt Diebner showed the *Nature* report to Field Marshal Wilhelm Keitel's scientific adviser Erich Schumann. With the Fuhrer about to make war Colonel Schumann had no time for abstract discussions. "Can you not finally put an end to your atomic poppycock?" he asked Diebner. Hamburg physicist Paul Harteck was more convincing. He persuaded Schumann that, "This newest development will probably produce an explosive many orders of magnitude more powerful than the conventional ones. The country which first makes use of it has an unsurpassable advantage."

The French team also faced skepticism. In May they applied for patents on five steps they had taken towards the design of a nuclear reactor. They immediately signed over these patent rights to the National Centre for Scientific Research. Postwar the centre transferred them to the French Atomic Energy Commission.One of the patents covered their calculation for the "critical mass," the workable reactor size to sustain a chain reaction. It was about forty tonnes of uranium in a sphere 2.7 metres in diameter. Edgar Sengier, whose Union Miniere du Haut Katanga shared global radium markets with Canada's Eldorado, supplied the Paris lab with seven tonnes of the radium by-product, uranium oxide, and armaments minister Raoul Dautry secured a quantity of graphite for their research. When the graphite failed to slow neutrons to an atom-splitting pace, the minister ordered heavy water from Norsk Hydro at Rjukan, Norway.

"Can the energy in the atomic nucleus by exploited on a technical scale?" asked Siegfried Flugge in *Naturwissenschaften* in June 1939. The energy in a cubic metre of uranium oxide weighing four tonnes would lift a cubic kilometre of water — weighing ten million, million kilograms — twenty-seven kilometres in the air, he figured. At the end of August *Deutche Allgemeine Zeitung* carried a lengthy interview in which Flugge reported the German quest to harness nuclear energy. That was the last nuclear story for public consumption in the Third Reich. Within a week Hitler's armies crossed the Polish corridor enroute to Armageddon. That week refugee scientist Leo Szilard in New York got Albert Einstein to sign a letter to the American president warning that "extremely powerful bombs are conceivable." In Britain Winston Churchill was dubious. Noting Sunday newspaper speculation he wrote Air Minister Kingsley Woods, "There is no danger that this discovery, however great its scientific interest and ultimate practical importance, could be put into operation on a large scale for several years."

The march to war caught French, British and German scientists in its train. Fears and hopes, dreams and nightmares, intellectual zeal and much wishful thinking, honest patriotism and the realistic pursuit of their professions, all merged in ambivalence. The reality of nuclear power seemed so close they could feel its vibrations. For countries already at war, however, nuclear research was not a priority. Knowledge pursued for its own sake — as it had been for three centuries — was a peacetime luxury. In wartime research must have a practical and preferably short-term goal. "In the autumn of 1939 atomic physics seemed frivolous in a nation embarking on war and badly prepared for it. There had been a flush of interest earlier in the year but it was put out of mind by the urgent tasks of military preparation," said George C. Laurence, the first Canadian to embark on nuclear-reactor research and still at it nearly a half-century later.

Undaunted, he spent his off-hours in the early war years trying to assemble a nuclear pile of uranium and graphite that would approach a chain reaction. Like similar piles initially attempted in Paris, Leipzig and Chicago, Laurence's bin full of little packages of uranium imbedded in coke (in lieu of pure carbon) failed to generate a neutron chain. For one thing his materials were too impure. For another, his approach oversimplified matters. Theoretically, tapping the power in uranium atoms should have been as simple as making fire. In fact the engineering proved incredibly complex. It took three years to refine the ingredients to a level of purity that would sustain a chain reaction. That is what the $2.6 billion Manhattan District Bomb program with its 150,000 scientists, engineers and technicians was all about.

"VAST POWER SOURCE IN ATOMIC ENERGY OPENED BY SCIENCE — Germany Is Seeking It — Scientists Ordered to Devote All Time to Research — Tests Made at Columbia," reported the *New York Times* on May 5, 1940. The front-page story was based on the isolation of uranium-235 by American scientists; a substance which science writer William L. Laurence said, "might yield such energy that one pound is equal to the power output in five million pounds of coal or three million pounds of gasoline." (Canadian utilities that use uranium to fuel electric-generating stations today get about twenty-four million times more energy from it than from coal; eighteen million times more than from fuel oil on a pound-for-pound basis.) With news of the US discovery, said *The Times*, "every German scientist in this field has been ordered to drop all other research and devote themselves to this work alone."

Pursuing *The Times* story, the *Ottawa Citizen* queried George Laurence at the National Research Council. He responded with a nice mix of reality, vagueness and obfuscation. "For the first time it is conceivable that it might be possible to use this energy as a source of power to operate machinery. It has been suggested there is a possibility of releasing the energy with explosive violence. While this might prove true our present knowlege would make it appear very doubtful." Dean Mackenzie had no such doubts; he was keeping Laurence apace of every step the British and American research scientists took.

In Britain, France and Germany, nuclear projects were now subject to military priorities while the Soviets pursued their research in a peacetime environment. Apace with the Americans, A.I. Brodsky in Leningrad worked to separate the rare uranium isotope. He estimated that just a few kilograms of U-235 would sustain a chain reaction. The Soviet Academy of Sciences sponsored a public conference on nuclear physics and Kurchatov developed a crash program for nuclear research. With Jaroslav Frenkel, dean of Soviet physicists, Kurchatov gave a detailed explanation of the fission process at the same time that Otto Frisch, Nils Bohr and John Wheeler were doing so in the Western world. In its 1940 New Year edition, *Izvestia* predicted: "Mankind will acquire a new source of energy surpassing a million times everything that has hitherto been known. We shall have a fuel which will be a substitute for our depleting supplies of coal and oil and thus rescue industry from a fuel famine. . . . Human might is entering a new era."

In June 1942 the British government asked that Canada take control of Eldorado's uranium resources. "The whole business was very secret but it was represented to me that whichever country possessed this mineral would in time unquestionably win the war," Mackenzie King told his diary. He was by nature and training a sociologist, philosopher and spiritualist ill at ease in the hard world of reality. He left such matters to his wartime supply minister Clarence Decatur Howe and to Dean Mackenzie. A hard-nosed engineer without a colonial reflex, Howe agreed to take over Eldorado. But to the dismay of the Brits, he did so unilaterally and told them afterwards.

A week before the German invasion of Russia, US President Roosevelt approved the Manhattan District program to build the Bomb. He named Brigadier-General Leslie Groves of the US Army Corps of Engineers to run the project. Ten days earlier Germany's Nobel Prize-winning physicist Werner Heisenberg had briefed Hitler's supply minister Albert Speer on the Bomb prospects. "Definite proof has been obtained that the technical utilization of atomic energy in an uranium pile is possible. Moreover, it is to be expected on theoretical grounds that an explosive for atomic bombs could be produced in such a pile," he said. "Investigation of the technical side of the atomic bomb problem, for example the critical size, has not been undertaken, however. More weight has been given to the energy developed in an uranium pile which could be achieved more easily and with less outlay." Thus having damned the Bomb's prospects with faint praise Heisenberg got the response he must have expected. "Speer ruled that the work was to go forward on a comparatively small scale. So the only goal attainable was the development of an uranium pile producing energy. Future work was directed entirely towards this one aim." Speer mentioned the idea of a nuclear bomb to Hitler who was unimpressed.

With the German invasion Igor Kurchatov and his boffins abandoned their nuclear research to cope with the tremendous problems of wartime production in the USSR. "The Russians made no attempt to conceal the fact that they had stopped atomic research and they apparently did not assign priority to atomic energy in their foreign espionage," said the Rand Corporation, a US corporate think-tank in a 1956 study. "By 1943 the Russians resumed an atomic development program with the apparent intent of trying to acquire nuclear weapons." That year Kurchatov moved his nuclear-research team to Moscow to organize the Soviet Bomb project.

The slow-neutron reactor concept developed by the Paris team, or "Halban's boiler" as the Brits called it, was essentially a furnace fuelled by natural uranium. It would convert a small amount of spent nuclear fuel to plutonium but the potential of this nuclear boiler to raise steam to generate electricity was evident from the outset. It was the plutonium output that justified the expensive development program in wartime. With the fall of France, Halban and Kowarski escaped to Britain, bringing with them the world's supply of the heavy water. The 162 litres, which had been spirited out of Norway just before the German invasion and then from Paris days before the city fell, was the ingredient to slow neutrons so they would create a chain reaction in natural uranium. Bureaucratic red tape and American-British hassling kept most of heavy water in its original twenty-six stainless-steel cans for nearly five wartime years. By the time the Anglo-Canadian team could fully use it, the Americans had begun to make heavy water in quantity at Trail, BC. Yet in a very real sense Canadian, British and French nuclear-energy programs were primed by the 162 litres of heavy water with a double atom of hydrogen in each molecule.

In the spring of 1944 the American, British and Canadian governments agreed to develop Halban's boiler into a natural uranium/heavy water nuclear reactor. It was ostensibly a part of the Bomb program and it reflected the ability of General Groves, Britain's James Chadwick and Dean Mackenzie to accommodate very different national goals. To General Groves the Manhattan Project was a military assignment; to James Chadwick it was a scientific challenge. To Dean Mackenzie the project to build a pilot nuclear plant was Canada's chance for high technology. He had watched countrymen wood-hewing and water-drawing for fifty years; he figured there were better things for Canadians to do in the twentieth century. He spelled it out in a memo that C.D. Howe took to cabinet in mid-April 1944. They were a formidable pair, these two. Mackenzie packed the snowballs tightly and the minister threw them with resounding impact.

"Atom for atom the energy released in radioactivity is 100,000 times that in the most modern high explosives," Dean Mackenzie wrote. "It is now certain that a bomb can and will be made that will be at least hundreds of times more powerful than anything yet known. It is also certain that power units will be made in future for aeroplanes, ships and submarines. Canada has a unique opportunity to become intimately associated with a project which is not only of the greatest immediate military importance but which may revolutionize the future world in the same degree as did the invention of the steam engine and the discovery of electricity. It is an opportunity that Canada as a nation cannot afford to turn down."

Howe briefed the prime minister. As Mackenzie King understood it, "The processes will not only have terrific destructive powers but may be used for many purposes for which electrical power is used. Howe mentioned that a fountain pen filled with the desired substance would propel a steamship across the Atlantic." The prime minister would be glad when the war was over and he could return to less complicated affairs. "It is a solemn business dealing with matters of this kind," he told his diary.

With the arrogance that cost them the Empire, Britain's high commissioner, Malcolm MacDonald, passed a note in to C.D. Howe. The son of Britain's one-time Labour prime minister, Malcolm spent the wartime years soothing his insecurities like aching feet in Ottawa's cool colonial waters. The time was 11:30 Monday morning, August 6, 1945. Canada's munitions minister was attending a federal-provincial conference. "Dear C.D., The thing has gone off and the President's statement has gone out. Stimson's will be issued in about ¾-of-an-hour and yours should go out about ½-an-hour after that. Could you come out of the Conference for a few minutes as there are two or three points I should like to discuss and one or two ways in which we should like to help you," Howe was told.

The note was as redundant as it was presumptuous; Howe filed it as a momento of post-imperial delusion. He had been told a month earlier of Truman's decision to use the Bomb and he had carefully developed his own statement in collaboration with Dean Mackenzie. Now his man in Washington, George Bateman, was keeping close contact with both the White House and the Pentagon. At mid-morning Howe left the conference to King. With Mackenzie beside him, he watched the teletype printer spell out history line by line. At noon he summoned press-

Canapress Photo Service

This helicopter view of the southeast end of the Chernobyl reactor building, below chimney centre, shows that nearly fifty metres of the fuelling hall above reactor No. 4 and the west side of the structure were destroyed by explosions that rocked the Soviet nuclear-power station in the early morning of April 26, 1986.

Map of the Chernobyl area.

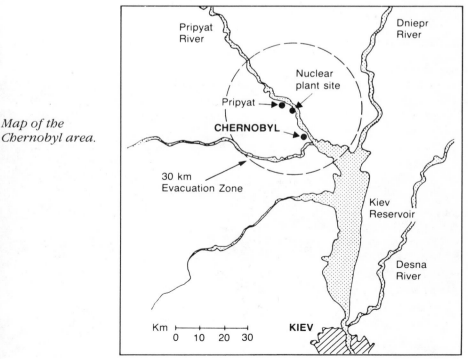

Soviet helicopters flew round the clock in the first days after the Chernobyl disaster to decontaminate the wrecked reactor building by spraying it with plastic sealing material.

Radio-controlled bulldozer tractors are tested on an improvised ground just outside the station prior to being used to remove rubble from the base of the razed reactor structure.

Shift leader Viktor Gladenko measures radiation level above the Chernobyl No. 1 reactor prior to its resumption of service.

Nuclear operators are pictured in the control room at Chernobyl.

Fotokhronika Tass

Politburo vice-chairman and head of the Soviet commission on Chernobyl, Boris Shcherbina was on the scene from the first day to direct the decontamination, rehabilitation and inquiry of what went wrong.

The Kirov settlement near Gomel is one of the near-instant villages built in the latter half of 1986 to house families evacuated from a thirty-kilometre area around the Chernobyl nuclear station.

The world's first uranium mine at Jachymov, formerly Joachimsthal, Czechoslovakia, now supplies radon-rich mineral water to a large sanatorium, part of the major spa facilities.

Two members of the decontamination crew at the NRX reactor in 1952 pictured in protective clothing.

Building at 103 Church Street, Toronto where a radium spill during World War II triggered a coast-to-coast cleanup by the Atomic Energy Control Board of contaminated properties.

A pinpoint fragment of Cosmos-954 is pictured alongside a Canadian penny in this much-enlarged picture.

Canada NAST team member measures the radioactivity of a large fragment of Cosmos-954 which had partially melted into ice on Thelon River, Northwest Territories.

Ontario Hydro Pickering A & B units.

Control room at Ontario Hydro's Pickering B station.

gallery members and passed along word to the prime minister.

Unawed by men or events, C.D. Howe took Canada into the nuclear age. "At a single stroke an atomic bomb destroyed a large part of the great Japanese army base at Hiroshima. The conception of a bomb one million times more effective than the most modern high explosive is staggering. However, pound for pound, that is the measure of the energy released in an atomic bomb. The magnitude and effectiveness of US effort has been unparalleled in the history of science," Howe said. Britain and Canada had begun a joint nuclear program in 1942. "While the first application was for purposes of war, the prospects for peace challenges the imagination. The present situation is comparable to electric power when Faraday made his classical discovery of the electromagnet. However, years of research and development must elapse before commercial power applications become a reality."

The wartime program at Montreal and Chalk River concentraed on developing Halban's boiler into the NRX reactor. The *raison d'être* for the NRX was to produce plutonium for the Bomb. It was, however a major step towards commercial power reactors and a research facility to achieve them. With the most powerful neutron flux (atom-splitting ability) of any reactor in the world the NRX spawned a rich array of radioactive isotopes. These radiating elements were chemically identical to stable sister elements except for the radiation they beeped out. A single neutron removed or added to the nucleus sent the atom into oscillation.

Isotope atoms became sub-microscopic power sources, tiny batteries in effect. Electronic detectors could readily track them through chemical and bodily reactions, through industrial processes and research experiments. They could also beam cancer-killing gamma radiation with laser-like precision. Within half a dozen years NRX-made isotopes were energizing Canada's "cobalt bomb" cancer-treatment machines worldwide; tracking body fluids in medical studies; tracing microbes' movements and killing weevils in stored grain; sterilizing foods and drugs; X-raying the dense depths of industrial components and the welding of submarine hulls.

Canada had provided more than half the 350 scientists and engineers on the Anglo-Canadian team at Montreal. Others were working at the NRC's labs in Ottawa and on specific atomic-science projects at McGill, McMaster, Queen's and University of Toronto. Just as Rutherford's McGill lab had been the hub of atomic science at the century's turn, the wartime team became the core and catalyst for Canadian postwar technological development. At Chalk River, a forty-square-kilometre site soon housed industrial facilities and research labs. Deep River, a dormitory town of 2,200 nearby, would soon boast more people with postgraduate degrees per capita than any other community in North America. As Howe pointed out, "For the first time a sizeable group of Canadian scientists under government auspices has had an active part in pioneering one of the major scientific developments in history."

Across the world the Bomb burned other images in other eyes. A sociologist with the Toronto Board of Education in recent years, Setsuko Thurlow remembers how it was with her that day in Hiroshima. When they dug the eleven-year-old from the wreckage of her school she went up on a hillside with a few others to try and ease death for the many. "Everybody wanted water, water, water. But there was nothing in which to carry the water. So when we got to a nearby stream we would rip off a blood-stained glove or whatever, soak it in water and take it back to let them suck out the moisture." When she summons that memory from dark depths Setsuko Thurlow's voice takes on a macabre tone. The words transcend experience; they stand naked of emotion, stark as those human shadows imprinted on the Sumintomo Bank steps when the fireball melted roof tiles half a mile away. Thirteen thousand kilometres and nearly a half-century removed, Setsuko Thurlow invites your comprehension. "Can you imagine that kind of primitive effort to make their deaths easier?" she asks. None answer and she has a final comment. "Remember that there was an outside world then to send in foodstuffs and medical supplies after about ten days. There won't be an outside world next time."

Prometheus, god of fire, gave earthlings a source of heat, energy and explosive power but not the wisdom to control them. When the Hiroshima and Nagasaki Bombs were dropped, the American nuclear armoury was empty. While the United Nations contemplated a nuclear world at peace the US built just thirteen atomic bombs. But said Soviet foreign minister Vyacheslav Molotov in November 1947, "the secret of the atom bomb has long ceased to exist." Said his comrade Andrei Vyshinsky a year later, "It is a mistake to think there is just one state which has a monopoly over atomic energy and the atomic bomb." By 1950, however, the Americans had made seven hundred of them. Then the H-Bomb — which used an A-Bomb to trigger the sun-like fusion of hydrogen atoms — boosted explosive power a thousand times. By 1960 the American nuclear arsenal was estimated to hold perhaps a million times the TNT equivalent of the Hiroshima Bomb. By that time the Soviet Union, Britain and France were making H-Bombs as well. A quarter-century later China joined the Bomb-rattling game.

"Even more devastating bombs are being, or could be, developed which will be to the present bomb as a machine-gun was to a breech loader," Lester Pearson warned. International control was the only alternative to "the most bitter and disastrous armament race ever run." Pearson had co-authored the three-nation declaration signed by Harry Truman, Clement Atlee and Mackenzie King on November 15, 1945. They had declared their "willingness to exchange fundamental scientific information, scientists and scientific literature, for peaceful ends with any nation that will fully reciprocate." A day later General Groves and Sir John Anderson made secret recommendations less altruistic. They aimed to control uranium supply worldwide. C.D. Howe had already rejected Canada's participation in this scheme. "The truth is that no system of safeguards can of itself provide an effective guarantee against the production of nuclear weapons by a nation bent on aggression," Mackenzie King told the House of Commons.

Bled white by war that killed twenty million of its people and scorched two-thirds of the wealth from its European territory, the Soviet Union had no warlike intentions. Confronted by American and British hostility and Joseph Stalin's paranoia, however, the Soviets moved quickly to build the Bomb. The first requirement was a nuclear reactor to brew plutonium; they quickly developed one. On Christmas Day 1946 Igor Kurchatov announced that a low-power uranium and graphite pile had "gone critical" at his Moscow labs. This was just three months after Canada's zero-powered ZEEP reactor began operating at Chalk River. The NRX went into service in July 1947. By this time Kurchatov had the Soviet nuclear program in full swing.

In the eastern provinces of the USSR thirty-two mining complexes were now producing uranium. The Podolsky plant near Moscow had begun to extract the elusive one per cent of uranium-235 from natural uranium. The plant, said American intelligence, was based on the uranium-separation facility built at Oak Ridge, Tennessee just four years before. Facilities to convert uranium oxide to uranium hexafluoride and then enrich it in uranium-235 content had been built "in the second half of the 1940s within a very short period of time," the Soviets have said. Five major industrial sites were producing reactor components and three commercial-size reactors were under construction to make plutonium by the summer of 1947. Ballistic-missile carriers were tested on the Soviet's Kazakhistan range that October.

In May 1948 Canada's NRX reactor power was increased from five thousand to eight thousand kilowatts. By summer the British were running their BEPO (British experimental pile operation) at four thousand kilowatts. By the year end the French had their first reactor going. It was the 150-kilowatt ZOE (zero energy) assembly modelled on Lew Kowarski's design for ZEEP at Chalk River. By then Soviet nuclear engineers were reprocessing spent fuel from plutonium. By January 1949 NRX was operating at 20,000 kilowatts and by spring the Soviets had a five-hundred kilowatt research reactor in service. In August they tested their first atomic Bomb at the Moskva proving site where the Kirgiz Steppe meets the old Mongolian border. They called it *"Tykwa"* for its pumpkin shape. To the Western world it symbolized a bitter harvest. Just a year and a half earlier US intelligence had doubted that the Russians could build an atomic Bomb before 1953.

The Americans first tested an H-Bomb, a weapon a thousandfold more explosive than the Hiroshima Bomb, in November 1952. The Soviets did so nine months later.

10

Big Spill, Small Fragments

"Mr. Spade who did the work before me apparently had a big spill. He left in a hurry and joined the navy."

— NICHOLAS TCHERNOUSSOFF TO AECB INVESTIGATOR,
FEBRUARY 1975

"The four thousand Cosmos-954 particles recovered would weigh less than five grams. Their distribution was probably one particle for every four thousand square metres."

— HUGH SPENCE, AECB, MAY 1980

WILHELM ROENTGEN DISCOVERED X-RAYS when he unwrapped a package of photo film and found it had been exposed to the invisible light. Henri Becquerel made a similar discovery a few weeks after when uranium rays fogged film in a dark cupboard. Nearly a century later, in the first week of February 1975, Toronto photographer Ray Erickson realized he was having the same experience.

Erickson's office and darkroom were on the third floor of a five-storey structure built at the corner of Church and Richmond Streets in Toronto's bygone days to accommodate business expansion a few blocks east from Yonge Street. During World War II it housed a mixed bag of retail, commercial and light industrial activities. Suite 302 in the war years was a radium-paint laboratory.

"Most photographers know that radiation can fog film. If the source of radiation is some distance away it's a gradual process. I had been at that location for about a year and a half when the fogging became significant. I had to get to the bottom of it," Erickson recalled. He talked with a nearby photo supply dealer; checked the film in his darkroom with that he kept at home. He double checked the packaging: "When I had boiled down all the information I phoned the Ontario Ministry of the Environment and told them I had fogged film. To my way of thinking there was probably radiation in the building and I wondered if they would be interested in sending somebody over to look for it." They did.

When Erickson's February 14 query was shuttled through the myriad provincial government corridors that approach, touch and transcend environmental pollution it landed on the desk of Dr. J. Harry Aitken at the health ministry. Aitken dispatched an inspector to monitor the premises. It took four days to get someone on the scene but only one more day to shuffle responsibility from Queen's Park to Ottawa and from Canada Health and Welfare to the Atomic Energy Control Board. The AECB, in turn, appointed senior technicians of the Ontario and federal health ministries as the board's official inspectors. Duly authorized, they evacuated the third-floor tenants at 103 Church Street. Thirty inches above Erickson's darkroom floor the radiation measured 200 milliroentgens an hour. The photographer was getting an average year's exposure every forty-five minutes. When the floor tile was stripped off in the next room and a 2.5-centimetre thick layer of concrete was chipped away with air hammers there was one spot radiating up to 1,000 milliroentgens an hour. It was twice as radioactive as the turbine building adjacent to Chernobyl units 1 and 2 a month after the world's worst nuclear accident.

The AECB's investigation established that the hot spot in the darkroom floor had been caused by spilled radium in 1943. "When I took over I found the place contaminated and immediately proceeded to clean and wash everything there. We recovered over a gram of radium from the washing concentrates, paper ashes and towels we used," Nicholas E. Tchernoussoff who had been in charge of the "high radiation lab in the middle of the third floor," told an investigator. "Mr. Spade who did the work before me apparently had a big spill. He left in a hurry and joined the navy," Tchernoussoff said.

"Radioactive Toronto office potentially lethal thirty years," said the *Globe and Mail* over a modest page-one story on February 22. "Radiation lethal, officials seal off downtown office," said the *Toronto Star* over an unsensational report the same day. *The Star* ran a picture of the radiation warning posted in the building. The stories were based on news releases from the AECB and Ontario health ministry. Nobody was hiding anything. "We issued a news release on February 21, the same day the third floor was closed, asking that any person who may have worked there for more than three months contact health authorities. Considerable publicity was given in order to find those who may have been exposed," said AECB health physicist Geoffrey B. Knight. In seventeen years with the AECL, Ontario Hydro and the control board, Knight had learned how to use the news media constructively. Within a week more than a hundred former employees of the radium company had responded. There was little further news coverage for four months when both the *Globe and Mail* and *The Star* reported that the AECB was still trying to establish who owned the building before it undertook the expensive decontamination work.

That press coverage was a bench mark; it demonstrated a modest interest in radioactive contamination in the spring of 1975. For one thing Knight and his colleagues talked about old, familiar, cancer-treating radium; they never mentioned the trigger words "nuclear" or "atomic radiaition." For another, the Porter Royal Commission on Electric Power Planning in Ontario was not established until a month after the second story about 103 Church Street. By the time the building had been decontaminated and a federal-provincial task force had recommended the cleanup of 109 other radium-contaminated properties across Canada, the Porter Commission was generating a full-fledged nuclear debate. But in mid-May 1975, a month before the Porter Commission turned radiation hunting into show business, responsible authorities were already concerned about the mental health impact of nuclear news which the AECB anticipated — correctly — might be more damaging than the actual exposure.

Geoff Knight discussed this problem with his boss, AECB director-general Jon H. Jennekens, and Gordon Jack of Canada Health and Welfare. What should they tell former employees of the Church Street radium lab a generation after their exposure? Knight put their concerns in a letter to Harry Aitken at the Ontario health ministry on May 12. "The exposure rates were far from uniform and there is some doubt about how constant the exposure was. There is likely to be considerable uncertainty in individuals' memories of when and where they occupied areas on the third floor," he wrote. At the same time "members of the public are very likely to have difficulty comprehending the meaning and significance of dose data especially when there is a very large margin of error involved."

Knight felt an indisputable responsibility "not to cause unnecessary worry to members of the public." Harry Aitken and Jan Muller at the Ontario health ministry agreed that the former lab workers should be given "qualitative" information. Dose estimates in hard numbers would be provided to their physicians along with "an explanation of the limitations and interpretation of the figures."

The AECB and Ontario health officials were trying to walk softly while applying their authoritative clout. News editors and reporters had no such hesitation about using hard numbers. They understood neither basic statistical practice nor the art and science of interpreting medical data. They had not the slightest idea of the scientific concepts involved in radiation health protection. Yet they could always rationalize that their only business was to report what the experts said. With the advent of the Porter Commission hearings there was no shortage of "experts." Pick a high-sounding name for a would-be institute — preferably one that made a catchy acronym — order stationery at the instant-print shop, testify at the Porter Commission and you were a nuclear-radiation authority in the media's eyes. People with doctorate degrees in mathematics were particularly popular. Dr. Gordon Edwards and Dr. Rosalie Bertell, for example, gave an authoritative stamp to their pronouncements. Their emotional commitment lent conviction to their testimony. Their freedom from scientific affiliation, from the discipline of a licensed professional body, from peer review, left them unrestrained, uninhibited and unfettered. They had no responsibility for the consequences of what they said. These anti-nuclear experts had no establishment bias and they were always available. Instant experts could make instant judgments on nuclear events. That's show business. The news media loved them.

Always restrained by a meagre budget and skeleton staff, the AECB made no move to clean up the Church Street premises until the owner was prepared to pay for it. By the fall of 1975 the AECB had the building owner's commitment to pay for the decontamination and they engaged a ten-member AECL crew to work on the third floor. It was soon evident that the radium lab people had frequently flushed contaminated cleaning water down the drain. Drain pipes had to be replaced right down through the basement floor. Radium, itself, is solid and static but it disintegrates to radon gas. The gas had travelled up and down stairwells, the elevator shaft and ventilation ducts for thirty-three years. It took the AECL crew three months to decontaminate the major sources of radioactivity. All walls and partitions on the third floor had to be removed; contaminated surfaces were shipped to Chalk River for burial. Concrete floors were scarified or chipped away with air hammers.

Ceilings, walls, window frames, metal stair treads and brick work were sandblasted. A section of roof was cut away, safely disposed of and replaced. In May 1976 a joint inspection by the AECB and Ontario health authorities showed further work was necessary and it was done. Then a private contractor installed improved ventilation facilities in the building basement to bring the radon concentration down to a tolerable level.

At the outset Knight converted a small room at the southwest corner of the third floor to an office. From here he monitored every move that the decontamination crews made. Curtains and air pumps made the scarifying, air hammering and sandblasting tolerable. Respirators, safety glasses, safety shoes and white cotton coveralls were mandatory. Every expendable supply from ear plugs to safety goggles was kept under inventory control until ultimately disposed of in low-level radioactive waste canisters at Chalk River. Every piece of equipment from hard-hats to jackhammers was decontaminated before movement off site. Knight spent 350 hours supervising the first phase of the work. Added to his twenty years of health physics experience it was the basis of his recommendations for a cross-Canada cleanup of long-neglected radioactive contamination by a subsequent federal-provincial task force.

Backtracking through AECB's wartime license records Geoff Knight located the proprietor of the wartime radium lab at 103 Church Street. He was Carl Burton French and in mid-May 1975 Knight, Harry Aitken of Ontario's health ministry and Gordon Jack of Canada Health and Welfare were on his Toronto doorstep. The AECB records showed that the radium had been handled at the Church Street lab, around the corner at 54 Lombard Street and at a Scarborough farm on the outskirts of Toronto. French provided other addresses. There was a third one in Toronto, two Montreal locations, a farm west of Toronto and a Port Hope building that Eldorado refinery manager Marcel Pochon had used as a laboratory after retirement. The investigators readily located Pochon's old lab structure. The trail was still radioactive enough after thirty years it could be readily followed with a detector in hand. It took them initally to thirty-seven other Port Hope properties, including a school, which had been terraced and landscaped with dirt, debris and rubble from the Eldorado refinery site. Recently hired as the company's health physicist, Stan Frost's first move was to trace the disposal of refinery waste in past years. When the refinery was rebuilt in 1954, he told Geoff Knight, "The buildings were gutted and all contaminated materials, including three radium laboratories were buried at a disposal site near the village of Welcome." Recent radiation measurements at the site about four miles north of Port Hope gave exposure rates of up to one milliroentgen an hour at the disposal area fence and a tenth that much at the property line.

The AECB and Ontario health ministry focussed on the more immediate problem in town. As a long-time resident and the indefatigable voice of local concern, Mrs. Patricia Lawson duly noted: "Who was to guess the possibility of long-term danger to health and home that might lie in an innocent order with Oliver Cartage for a load of fill for the driveway?" A lot of residents had not. Eighty-five per cent of Port Hope's approximate thirty-five hundred homes had measureably high radon levels; about four hundred of them required decontamination. The work ranged from replacing actual contaminant building block and construction materials to carting away front lawns and underlying topsoil and replacing it. A subsequent $7 million decontamination program, conducted by an engineering firm under AECB direction, made these properties safe for occupants. But the interaction of concerned citizens, opportunist politicians, Toronto and Montreal-based anti-nukes with the news media fed a decade of controversy. That actually *prevented* the resolution of Eldorado Nuclear's waste-disposal problem at Port Hope.

That controversy followed on Geoff Knight's heels in the spring of 1975. Alerted by the AECB's newspaper appeal for former radium workers at 103 Church Street, two "researchers" were on his trail. One was William Peden of Energy Probe; the other had a similar job for the CBC television program "This Monday." Research scientists in industry and established government agencies pursue nature's truths in the innovative, but disciplined, manner that Roger and Francis Bacon ordained centuries ago. Energy Probe and TV researchers follow a simpler procedure. They clip newspaper reports, find phone numbers for the people involved, contact them and rehash others' findings. About ten days after Knight's first Port Hope inspection tour with Stan Frost, Bill Peden and a CBC-TV crew "discovered" the Welcome dump site. Much of the land around it would be unfit for farming for four thousand years, they told viewers. Hold a public inquiry immediately, MP Allan Lawrence demanded. The dump was emitting radiation a hundred times higher than normal background, as Knight and Frost had already established. It would not have been hazardous to anyone not living at the property fence 8,760 hours a year but it was still more than radioactive enough to energize the needle of a radiation counter into a menacing leap for an enterprising TV crew.

In May 1983 Energy Probe researcher Norman Rubin recalled the Port Hope affair in a newspaper article. "In 1975 a massive cleanup of radioactive contamination in Port Hope was triggered, not by AECB action — although the board had been warned of local hot spots nine years earlier — but by the discovery and disclosure of contamination by Energy Probe and the Canadian Broadcasting Corporation." His account, to put it politely, was absolutely wrong. Cynical readers who might doubt the AECB and Eldorado records — available to Rubin if he had sought them as diligently as I did — might refer to Penny Sanger's *Blind Faith* published in July 1981. "In 1974 revised Atomic Energy Control Board regulations became effective requiring that all residue-disposal areas operated by Eldorado become licensed. The company was required to track down places where waste had been dumped," Ms. Sanger wrote. That, in fact, had prompted Stan Frost's retrospective search for Eldorado waste sites. "During the previous winter... the board's health physicist Dr. Geoffrey Knight was on the trail of forgotten waste dumps throughout the province," said Ms. Sanger of the winter of 1974-75. "Alerted by these scattered events a CBC-TV newsmagazine team turned its attention to the town where the wastes had originated.... Viewers on June 23, 1975 saw dead trees and scarred vegetation at Port Granby."

A year later, with a federal-provincial task force under AECB aegis focussing several agencies' attention on long-neglected radium-waste sites across Canada, Geoff Knight observed: "Due to considerable publicity, the AECB is finding that decisions and choices are subject to political pressures and that reasonable technical and economic information is no longer sufficient. Thirty-five years ago there were no regulations controlling the use of atomic energy and public interest in the environment was minimal. Previously the AECB has dealt with well-identified licensees but this is no longer true when radioactive contamination is found in a private citizen's backyard. The AECB and other regulatory agencies now find they are facing problems which, with the publicity given to these 'discoveries', all cry at once for immediate solution."

It is ironic that the TV news and anti-nuke discoverers failed to follow the AECB's remarkable recovery of more than four thousand radioactive fragments of a Soviet satellite from some sixteen thousand kilometres of Canadian Arctic tundra. That project was virtually ignored by the media. It was completed in the first nine months of 1978 coincident with the wind-up of the Porter Commission nuclear inquiry and the Ontario legislative select committee's high-profile probe of Hydro's nuclear expansion. In May 1980 the AECB published a graphic account of the Cosmos-954 cleanup. But that was a year after Three Mile Island and the China Syndrome had captured public imagination. When you could shudder, shake and palpitate with Jane Fonda over the prospects of a nuclear reactor melting to a molten blob and burning its way through the planet clear down to China, who wanted to read about picking radioactive particles from Inuit country? The first radioactive fallout from the Soviet Union was heralded on arrival but its cleanup was generally considered a non-event.

One of thousands of satellites in earth orbit — but only one of a half-dozen with nuclear power on board — Cosmos-954 burned out in the Canadian sky on the morning of January 24, 1978. Travelling at twenty-seven times the speed of sound it hit the earth's atmosphere at a shallow angle and bounced around the world again. When it re-entered the upper air its speed was too slow for disintegration, still fast enough to be scorched and buffeted to fragments. Like stones flung by an angry god, satellite pieces fell across more than a hundred-thousand square kilometres of Inuit hunting and fishing lands. The larger fragments tracked a hazardous path in the snows of the Barrenland from Wood Buffalo Park to the Thelon River. About fifty radioactively hot chunks, rods and cylinders fell in a narrow path on the ice of Great Slave Lake. The debris extended northeasterly; the last and most conspicuous piece, a twenty-three kilogram assembly resembling caribou antlers, was found in the Thelon Game Sanctuary.

Cosmos-954 carried a small nuclear reactor to supply about a hundred kilowatts of electricity for communication. When it fell from orbit it was generating about a half-million curies of radioactivity, not more than a twenty-millionth part of Chernobyl's radiation. Most of it was in the fifty sizeable pieces recovered in the first dozen weeks of the winter search. But thousands of radioactive particles had fallen down-wind over a vast snow and ice-covered area. More than four thousand of these fragments, with a total weight of only five grams, were recovered. An Atomic Energy Control Board analysis showed that each of these pinpoint bits generated more radioactivity in an hour than Canadians would normally encounter in a month. "If an average particle was consumed up to mid-1978 it could give a radiation dose equivalent to a conventional stomach X-ray," the AECB warned. Inuit and their caribou herds roam these lands, the people fish these waters. "Our footprints are everywhere," the Inuit say. The control board recognized its responsibility to recover as many of those radioactive particles as the most advanced radiation-detection equipment could locate.

Several agencies cooperated in what was the most remarkable decontamination job prior to Chernobyl. Always operating with a minimal staff, the AECB relied heavily upon the expertise and facilities of the Geological Survey of Canada (GSC) and Atomic Energy of Canada Limited (AECL). While the board had responsibility for the location, recovery and safe disposal of Cosmos-954 debris the Department of National Defence did the logistical planning, the transport and supply. It was typical of the Canadian government's attitude that it dispatched just eleven AECB personnel and thirteen GSC experts, supported by 250 Canadian Forces members to do the job. The Americans sent 120 observers including their seventy-three-member nuclear search team. While AECB and GSC specialists manned the airborne detection equipment a twenty-five-member Canadian Forces Nuclear Accident Support Team (NAST) undertook the ground searches in Yellowknife and remote communities south of Great Slave Lake. There are a dozen NAST squads at Canadian Forces bases across the country. They originated when Armed Forces members were first recruited to help the AECB and AECL clean up the NRX and NRU sites in 1952 and 1957. Each NAST team embraces a radiation-monitoring unit, a security section trained to cordon off and isolate a source of radioactivity and a medical section including a medical officer and corpsmen trained to treat radiation victims. NAST members volunteer to participate in the training and ongoing drills. Their prime role is to locate and contain a nuclear weapon if one goes astray on Canadian soil.

Three months after Cosmos-954 was launched it began to wobble and NORAD advised Canadian authorities it would likely fall in January. When the satellite made its fiery re-entry the Control Board had been expecting it for twenty-four hours; the Geological Survey and AECL experts were ready at the Chalk River and Whiteshell nuclear labs. Regional army commanders had put their NAST squads on alert some days before. But in a sense Canadian agencies had been assembling the expertise and airborne equipment to detect pinpoint sources of radiation across the trackless tundra for nearly sixty years. With a fair amount of the world's surface in our backyard, Canadians practice global logistics with casual mastery. In the nineteenth century we cut portages from the Great Lakes waterway and built continental railroads. After World War I, when others were wing walking and barnstorming the fall-fair circuits or playing war games in Schneider Cup aircraft, our flyers were pioneering commercial aviation across the Barrenland. Amphibious Vickers Vikings, businesslike Fairchilds, workhorse Fokker and Ford tri-motor planes trundled northern skies like winged wheelbarrows. Aerial surveys were begun in the summer of 1919, prospecting by air a year later. A decade after that uranium prospector Gilbert La-Bine flew north to track radioactive outcrop on the shore of Great Bear Lake. Within a year or so other mining engineers, geologists and prospectors were radiologically mapping potential uranium fields throughout the territories.

The prevalence of uranium-bearing rock in the search area for Cosmos-954 debris was a mixed blessing. It had stimulated comprehensive mapping and radiological measurement. But radiation from uranium ore could mask that emanating from satellite particles unless very sophisticated equipment was employed. Natural background radiation in North America averages about ten microrems an hour in most localities. Where uranium exists it may be two or three times as high. But there were pitchblende deposits at the easterly end of the Cosmos-954 search area where readings a hundred times the nominal background are encountered. Such deposits encouraged the development of airborne detection equipment capable of distinguishing between a wide range of radiation levels. Some of the technology used by the AECB to track down the Cosmos-954 fragments orginated with LaBine's wartime exploration program. His crews moved out from Eldorado's Port Radium mine with advanced portable Geiger-Muller radiation counters and a proposal to use helicopters for the geological survey. A portable radiation counter, developed at the National Research Council in collaboration with the Geological Survey, was soon in use as far afield as South Africa. It was the first of a long line of radiation-detection equipment jointly developed by the NRC, GSC, AECB and AECL nuclear instrument makers.

Within days of the Cosmos-954 burnout the combined Canadian team was flying a half-dozen advanced scintillator gamma survey meters, several other sensitive detectors, an air sampler and a scintillometer on search tracks. The searchers' prize resource was a $250,000 spectrometer, a device developed just four months earlier by Quentin Bristow at the Geological Survey of Canada for use in detecting and mapping uranium deposits. A spectrometer catches radioactive rays in sodium-iodide crystals, sorts them out and identifies them with electronic blips and squiggles that are characteristic of the source. Pitchblende ore, for example would emit only the radiation identifiable with its uranium and radium content. Cosmos-954 particles radiated such products of nuclear fission as the tell-tale niobium isotopes fathered by plutonium. The heart of Bristow's machine was a crystal array 50,000 cubic centimetres in size. There was nothing else quite like it in the world. A physicist and mathematician by training, Bristow had begun his career at the Department of National Defence designing instruments for weapon testing, then he spent five years at the AECL on design of nuclear controls before taking his expertise to the Geological Survey of Canada. Said the makers of NOVA, the computer which coordinated navigational data with the GSC machine's findings to pinpoint the location of the satellite fragments: "As a computer programmer Bristow was not just conversant, but eloquent in assembly language. During the Cosmos-954 operation he had to devise quick interface with microwave navigation systems, even to turn the spectrometer's programs inside out to process the data in less than elegant facilities."

Bristow's work area was the cargo hold of a Canadian Forces four-engine, turbo-prop C130 Hercules where he mounted the three-quarter-ton, eight-foot gamma-ray machine back to back with the navigator's radar and electronic air-plot equipment. Like other search personnel Bristow watched his instrument's dials and strip-chart recorder through twelve to fourteen-hour flights thankful that the aircraft was well heated in the -40 degrees Celsius weather. The four Hercules heavy transport planes, four bush-flying Twin Otters, three Twin Huey helicopters and two big Chinook helicopters which worked the search area for the next twelve weeks were fitted for winter flying in Arctic terrain and their Canadian Forces crews were accustomed to it. They were sympathetic to the members of the American nuclear-emergency team who arrived in two cargo planes from their Las Vegas, Nevada base equipped and accustomed to a sunny climate and hospitable terrain.

Robert Grasty was at the spectrometer console when it located the first radioactive piece of the satellite on the snow-covered ice of Great Slave Lake. A geophysicist with ten years experience on airborne geological surveys with the GSC, Grasty was the first expert dispatched from Ottawa. Four hours after Cosmos-954 broke up over Canada, Grasty's boss Arthur Darnley called him to a meeting at the AECB's Albert Street offices. "We've got a problem out near Great Slave Lake and that's where you're going," Darnley told him. The sole passenger in a Falcon jet that whistled him to CFB Nanaimo, just north of Edmonton, Grasty arrived there in mid-afternoon Tuesday. As he entered the terminal building seventy-three US scientists and technicians came in all the other doors. "These Americans had been standing by all over the States for two weeks and they had all these airborne detectors, high-power cameras, infra-red scanners and computer equipment. Wonderful stuff," Grasty recalled. The problem was their equipment was designed for use in a warm climate over relatively flat terrain. "In any case

I did think Colonel Garland should know our system was twice as sensitive," Grasty said. He convinced the NAST commander Colonel David Garland that Bristow's device should be brought from Ottawa.

Grasty, Bristow and a third GSC air survey expert, Peter Hallman, worked through Wednesday night installing the spectrometer. Then Bristow flew with it for fourteen hours. But no high source of radioactivity triggered squiggles on the recorder paper. Grasty does not recall whether he slept at all Thursday night. He does remember an early-morning discussion with the Hercules navigation officers who were plotting search-and-rescue style flight patterns over the trackless Barrenland for twenty-five kilometres either side of the Cosmos re-entry route. "This was a military operation and for a civilian like myself it was rather difficult to have any input." But by that evening he had convinced the Forces airmen they should use larger-scale maps. Also at his suggestion Marine Command Argus submarine-tracking aircraft were brought in to overfly the Hercules and keep them on course. A day or two later two Forces helicopters were assigned to leap-frog the search aircraft, picking up and moving ground beacons of a microwave location system to keep the electronic searchers on precise pathways above the featureless, snow-coated tundra.

Grasty and Hallman sat through a fourteen-hour flight Friday watching vainly for blips on the spectrometer screen. At 7:30 p.m. they were rolling up chart paper when they caught sight of a notably high signal recorded a few minutes earlier. Eyes dimmed by fatigue they had missed it on the visual screen. When they landed Grasty did a quick backcheck. Time and ground speed put the suspect signal back at the eastern tip of Great Slave Lake. Computer experts double checked the recording tape with electronic precision. By noon Saturday Bob Grasty had confirmation. A NAST squad was flown by helicopter to the indicated site. There, a dozen miles from Fort Reliance, they found two pieces of the Soviet satellite on the snow-covered ice. Bob Grasty slept fitfully for a few hours Saturday. Then he went into the Combined Forces mess at Nanaimo base and got drunk. "I hope the deputy minister wasn't offended but I really did have to let down. It had been a tiring week," he told me.

By February 5 all the Canadian servicemen and the radiation-detection specialists were operating on twelve-hour shifts. Day in and day out the search crews flew three Hercules aircraft in an inverted-V formation at 250 metres above ground. Guided by microwave beacons the aircraft centred on imaginary lines that took them over trackless land on paths precisely 500 metres apart. Most of the debris, the larger fragments, were located and recovered from 40,000 square kilometres in a narrow path between Great Slave Lake and the Thelon River over a dozen weeks search. But weather data quickly established that the prevailing wind would have carried the smallest particles of radioactive satellite debris as far as 350 kilometres to the south. Irradiating pinpoints might have fallen in the settlements of Hay River, Pine Point, Fort Resolution and Rocher River on the south side of Great Slave Lake. They had. Lethal radioactive bits from Cosmos-954 might have been anticipated down through Wood Buffalo Park as far south as Fort Chipewyan, Alberta. They were. How many of these fragments fell in that vast area will never be known. But the combined recovery operation retrieved more than four thousand particles none of which weighed more than five-thousandths of a gram. Some weighed less than a hundred-millionths of a gram. Each of these miniscule bits was located by airborne detectors and computer-aided navigation on the leading edge of technology. Geoff Knight's survival skills in political territory were recognized by this time and he was given a key role in negotiating with Soviet officials to recover more than five million dollars towards Canada's costs in cleaning up Cosmos-954. In the process Geoff Knight gave his Soviet counterparts a comprehensive account of the high-tech expertise involved. Soviet experts would recall that when AECB, AECL and Ontario Hydro engineers outlined the facilities and know-how they had available after Chernobyl.

Quentin Bristow, Robert Grasty and their colleagues refined their spectrographic detectors and recalibrated their electronic instruments to even more precise parameters. When another Soviet nuclear-electrified satellite, Cosmos-1402, began to wobble in orbit five years later, the AECB had a contingency plan based on Cosmos-954 experience. The AECB would again be responsible for recovering debris and the Department of National Defence for logistics. But Cosmos-1402 did not fall in Canada so the authority of the AECB and of National Defence to mount another such recovery operation was an academic question.

But by then their authority to decontaminate radioactively polluted property in Canada had been challenged. The Appeal Court of Canada had decided that neither the ministers of defence nor energy had the statutory authority to finance such activity from their departmental budgets. Neither minister made a move to appeal that decision nor to pass enabling legislation. Anti-nuclear activists, labour organizers, environmental lawyers and NIMBY neighbours had forced the government agencies out of the controversial nuclear cleanup business in Canada. Good riddance, the ministers said. Why fight it?

11

Myths and Metaphors

"Myths and legends are being born before our very eyes."

— YURY SHCHERBAK, *LITERATURNAYA GAZETA*, JULY 23, 1986

"Different world views cannot be expressed except in terms of myths or metaphors."

— GORDON EDWARDS AND RALPH TORRIE,
TO PORTER COMMISSION, 1979

MYTHS ARE WISHFUL THINKING IN retrospect; metaphors sidestep reality. When Chernobyl opened the Iron Curtain a little wider each side had a chance to see how the other dealt with them.

"Myths and legends are being born before our very eyes. Sometimes I had the feeling that a time machine had transported me back to ancient Kiev when the irrepressible, vivid imagination of its inhabitants created poetic images," Yury Shcherbak wrote in a Soviet literary journal a few weeks after Chernobyl. A women evacuated from Pripyat was convinced that "right after the reactor exploded, night turned to day lighting the sky with strange tinges of colour, the air become unusually hot and all the flowers and trees in this cool region suddenly burst into blossom." Believing it herself she would tell this story to her children and grand-children. "Perhaps a thousand will tell it to each other and it will make its way throughout the world in various versions as an atomic-era legend."

But in his own recollections, Soviet writer Yury Shcherbak sorted fact from fiction. "My memory suddenly pulls out a picture from 1941, the wartime evacuation of Kiev. I remember how my first teacher gave me shelter, a seven-year-old Ukrainian boy in faraway Syzran. All the same I remember a constant sense of anxiety, of separation from home and the unnaturalness of what was happening. All this, of course, left its imprint on the children of the war who came to know the burden of evacuation," Shcherbak wrote. "That is why all of us should begin thinking hard about the children of Pripyat, Chernobyl and the many villages around the atomic-power station. Their health after all is our future, the life of our people in the twenty-first century. We should be thinking how to mitigate the consequences of the psychological trauma that has been inflicted on the children. The problem cannot be solved only with gifts and volunteer work in Young Pioneer camps. The children write about the hospitality and warmth with which they were greeted but confusion and uneasiness over the fate of their homes is constantly woven into their message."

Gordon Edwards is a mathematician; Ralph Torrie a physicist. But the tone of their seven-thousand-word summary argument to the Porter Royal Commission in 1979 was rhetorical. Their message was redolent of smoke and mirrors. They entitled it *A Metaphorical Framework*. As they explained, "It is impossible to understand the nuclear debate without understanding the different world views which underlie the two sides of the debate.... Different world views correspond to different visions of reality or different axiomatic systems which lead to mutually contradictory conclusions.... Different world views cannot be expressed except in terms of myths or metaphors." Edwards and Torrie were spokesmen for the Canadian and the Ontario Coalitions for Nuclear Responsibility at the Porter hearings. In testifying, arguing and cross-examining other witnesses they aptly expressed the anti-nuclear viewpoint, those "axiomatic systems" which the latter-day metaphysicians materialized out of the Hiroshima cloud. Pursuing mythical environmental laws, and the metaphors of self-elected public activists, they had no time to be concerned about uneasy children.

In the Middle Ages metaphysics — the philosophers' attempt to soar above reality — produced soothsayers, alchemists and charlatans. It was these and their mythology that Roger and Francis Bacon sought to disabuse. In the years after World War II the rejection of the Bomb's reality created a new crop of metaphysicians. They produced social scientifica, pseudo-science, myths and metaphors, talk fests and con games; they fostered opinion-poll leadership, government by public hearing and other verbal anarchy, self-elected public-interest advocates and environmental lawyers. They ploughed the depths of our public psyche where the repressed demons of the Bomb still lurked. They worked the ragged ranks of losers; they exploited the righteous anti-war activists, the rationally fearful and latter-day Luddites. They wooed opportunist politicians, the TV-light blinded and the ego freaks. There was no time to think about frightened kids.

The mass media loved them for the flood of entertainment they brought to a bored world. Their style was metaphorical, often ponderous as ancient Greek, disputatious as medieval monks arguing the number of angels dancing on a pinhead. Yet they affected a scientific manner and chanted their own mumbo-jumbo — "impact assessment," "institutional feedback," "accountability mechanisms." Their aim was to uninvent the wheel, windmill power the economy, make solar collectors a cottage industry, replace microwave ovens with dung-burning stoves. For fifty-five months in the 1975-1980 period the Porter Royal Commission was their stage in Canada. Then some of the same performers played in the Malvern drama that began with the media's rediscovery of refinery crud in fifty suburban backyards. The scenario reached a climax with the Federal Court's Borden ruling that emasculated the Atomic Energy Control Board. The Malvern affair and Borden case left some very disturbed children in their train.

In the summer of 1975 the Ontario government put Dr. Arthur Porter, electrical engineer and professor of engineering, into show business. He was commissioned to chair an inquiry into electrical-power planning in the province. Naively convinced of universal goodwill and intellectual honesty, creative and gregarious himself, he conducted an endless repertoire of pubic meetings, adversarial hearings, debates, guest panels, seminars and symposia that threatened to outrun the longevity of *Hello Dolly*. The commission quickly became a lightning rod for the nuclear debate in Canada. Anti-nukes swarmed from the woodwork like fireflies to tall clover. Hydro engineers, nuclear experts and brief-laden authority chased every spark with a net of science. But they never caught up with the environmentalist rhetoric.

The commission's mandate was to ventilate public concerns about Ontario Hydro's "environmental and socio-economic factors, load growth, system reliability, interconnections" and such. But you don't give the audience Shakespeare when they want a skin show. The commission shuffled most of the dull, weighty issues over to the legislature's all-party select committee on Hydro affairs. With the media and mass audience clamoring to be entertained, Arthur Porter played impresario to the nuclear debate. First season press notices were encouraging; TV lights glowed and cameras clicked. University lecture halls had never been like this. There was really no business like show business. Pausing to bring the "larger issues into preliminary focus" with cartoon illustrations, Porter launched his second season. Performers pro and con leapt to the freest-wheeling platform in Ontario since pre-war premier Mitchell Hepburn mounted a manure pile to harangue a fall-fair crowd. In 1976 Ontario Hydro, alone, deluged the commission with fifteen volumes of memoranda. Shaken by an air crash that killed the commission lawyer and seven government officials (a quarter of Chernobyl's death toll), the members went on a European tour. They were back in time to stage symposia at Christmas-pageant time.

Dr. Porter had found the key to the limelight in the 1970s. Nuclear was a dirtier word than sex; it got newsroom attention. The pre-Christmas symposia prompted further nuclear debate. Eminent nukes and anti-nukes were flown in from the States and from Britain for panel discussions the following summer. More eminence, pro and con, was presented in the fall. Originally expected to finish in October 1977, the "final" hearings were merely a pause for breath after 306 hours of debate, 829 cross-examinations and 700 hours of testimony that covered 26,000 pages of transcript. Then "new and compelling information required further investigation," Porter claimed. "The first matter encompassed serious concern about the safety of existing nuclear-power stations in Ontario." A second matter concerned a Canadian nuclear-industry study of where their next meal was coming from. These matters bought the commission two and a half years more tenure but the chairman was sharply rebuked for airing unfounded concerns. The "new and compelling information" turned out to be a swath of on-going correspondence that Ontario Hydro had maintained with the AECB since the 1960s. The safety of Canadian nuclear plants was re-affirmed by the federal and Ontario energy ministers and by the control board president.

"Perhaps I exaggerated a bit. I'm so innocent, so naive," Arthur Porter agreed. The impresario had reached too far over the footlights to embrace the audience and had fallen into the pit. Still the show must go on and it did. Moreover, it won applause from both sides. Its report on nuclear power, titled *A Race Against Time,* graphically illustrated the technology involved and it put complex nuclear issues in clear and forthright language. The 224-page report with its neat flow charts, graphs and tables should have gone into every secondary-school classroom in Canada. But that would have ended the controversy. The Porter Commission concluded that nuclear industry was a good thing for Canada and that it was relatively safe. "The absolute safety of any industrial process or human activity cannot be guaranteed," they said. In the case of the Candu reactor we believe that the likelihood of a major accident is extremely small. Within reasonable limits the reactor is safe. However, the need for continued vigilance and reassessment of reactor safety systems by Ontario Hydro cannot be over-emphasized." They recommended an ongoing committee of ecologists to keep both the AECB and Ontario's environment officials posted on the containment of uranium-tailings piles. They were confident that Eldorado and AECB would remain vigilant on the Port Hope waste-disposal problem.

The even-handed report did decisively part company with Energy Probe and the Canadian Environmental Law Association in one important matter. Both of these anti-nuclear groups had mounted public-relations campaigns and fought long and costly court battles to try and pack the Atomic Energy Control Board with members from organized labour, environmentalist and non-nuclear engineers and social scientists. "Vested interests" should be excluded until they had been inactive in Canadian nuclear matters for at least five years said Energy Probe and CELA. The Porter Commission members disagreed. "The complexity of the technology and the engineering, scientific, medical research and evaluation that must be conducted require the knowledge and skills of experts in nuclear matters. Given the limited number of nuclear experts in Canada, we accept that a close working relationship must exist between the regulator and the regulated," they said. The commission had entertained the public, stroked the anti-nukes and fed the press. But they were not prepared to entrust nuclear safety to amateur scientists.

The Porter Commission reinforced the nuclear industry and the AECB *vis-à-vis* the increasingly bitter assault by an anti-nuclear alliance embracing the New Democratic Party, organized labour, environmental lawyers and zealous crusaders who had become professional activists. At the same time the Commission funded the self-proclaimed public interest groups. Moreover, for five years it gave their spokesmen credibility, an aura of expertise and more publicity than these young pseudo-scientists and amateur advocates would have dreamed of before Arthur Porter brought them on stage. Gordon Edwards' Canadian anti-nuclear coalition lacked funds and identity when the Porter Commission began its hearings; Energy Probe needed all the help it could get in meeting its annual quarter-million-dollar budget. Ralph Torrie and his wife, an environmental-science graduate, launched a consultant practice based on his Porter Commission performance. The Porter

Commission provided some $346,000 to about two dozen organizations. The Canadian and Ontario Coalitions for Nuclear Responsibility got $40,000 of that in the first two years then they regrouped with Greenpeace and three other organizations to have Edwards and Torrie cross-examine establishment witnesses on their behalf. The Commission paid the coalition another $13,000 a year for that service. They gave Energy Probe $50,000 funding in three years. The Bates Commission, probing the possible hazards of uranium mining in British Columbia, funded twenty-eight organizations to a total of $219,000. Ralph Torrie and his wife represented four citizen groups in proximity to the proposed uranium development. They received $25,000 of funding for six months work before the BC government summarily closed down the inquiry in mid-February 1980. "We could have gone on until the end of March but all the other groups were at the end of their budgets and everyone was trying to find additional money," Torrie said with customary candor.

Until two journalism students rediscovered radium crud in the backyards of Malvern, a Metro Toronto subdivision, in 1980 this nuclear debate was relatively harmless. Social scientists might say it was a healthy ventilation of public dissatisfactions. The hearings cost millions of taxpayer dollars yet it was better to fund the interveners and their lawyers than have them rake leaves in the park. But Malvern added two new elements to the cost. It destroyed the Atomic Energy Control Board's authority to assemble, coordinate and direct what was probably the most expert radiation detection and decontamination program in North America. And it did grievous harm to the children of McClure Crescent in the Malvern subdivision. "We should be thinking how to mitigate the consequences of the psychological trauma that has been inflicted on the children," said Soviet writer Yury Shcherbak after Chernobyl. "As a precaution several thousand children were hospitalized. Like a number of older people they had to be calmed down," Leonid Ilyin told us at Vienna. No one said anything like that in Canada after the Borden case.

Keen, enterprising and knowledgeable, journalism students Janel Glassco and Frank Giorno followed the flickering needle of a Geiger counter around McClure Crescent one mid-November day in 1980. They were after a story as a term project. The lead had come from a chemist who had worked at 103 Church Street. He told them of a shack on a Scarborough farm where refinery waste and cleanup materials had been incinerated. A nuclear scientist who measured the radiation at that shack as part of an RCMP wartime investigation in June 1945, Leslie

Cook, had vainly urged both federal and Ontario health officials to decontaminate the site. Thirty years later the ten-acre farm was stripped of its topsoil to make way for house building. Then the dirt had been bulldozed back to form home-site yards. In 1975 Geoff Knight sampled the soil at twenty-four places and found nothing alarming. Nine years and several examinations later and AECB radiation expert Roger Eaton examined 109 houses on McClure Crescent. None had radon-daughter levels of radioactivity above established health standards. Four did have above normal concentrations of radon gas comparable to hundreds of homes in mining communities where small ventilation fans readily remove the excess.

The *Globe and Mail* headlined and front-paged the Ryerson students' findings for three days in November 1980 but did not suggest that the Malvern families' health was endangered. "Traces of radioactive waste have been located in the middle of an Ontario Housing Corporation subdivision in Scarborough and unofficial tests indicate the level of radioactivity is above acceptable levels set by the federal government," they said. Those who read two paragraphs further on would learn that the above-normal readings were found in two McClure Crescent backyards and that Roger Eaton "expects to remove some contaminated soil from the two properties." Readers who persisted to the tenth paragraph were told by a university physicist that the radiation a metre above ground at the two hot-spots was one ten-thousandth of a rem per hour or twice the level federal authorities say is safe for long-term exposure.

"There is not a serious immediate health hazard associated with low concentrations of radioactive materials," Geoff Knight had been saying for five years. The solution was to remove the contaminated soil and/or ventilate basements to avoid radon concentration. In Port Hope he was dealing with the occupants of a nuke town familiar with radioactivity and with a local newspaper not inclined to upset the industry that employed one wage earner in six. Yet even in Port Hope the AECB had found "that decisions and choices are subject to political pressures." The Malvern community, developed under the provincial government's Home-Ownership-Made-Easy plan and a news target for half a dozen daily newspapers and television stations, was a considerably more volatile community. Within a week the AECB invited two hundred Malvern residents to a meeting in the local high-school auditorium. Roger Eaton said the hot spots would be eliminated. Scarborough medical health officer Keith Fitzgerald told them he was not "unduly excited;" the Burrows Hall junior public school, more than a thousand yards from the contaminated soil, was unaffected, he said. The area's alderman Joe deKort had a graduate degree in nuclear physics. He did not think it was a serious problem.

But Scarborough Major Gus Harris was already concerned about how and where the cruddy soil would go. More than a generation removed from the working-class community of an English mill town, Gus Harris was chief magistrate of a big metropolitan borough in which he still visualized "us" and "them" on opposite sides of the tracks. Harris voted with the New Democrats, the labour unions, and they with him. The NDP, with support from organized labour, was decidedly anti-nuclear, so was Gus Harris. Nuclear technology and engineering are high-tech fields demanding highly skilled and well-educated operators. They are unionized but they are out of step and ill considered by the big union leaders and by labour's political voice, the NDP. Technology is as suspect to the NDP-labour-Energy Probe coalition today as steam-powered textile mills once were in north England.

Among labour and NDP leaders this Luddite fear of the nuclear industry is long-standing. The NDP's predecessor party was the CCF for Canadian Commonwealth Federation. In the spring of 1957, the CCF member for Nanaimo, BC, Colin Cameron told Parliament that the government's pursuit of the peaceful atom "can only lead to catastrophe to the human species." At the NDP's national policy convention in 1979 they urged a moratorium on all nuclear development in Canada. The loudest nuclear critics were from British Columbia. But Saskatchewan and Ontario delegations were notably split on nuclear issues. An NDP government in Saskatchewan had built a Crown company, Saskatchewan Mining Development Corporation into the world's biggest uranium producer. Once out of office they railed against SMDC but stopped short of opposing its continuing operations. In Ontario, where nuclear and uranium industries provided more than twenty-five thousand jobs, the NDP steered a hectic course between outright class warfare against these industries and endorsement of their high-wage employment.

At that convention there were two notable exceptions. "We may have enough nuclear power but to say that we shouldn't mine any more uranium is nonsense. It is the sort of emotional breast-beating we sometimes get ourselves into," the former NDP national leader and past premier of Saskatchewan Tommy Douglas told me. The even-handed chairman of Ontario's all-party leigslative select committee which had recently declared Ontario Hydro nuclear plants "acceptably safe," Donald Macdonald told fellow delgates: "If I was in BC or Manitoba or Newfoundland I would be totally opposed to the nuclear establishment because those provinces enjoy the luxury of water power and Alberta can produce electricity from coal. In Ontario 34 per cent of our electricity is nuclear. Do you want the whole province to be in a blackout?"

NDP delegates were shown a thirty-minute anti-nuclear television film jointly produced by NDP MPP Evelyn Gigantes, a former broadcaster, and Energy Probe's Norman Rubin. Ms. Gigantes had been the most indomitable member of the select committee. She was invariably the one who asked the right questions. Militantly anti-nuclear she was still too intellectually honest to distort, misquote or misrepresent the evidence. Her collaborator, "nuclear researcher" Norman Rubin was not so inhibited. A self-styled "professional anti-nuclear activist," and "card-carrying peacenik" who found sanctuary in Canada while of draft age, Rubin made no attempt to cover his contempt for Canadian nuclear expertise. "If Ottawa and Queen's Park decide to keep propping up an unviable Candu industry we will all have to be ready for more mushroom clouds with the maple leaf on them," he insisted. In Scarborough, where fifty families on the Malvern community's McClure Crescent faced years of anxiety and harassment by anti-nuke zealots and overly zealous reporters, Gus Harris prolonged the ordeal by steadfast opposition to having the mildly contaminated dirt temporarily stored anywhere in the municipality no matter how benign the crud or remote the site.

The control board moved quickly. One week after the initial *Globe and Mail* story, Roger Eaton, of the AECB, opened an office in the Malvern community to handle resident queries. A fortnight later AECB officials and a member of the Malvern Community Association met with Scarborough and Ontario representatives to discuss removal of the contaminated soil. Opposition first caught up with the AECB a week before Christmas. Roy Paluoja of the Malvern Community Association was told that Scarborough's Beare Road garbage dump had been mentioned "but approval would be a problem." Later that week Ontario's Minister of Intergovernmental Affairs and Scarborough MPP Tom Wells said he didn't think the Beare Road dump was "viable." He suggested that it might go to Eldorado's leaking and interdicted Port Granby disposal site. Mayor Harris agreed; he had no hesitation in seeing this erstwhile Eldorado waste go back to Allan Lawrence's constituency. "Move it out of Scarborough fast," he said.

Prompted by concern for the badgered McClure Crescent residents, the AECB president Jon Jennekens proposed an abandoned mine site near Bancroft. "The amount of radium in the soil was very small but it had become a matter of mental anguish for the families who lived there," Jennekens recalled. "If we could have taken it to the Madawaska mine-tailings area [near Bancroft] it would have removed it from the Malvern subdivision and it would have promoted grass or other vegetation growth to contain the tailings. We outlined the various options in a news release and we discussed them with our Ontario colleagues. We talked to the Madawaska Mines people and they were happy to cooperate. We had some meetings with local township officials who accepted our assurances there would be no environmental contamination." So far so good. But the Bancroft council demanded a public meeting. "About 150 people attended; some were there for an argument," the AECB chief remembered. "They were there to say 'not in my backyard. I don't care how sound your technical arguments are.' At that point the Ontario government decided it didn't want any part of a controversial plan. If they had supported us as their officials had said they would, the Malvern problem would have been removed in the summer of 1981." Second-guessing himself Jon Jennekens regreted his capitulation to federal and provincial politicians. "You know if we had stood up to the two levels of government and said 'throw out all these nonsensical arguments, throw out all these confrontational tactics' it would have been inescapable that this is the way to go." If Jennekens had thumped their desks in anger the political bosses might have thanked him a year or two later. Instead he tried again to find a temporary Scarborough location. But the mayor of Scarborough said, "I won't have any of this, don't bother me with arguments."

So the AECB proposed temporary storage on an asphalt pad at a corner of the Camp Borden Armed Forces Base. Built to train air force pilots for World War I, the base was enlarged to eighty-five square kilometres and urbanized to house eight thousand residents after World War II. This major military base was still nominally under national defence control but times had changed. By the summer of 1981 the defence minister shared his authority with the Public Service Alliance of Canada which spoke for the thousands of civilian employees there. "I don't think the federal Liberals or the provincial Conservatives are clean on this whole thing. Borden was selected purely for political needs and I don't think any consideration was given to the geology or water table or anything else," Arthur Curtis, regional representative for the Public Service Alliance told me in September that year. He was right about the politicians but he should have included federal Conservatives, provincial Liberals and the NDP everywhere. He was wrong about the geology and water table. They were irrelevant.

What allied labour, politicians, anti-nukes and environmental lawyers at Borden was the NIMBY factor. "Our governments have agreed that the low-level radioactive waste in the McClure Crescent area must be removed," Ontario Premier William Davis told Prime Minister Pierre Trudeau on August 7. "Instead of the current plan by the AECB to move it to Camp Borden it is in the public interest that it be moved to the AECL waste-disposal site at Chalk River as quickly as possible." The Ontario government was "profoundly concerned" with the plan, the cabinet's management-board chairman George McCague telexed Energy Minister Marc Lalonde. McCague was the MPP for the Borden area. "It is offensive to me that Premier Davis feels the Upper Ottawa Valley ought to become the province's nuclear-waste disposal site," Sean Conway, MPP for Renfrew North which embraces Chalk River, told the premier. "It was a decision made strictly on a political basis to get it out of Scarborough where it was creating political problems for [federal Public Works Minister] Paul Cosgrove," Perrin Beatty, one of the two MPs embracing the Camp Borden area, advised. "Get it out of Scarborough," Ontario Intergovernmental Affairs Minister Tom Wells and Scarborough Mayor Gus Harris reiterated.

"The people who live in the Township of Essa, or many of them have expressed great concern not only about health but about the effect which radioactive storage may have on the economic value of their properties," Essa Reeve Charles Vernon Pridham testified in the Federal Court action which Essa and Tosorontio townships brought to stop the AECB. Reeve Pridham was personally concerned about the nearby Pine River which frequently flooded in the spring. He owned five tourist park sites including an arena close by and twenty-eight acres alongside Base Borden. The Nottawasaga Valley Water Control Advisory Board was concerned "that the deposit of the waste is anticipated to be at the heart of the Nottawasaga watershed within close proximity to the Pine River," said its chairman Ralph Rae Macdonald. "I am also in the construction business," he said. No builder eyeing the Malvern subdivision notoriety was apt to welcome the crud, and Luigi G. Biffis was another who didn't. As president of the Alset Construction Company he was about to develop a 105-lot subdivision of $50,000 homes in Essa Township close to the Borden base. "The plan of the Atomic Energy Control Board and the federal government to store radioactive soil at CFB Borden has created considerable anxiety in the area. Because of the anxiety and concern over a possible drop in land values caused by the plan I am now finding it uneconomical and difficult to proceed with the subdivision until the radioactive-soil storage is settled."

It would be difficult to determine who cast the first stone. Reeve Pridham said that by the time he and other municipal leaders were briefed by the base commander and by Roger Eaton of the control board on July 23 there were people protesting. "I was watching the television news on the August first holiday when I learned of the situation at Borden. People were picketing the base, demonstrating against the Malvern soil," Arthur Curtis recalled. As the Public Service Alliance of Canada representative in London, Ontario, Base Borden was within his bailiwick. Curtis called the Alliance headquarters in Ottawa; they sent him to Borden. "I got the feeling of the workers there and did some research. I got some background stuff on radioactivity. It was my first encounter outside of the little bit I got in school. Then I talked to Perrin Beatty, one of the two MPs for the area, and to Charles Pridham, the Essa reeve. Given the wishes of the people we decided to hold a demonstration on August 13," Curtis said.

Meanwhile Beatty headed a delegation to Ottawa. Energy Minister Marc Lalonde declined to see them but they did meet with MP Roy MacLaren, the parliamentary secretary who answered for energy in the Commons. "We were concerned about the hazard and with the principle," Beatty said. "If they could bang this thing into Borden within a month of announcing it would it be a political option the next time hazardous waste was found in a cabinet minister's constituency like Cosgrove's?" Beside all that, Beatty and the other Borden area politicians didn't trust the AECB. They didn't know if the control board could safely store the 3,600 tonnes of contaminated soil at the Borden base. "The only way people will be satisfied as to their safety would be if there was a full, public environmental-assessment hearing by a disinterested third party as opposed to reassurances from the AECB. The AECB are a proponent," said the MP. He felt that until there was a public hearing with input from other "experts" such as Energy Probe and the Canadian Environmental Law Association, for example, Energy Minister Marc Lalonde and Defence Minister Gilles Lamontagne were being dictatorial.

Beatty was worried that Base residents were being muzzled by military authority, but Arthur Curtis said there were always legal, evasive ploys. "Collectively, if you utilize the proper procedures you have the right. We held a demonstation in Angus plaza but the public servants themselves were not speaking. People like myself were the ones who did the talking. Public servants can attend a demonstration or hold a sign as long as they are not vocally criticizing a government department policy." In any case the Public Service Alliance members had the contractual right "to withdraw from an unhealthy environment until such time as Labour Canada and National Health and Welfare determine it is safe. More than 50 per cent are ready to walk off the Borden base. It's their individual right," Curtis explained.

Just to be on the safe side the base residents were transported in a convoy of thirty cars, trucks and a chartered bus eighty-five kilometres from Borden to the Ontario legislative buildings in Toronto, on August 9. It was a Sunday with nobody at Queen's Park to protest to or wave signs at. No one except the news media. Men, women and children paraded into camera range again and again. The signs were homemade. "Save us kids, you'll need our taxes," "Trudeau, are you sending us to an early grave?" "Fuddle duddle to Trudeau and the Just Society," they said. A two-year-old held her daddy's grasp with her right hand and clutched a sign with her left. "I may be LITTLE but I CARE," it read. The news media loved it. How thoughtful to bring the news to their doorstep on a dull summer weekend!

On August 12 Federal Court Justice Patrick Mahoney heard the application of the two municipalities adjacent to Camp Borden, the townships of Essa and Tosorontio, who sought an injunction to stop the Atomic Energy Control Board from transferring a hundred thirty-six-tonne truckloads of dirt from McClure Crescent backyards to the military camp within a mile and a half of rural homes. "The anxieties of residents of both townships are real and not unreasonable given the lay perception, which I share, of the implications of even the slightest threat of radioactive pollution of the environment in which one regularly lives and works. I accept that personal harm may result from anxiety, as here, and that economic damage can ensue if the anxiety is related to the safety of the locality," Justice Mahoney declared two days later. "However, the question in this case is whether the plaintiff will suffer injury from the actual escape of radon-222 from the site, not injury from fear or anxiety as a result of its storage there. . . . The court does not enjoy the range of options suggested as to the disposition of the contaminated soil. The court can only decide whether it should remain in a built-up residential area of Scarborough until trial or be removed to CFB Borden to be stored one and a quarter miles from the nearest residence. The choice is obvious."

It was obvious to Justice Mahoney but Premier Davis, managment board chairman George McCague and Intergovernmental Affairs Minister Tom Wells found the comparison politically odious. Store the stuff at Chalk River, they urged Marc Lalonde. "We find no compelling arguments to support your proposal," the energy minister replied. Borden area residents marched on Queen's Park again. Their protest was with Ottawa but Toronto had more TV and newspaper cameras to march into. "Radioactive dirt a political ruse, officials say," the *Toronto Star* reported.

The Township of Tosorontio appealed the Federal Court Decision. On September 11 Appeal Court Justice Louis Pratte reversed the Mahoney decision and granted an injunction not only against the AECB, the energy and defence ministers, but against the Borough of Scarborough as well where Mayor Harris certainly didn't want to keep the cruddy stuff. Justice Pratte seriously doubted that the government of Canada could authorize the AECB to do anything under the authority of the Appropriation Act, the government's funding mechanism, "even when it is read with the estimates to which it refers."

"Having lost the case the federal government felt frustrated in its attempts to do something that would serve the public interest and they said now, look Ontario, it is within your power to do something and Ontario has been endeavouring to do exactly that for the last two or three years," Jon Jennekens told me two years later.

"But when the government accepted the Appeal Court ruling didn't you feel that they were letting the challenge to AECB authority go as well?" I persisted. "Yes, very definitely," the AECB president replied.

"When the federal lawyers were instructed not to dispute the spending authority of the AECB were you, in effect, taken out of the the the decontamination business for all time?" "That's true, exactly," he agreed. But he was a civil servant subject to government authority. Neither subsequent Liberal or Conservative governments in Ottawa chose to restore AECB domestic authority and the NDP certainly would not.

"So it has now been clarified that the Atomic Energy Control Board really has no ability to remove this soil. They have no trucks, no people and no place to put it," Sister Rosalie Bertell told a CBC interviewer on March 26, 1984. She was commenting on her Federal Court testimony that week on behalf of Waste Not Wanted, yet another ad hoc group of a dozen families who had stopped yet another federal agency — the five-member, low-level radioactive-waste management branch of Atomic Energy of Canada Limited — from moving the Malvern waste to yet another temporary location, a government-owned site in a remote corner of Scarborough. Three years earlier Sister Bertell had offered to help lawyer Jack Futerman who was acting for four McClure Crescent families by arranging for urine and blood tests. Those tests inspired the myth of the irradiated McClure Crescent children.

Here is the anatomy of that myth: "Six Scarborough kids guinea pigs in radiation test," the *Toronto Star* headlined a story in mid-July 1981. Six children in a McClure Crescent home would undergo body scans at Toronto General Hospital to determine if there was any trace of radium in their bones. The tests were demanded by Sister Rosalie Bertell. "Kids radiation scans called inadequate," said *The Star* the next day. Sister Bertell said so and at least one McClure Crescent parent agreed with her. "Father skeptical about methods of testing children for radiation," the *Globe and Mail* reported. "Sister Bertell feels the urine test is better," said one of the parents, John Langcaster.

"Tests show no traces of abnormal radiation in three Scarborough children," said *The Globe* at the end of July. "Body scans are negative," said the *Scarborough Mirror* a few days later. Twenty children had been examined with no indication of radioactivity said medical health officer Keith Fitzgerald. "Final body scans find no trace of radiation," said *The Star* a day after that citing twenty-six children's results.

But after nearly a year's frustration John Langcaster met that fall with Sister Bertell, University of Waterloo chemistry professor Hari Dutta Sharma and Dr. Dermit McLoughlin, a radiologist associated with Physicians for Social Responsibility. They convinced him that blood and urine samples should be done on forty-one McClure Crescent children. "Malvern children found healthy but parents worried over A-soil," said the *Globe and Mail* in mid-September. "It's reassuring to know that they haven't found anything but the soil is still in our backyard. We want it elsewhere," said Judith Heighington, mother of six. "My children could be walking time bombs," her husband George added.

"Radiation expert wants more tests," the *Toronto Star* reported late in September. Dr. Sharma had found the urine analysis "inconclusive." A week later blood tests proved more newsworthy. "Kids in radioactive area have low white cell count," the *Toronto Star* said in a front-page story that quoted one parent. "Dr. McLoughlin cautioned yesterday that the high results may have been due to a virus and tests must be repeated at intervals before conclusive evidence can be drawn," said *The Star*. "Nevertheless Sister Rosalie Bertell finds the results disturbing because of the residents close proximity to the radiation."

The following summer, Sister Bertell revealed more disturbing news. "Child's level found forty-six times average," the *Globe and Mail* announced on June 26. "We're facing another summer where the children want to play in the backyards and the backyards are contaminated," she told the paper. A day earlier she had issued a news release from the Jesuit Centre for Social Faith and Justice to report: "One child in the McClure Crescent area of Scarborough had a level of radioactive lead in urine forty-six times the expected level for adults in the industrialized sections of North America. This finding may also indicate the child was exposed to forty times the investigative level set by the Atomic Energy Control Board." The child was one of four who had been retested a few weeks earlier. The release gave results of the four tests but no further explanation. In light of her Federal Court testimony in the spring of 1984 I queried her about that test which had turned up such startling results contrary to all previous findings.

Had the study ever been reported in a scientific or medical journal? Well no. Could I get a copy of her data, or see it? Well no. "Nothing has been written up. I've done this all free of charge in my spare time trying to help people out there because I thought it was incredible the way it was handled by government," Sister Bertell replied.

"There are some people who say, Sister, that your recent comments encouraged Waste Not Wanted to prevent the movement of this soil from Malvern and that your earlier comments to a group in the Beare Road area encouraged people to take action to stop it being moved from Malvern," I said.

"In actual fact I have gone to groups and asked them to accept it but also to demand that it be properly handled, properly packaged and properly isolated from the environment," she told me. Sister Bertell, with a doctorate degree in mathematics, considerable practice in analyzing statistics of cancer incidence, and much more experience in giving her analyses an anti-nuclear slant as a globe-trotting, professional witness, did not trust the AECB. Like Norman Rubin of Energy Probe she thought the control board was the mouthpiece of nuclear industry, of the power people, of big government. Like Rubin she did not trust Jon Jennekens. Sister Bertell and Norman Rubin would not understand that Canada's chief nuclear regulator and IAEA safeguards specialist, scientist and soldier, father of three, would be moved to tears by the anguish of the McClure Crescent families.

In the spring of 1985 a Scarborough social worker named Alvin Curling ran for election in the provincial riding that embraces the Malvern development. As so many politicians had done before him he promised to do something about the McClure Crescent home sites if elected. That summer he was named minister of housing in the Peterson government at Queen's Park. In October he announced that the government would buy any of the forty-one homes concerned. "Most of the problem was psychological. What we did was to disclose all the information for them to assess themselves. I didn't think they should make a decision under duress," he explained. By the end of 1986 twenty-four

145

McClure Crescent families had sold their homes back to the government, another nine were considering it. Yet others, made fully aware of the controversy and radiation surveys, were buying these same homes. The newcomers to McClure Crescent, however, had not been hounded by the news media. They had not been worried about blood and urine tests and body scans. The Malvern affair was over and their children would not be taunted in the schoolyard about radioactive urine.

"My youngest one who is almost four, he's never played in the backyard," said John Langcaster of 106 McClure Crescent that summer of 1984.

"I had a swing set in the backyard. They were constantly using it. We grew vegetables. We don't use the yard anymore. The swing set is just sitting there rusting," Royston Neil Jones of 52 McClure Crescent said.

"The stress is really there. It is all throughout the street. I wonder when someone's going to break. I really do," said J. Ross Stirling at 54 McClure Crescent.

"What can we do? My wife says 'When I go down in the basement it seems like some cloud is over my head.' There is a lot of stress," Tseng Tang said at 87 McClure Crescent.

"We removed the kids from the neighbourhood school and brought them downtown to work with us. After work we used to take them home. Every day we used to do that. We did it for one year. For two summers we sent them to their grandmother," said Doyne Senevirante at 50 McClure Crescent.

"If I let myself think about it I wonder what kind of guilt am I going to have if something happens to my children in fifteen or twenty years? Will I be able to say to them it wasn't my fault we moved here?" Lorna Weigand at 3 McClure Crescent asked herself.

"I was driving to work when I first heard about it on the radio. I thought Oh God I've spent my whole life struggling very hard, sometimes working two jobs at a time, so we and the kids could have a home, so they don't have to live in an apartment and play in a parking lot. And like suddenly all that just seemed to be going right out the window," Eileen Elford at 1 McClure Crescent remembered.

"My oldest son is under a psychologist's care right now. His grades have dropped tremendously. He's constantly being kidded at school. You know, 'You live on radioactive soil,' that sort of thing. He is a very emotional child," said another McClure Crescent mother.

"I am listening with the greatest attention to Pripyat teachers," Soviet writer Yury Shcherbak said. "They are talking about the selflessness of most teachers who did not abandon their children in a difficult time.

They also tell me about those who taught the children their first cruel lesson, the teachers who abandoned their pupils, who betrayed them. That was a lesson in faithlessness and it shocked the children's souls."

Yury Shcherbak would understand the children's anguish on Mc-Clure Crescent.

12

Glasnost and Doomsayers

"It's a great time to be a doomsayer."

—NORMAN RUBIN, *MACLEAN'S*, APRIL 9, 1979

"Glasnost is a political weapon used by the Soviet leader to light a fire under sluggish administrators and leaders and to overcome opposition to economic and political reforms."

— PAUL QUINN-JUDGE, *CHRISTIAN SCIENCE MONITOR*, SEPTEMBER 1, 1986

CHERNOBYL WAS A MOMENT OF TRUTH for the Soviet press. It was the catalytic event that transformed a servile media into a critical agent of Mikhail Gorbachev's new Soviet state. Chernobyl may have had a lasting impact on the Canadian media as well. It squelched the doomsayers.

To just equate the Soviet term *"glasnost"* with openness is an oversimplification said Paul Quinn-Judge, the *Christian Science Monitor*'s man in Moscow after Chernobyl. "It's a political weapon used by the Soviet leader to light a fire under sluggish administrators and leaders and to overcome opposition to economic and political reforms. The press was given a free rein in examining the performance of the Communist party and government bodies in responding to the accident. The heroism of troops, firefighters and workers has been given extensive coverage. But the leading papers also reported that senior members of the power station staff deserted the plant in panic soon after the

148

accident. A Western-style benefit concert was given a good play. But so was the fact that about thirty other concerts in the Chernobyl area were cancelled in May, presumably because artists were afraid to travel to the area."

Nor was the candid Chernobyl coverage "just a one shot deal," Lawrence Martin said in the *Globe and Mail* when the Soviet naval ministry called a Moscow press conference that fall to report the sinking of a Black Sea cruise ship. "It is a new tendency. There is an emphasis on changing our approach," a Soviet deputy minister told Martin. "Under the direct authority of Mikhail Gorbachev officials are beginning to show signs of *glasnost* or openness where reflex secrecy reigned before," Gordon Barthos agreed in the *Toronto Star*.

Glasnost was not immediately apparent; it took the Soviets more than a hundred hours to get their act together at Chernobyl. This was not an unreasonable delay considering the unprecedented situation that confronted Valery Legasov's experts. "People would do well to look back to the little accident at Three Mile Island. It was days, if not weeks before anyone could paint a reasonably clear picture of what had happened," Britain's *New Scientist* observed. But here was the world's worst nuclear accident happening and those frightful Russians were ignoring North American news deadlines. Response varied.

" '2,000 DEAD' IN NUKE DISASTER," screamed a *Toronto Sun* headline, based on a United Press International report from Kiev. *The Sun* editors cautiously put single quotation marks around the toll suggesting they doubted its validity. As it turned out the UPI report was 99.9 per cent wrong. A Kiev woman, Mrs. T.V. Yatsenko complained that on April 29 UPI correspondent Luther Wittington, "insistently tried to obtain untruthful figures on the supposedly large number of casualties. I answered that two people had died." UPI editor-in-chief Michael McCrohon apologized a month later: "UPI can no longer stand by its article. Subsequent developments did not confirm this report." By then, however, *The Sun* had found other cause for hysteria. "NUKE FIRE SPREADS, Second Soviet reactor believed melting down," it advised on May 1. "MOSCOW ADMITS WIDER NUCLEAR LEAK DAMAGE. New evacuation ordered," it reported on June 5. In fact, Ukraine Premier Alexander Lyashko had ordered ninety-five thousand people evacuated from farms and sixty-two rural communities a month earlier and there were no further evacuations. "The press," said *Toronto Star* ombudsman Rod Goodman, "is the catch-all term by which we are known. When one is out in left field with a story or headline we all carry the can." Goodman was commenting on the *New York Post* 's initial headline on Chernobyl.

"MASS GRAVE FOR 15,000 N-VICTIMS," it said.

No Canadian medium achieved that degree of sheer irresponsibility. But one or two vied for it. On the Sunday morning following the Chernobyl accident radio listeners who tuned to the CBC in the Toronto region about 9:30 a.m. would have heard: "This is Durham Region Police. An emergency warning is in effect. If you are outdoors please go inside immediately. Close all doors and windows. Tune your radio to Station CHOO or CKAR for further instructions."

"This is an emergency measures announcement," said a second male voice. "A radiation alert is in effect. There is no need for panic. Pickering residents with their own transportation are requested to proceed in an orderly fashion to Iroquois Park Arena quickly. If you require transportation please remain indoors and tie a white rag on all doorknobs that can be seen from the road." Those listeners who were not already headed for Iroquois Park or tearing up sheets for doorknob rags, would have heard a third man say, "Now, we continue our special programing. Our reporter has reached the Emergency Processing Centre in Whitby."

"Hello, Jim," a fourth speaker went on, "there are several hundred people here already with more arriving every moment. Teams from Ontario Hydro and EMO are checking for radioactive contamination as they come in. . . ." Listeners who tuned in on the "Durham police warning" heard eleven minutes of this puerile play-acting; adult broadcasters crying havoc for dramatic effect. No accidents or heart attacks apparently followed. Perhaps the George Orwellian folk who move about with walkman head-sets blocking out reality only listen to music. Maybe they don't comprehend the words.

None of the other media were quite that irresponsible. Most continued to have problems with epidemiological statistics, that is the postulated, statistically predictable, theoretically calculated, guess-estimated number of cancer deaths that might result from Chernobyl. "These are notional or statistical, not real deaths," said a British publication. "There is no direct experimental evidence that the radiation doses, in fact, lead to any cancer fatalities," Canada Health and Welfare cautioned. Southam Press correspondent Paul Koring probably said it best when he reported from Vienna that, "Thousands of people will eventually die of radiation-caused cancer from Chernobyl. But statistically they will be lost among the millions of cancer fatalities occurring naturally in the Soviet Union. Medical experts were careful to point out that no individual death from cancer could be traced to Chernobyl." Here is how three Canadian papers handled that story: "Nuke toll could hit 75,000," said a *Toronto Sun* heading over an Associated

Press report. "Chernobyl death toll may reach 24,000," said the *Hamilton Spectator* based on Koring's story. "Chernobyl toll expected to hit 6,500," the *Globe and Mail* advised with a Reuter's report.

Canadian papers validly reported what people told them. The news, of course, was dependent on whom they asked. Mulroney ministers were notably unavailable except for Health Minister Jake Epp, but at Queen's Park provincial leaders were forthright in their responses. "Chernobyl is going to put the nuclear industry under siege," said Premier David Peterson. "But I'm assured by everybody involved that ours is the safest system that exists. Certainly I have no fear of the Candu system." Conservative leader Larry Grossman suggested that Ontario should offer the Soviets its technical expertise, a suggestion that Hydro chairman Tom Campbell already had underway. NDP leader Bob Rae told the *Globe and Mail*'s Orland French he didn't want to overact; however, it was important "to recognize that there are limits to scientific knowledge." Canadian scientists agreed the Candu system was safe, Rae noted, "just as I'm sure Soviet scientists told Soviet authorities their system was foolproof." Energy Probe's Norman Rubin had said the same thing a day earlier.

At a Queen's Park press conference called by the NDP on May 6, their energy critic MPP Brian Charlton noted that both the Candu and Chernobyl reactors were based on a pressure-tube design. So are most non-nuclear steam plants, of course. In both Canada and the USSR there were a number of reactors located at each station, said Charlton, not mentioning that this was true almost everywhere else. Hydro and government had "resisted any attempt at public input concerning safety or expansion of the nuclear-power stystem," Charlton continued, ignoring the Porter Royal Commission and Select Committee public hearings that had exhausted these subjects in the 1975-1985 period. Described as an NDP adviser, Rosalie Bertell told the media that, "One of the underlying problems is the difference between the definition of safety by engineers and the definition of safety by the general public. Engineers regard 'legally permissible' and 'safe' as synonymous." Sister Bertell was using sly semantics. AECB engineers say that if it is safe it is permissible. News editors paid scant attention to the NDP press conference but several newspapers carried an article by Norman Rubin, "director of the non-profit energy watchdog organization," making the same points as Charlton ten days later.

The *Toronto Star* gave Rubin's demand for the shutdown of Canadian nuclear-power plants prominent coverage but matched his claims with equal comment from the Canadian Nuclear Association's vice-president

Ian Wilson. It was a significant attempt at balanced reporting and seemed to mark a new and more equitable attitude toward nuclear realities. A fortnight earlier *The Star* had devoted nearly a full page to the post-Chernobyl nuclear debate. It had quoted the anti-nuclear tirades of Rubin, Greenpeace and the American guru Amory Lovins, but *The Star*'s energy writer had also talked with Premier Peterson and spokesmen for the AECL and CNA president Norman Aspin. Three days before that *Star* columnist Frank Jones had sought out John C. Runnalls at the University of Toronto. Chairman of the nuclear engineering centre there and an Ontario Hydro director, Runnalls spoke from more than forty years experience and he put the Chernobyl accident in perspective. For a veteran *Star* watcher, this post-Chernobyl coverage was a giant leap towards unbiased reporting of the nuclear debate.

Maclean's coverage of the Chernobyl disaster was even more surprising. After a decade of near-hysterical reaction to the nuclear industry, the magazine had seen the world's worst nuclear accident happen and was not appalled. Its ten-page coverage of the Soviet accident was comprehensive, authentic, well illustrated and relatively balanced. It had sought out people who knew what they were talking about and took responsibility for what they were saying — Ernest Letourneau at Health and Welfare, Ken Reeves and Furrukh Ali in Ontario's emergency planning office, Mike Williams at Ontario Hydro, Hugh Spence at the AECB, Norm Aspin at the CNA. They still quoted Norman Rubin and Gordon Edwards but now *Maclean's* identified them as "critics," not as "experts."

Half a dozen years earlier a nuclear-power plant at Three Mile Island had emitted a radioactive cloud and Norman Rubin told *Maclean's*, "It's a great time to be a doomsayer." But the cloud over the Susquehanna River dispersed and there were no casualties. Now a power reactor in the heart of the Ukraine had exploded in the worst sort of accident that nuclear experts could conceive of happening and the sky had not fallen. Compared with the toll that industrial accidents take almost weekly around the globe, measured against the cancerous fallout from coal-fired generating plants, in news editors' terms Chernobyl was regrettable but not catastrophic, momentarily newsworthy but not memorable. They were in the doomsaying busines and Chernobyl had not spelled doom. Until Chernobyl a skilled doomsayer could work the circuit of TV, radio and daily-paper newsrooms with the timing and reception enjoyed by Apollo at Delphi. After Chernobyl, the anti-nuke, skyfall-callers lost credibility. The world held a lot more dismal things for news people to think about.

Acceptance of nuclear reality by the Canadian news media had been a long time coming. When Ernest Rutherford and Frederick Soddy advised McGill University colleagues in November 1902 that the atomic age had begun, Montreal papers gave the atom smashers scant attention. "They have established the existence of a new sort of matter quite unlike any other element yet discovered," said *The Gazette* under the single-column advice that the "Discovery Is Important." "Where this discovery will lead is yet quite impossible to say but taken in connection with the recently established existence of radium, thorium and uranium, an entire revolution in physical theory may be within reasonable distance. To the layman unused to regarding himself as an aggregation of air made of an inconceivable number of inconceivably small atoms rotating at an inconceivably rapid pace, this may seem of slight interest but X-rays and other important phenomena as yet unknown may be cleared up by the new knowledge." That said in three hundred words, *The Gazette* gave double the space that day to a report on the liquid-air pump that Rutherford and Soddy used in their experiments. It had been donated by a very important McGill benefactor. When Cavendish boffins split the atom in the mid-1930s the Toronto *Globe* shrugged. "ATOM IS DISRUPTED BUT WORLD GOES ON," it said.

Maclean's magazine caught up with atomic science early in the century and went on ranting and raving for decades. Reviewing a *Popular Science* piece in May 1920 Canada's premier magazine said: "It is a tremendous thing, so tremendous in fact that the lay mind can hardly conceive it. But it seems that in every atom of matter — even in our own bodies — there is enough latent power to do tremendous things such as propelling steamboats and trains." If *Maclean's* editors, for all their talk of lay minds and conception, had any other ideas on using bodily powers they were too polite to say so. They titled the story "A FORCE TO SHATTER CONTINENTS." It was the first of the hyperbolic headings and hokum that would periodically assault readers over the next sixty-five years. When Gilbert LaBine struck uranium at Great Bear Lake in 1931 *Maclean's* reported that, "At one stroke the northward thrust of civilization through the Northwest Territories to the borders of the Arctic Sea has been given an impetus and objective." The editors must have been out to lunch when that ecstatic efflux crossed their desks.

During Pierre Berton's more sober tenure at *Maclean's* I was allowed to write of Rutherford's discovery at McGill without expostulation or a god-forgive-me. But, as if to make amends for such apostasy, latter-day editors writhed with revulsion. In January 1978, I suggested a half-dozen stories on Canada's many-faceted nuclear enterprises to Peter

Newman. His mind on more esoteric things he shuffled me into the office of a young woman editor. Her cheeks flushed red with anger at the very word "nuclear"; she wanted no part of the frightful subject. "FEAR AND LOATHING IN THE LAND — Nuclear fallout throughout the nation and one very closely watched train," *Maclean's* reported in June 1981. That outburst described the passage of twelve railway carloads of milled uranium ore from Australia enroute to Eldorado's Port Hope refinery. The refinery is one of five worldwide which upgrades uranium to fuel for nuclear-power plants. It had handled such material for forty years without incident. But Greenpeace Canada was into a month-long publicity campaign to encourage donations. Greenpeace publicists organized well-timed media fests and "picture opportunities" at railway stops adjacent to major urban centres. The little golden folk stared solemnly into the TV camera eye and with tremulous voices implored the Canadian nuclear industry to shut down. *Maclean's* coverage of Greenpeace's harassment of a trainload of uranium was hysterical.

In the wash from Three Mile Island the magazine did turn to one of the world's best authorities on safe nuclear design, the co-designer of Candu and Ontario Hydro's vice-president for development, William Morison. He was reassuring but not complacent. So far so good. Then they irresponsibly accused the AECB of planning to relax safety regulations. They made no attempt to contact the control board; they simply accepted the word of nuclear "watchdog" Norman Rubin. A fortnight after Chernobyl the *Maclean's* cover showed a nuclear bomb exploding from a power-plant cooling tower. Very clever but quite misleading. "A NUCLEAR NIGHTMARE, The Terror of the Chernobyl Meltdown," they said. But suddenly their coverage was evenhanded.

The era of bad nuke news began with the Bomb. The subject arrived in the public domain with the daily papers on Tuesday, August 7, 1945. "ATOMIC BOMB ROCKS JAPAN," said the *Globe and Mail.* "ATOM BOMB DEVASTATING — JAP," said the *Toronto Star.* "ATOM MAY END ALL WAR," said Toronto's *Evening Telegram.* C.D. Howe and Dean Mackenzie tried to explain it all in forthright terms. Veteran newsmen listened attentively, soberly. But for my generation, taught that atoms were solid, impenetrable little balls a billion times smaller than marbles, it was very difficult to fathom. "New Weapon Equals 20,000 Tons of TNT," "Pill Bottle May Hold 50 Years House Heat," "Power of Solar System Released for Man's Use," we were advised. The concepts shattered imagination. The numbers were incomprehensible. We were expected to understand that a nuclear cross section was a millionth, billionth, billionth part of a square centimetre. It was called a "barn," said the boffins, because, "hitting that area with a neutron was like firing a bullet into the side of a barn. You couldn't miss."

One Friday afternoon in 1952 when 10 per cent of the steam channels burst and the fuel melted in Canada's NRX research reactor at Chalk River, the newspapers were disarmed by the country's chief scientist and nuclear industry founder C.J. Mackenzie. "CHALK RIVER PLANT EVACUATED; ATOMIC PARTICLES POLUTE AREA," said the *Globe and Mail* over a bare-bones story. They reported correctly that, "an abnormal amount of radioactive particles were discovered in the plant area." *Toronto Star* correspondent Robert Taylor was more explicit. "Radioactive material — potential death dust — seeping in mysterious fashion from the world's most powerful atomic reactor yesterday forced the evacuation of one thousand workers from the hundred-odd buildings at the Chalk River plant site," he wrote. But by Monday morning the short-lived fallout had been cleaned from work places and a massive decontamination job was about to begin.

Decontaminating the radioactively drenched reactor building involved nothing more than "a surgeon sterilising his hands," Mackenzie told reporters, and editors dismissed the story in a few sentences. In a rare lapse of judgment Dean Mackenzie had diverted them from covering an exceptional technological success story. In fact, 4.5 million litres of water containing eight thousand becquerels of radioactivity per litre had to be pumped out and safely disposed of on the Chalk River site before they could even begin to dismantle the reactor plant. No one had ever attempted to take such a powerful nuclear furnace apart before. Robot tools and remotely-operated devices had to be developed to safely remove and replace the "calandria" core of the NRX. The work took eight months and it was of worldwide interest to the nuclear industry. The rehabilitation of the NRX reactor would have a major impact on Canadian-Soviet nuclear-trade potential a generation later. Quick-acting shutdown rods designed on the basis of the NRX meltdown, automated devices, operator training and procedures that evolved from that experience took on new significance after Chernobyl.

"Sufficent information is now available to permit any country to undertake a program of nuclear-power development assuming it has the required scientific, engineering and industrial competence," Atomic Energy of Canada Limited president Bill Bennett told the managing editors of Canada's daily papers back in February 1956. "The problem which faces us today is not a scarcity of information but one of interpretation." He urged the editors to put reporters with "at least some elementary science knowledge" on nuclear stories. Over the years the *Montreal Gazette*, the *Globe and Mail*, the *Financial Post* and Canadian Press usually did so; CBC radio frequently and CBC-TV occasionally provided accurate and meaningful coverage. For the rest, reporting the nuclear industry and technology in Canada was a sad mix of disinterest, penny-pinching and often irresponsible journalism.

In 1971 Ontario Hydro commissioned the first of eight nuclear plants on Metropolitan Toronto's doorstep at Pickering which would lead the worldwide commercial nuclear-power field with near-faultless performance for nearly a decade. Within three months the *Toronto Star* launched a campaign to discredit the Candu reactor and shake public confidence in its joint development by the AECL and Ontario Hydro. "OTTAWA, HYDRO GAMBLE MILLIONS ON NUCLEAR POWER," *The Star* began. "Candu has its supporters and also its critics who argue from the sidelines that patriotism won't count for much if the whole project becomes a colossal flop. They also claim that Candu is less safe; that it's far more complicated and that its development here is far behind nuclear systems being developed in other countries. They say it has yet to be proved economically sound."

Who were these critics? The main one was a brilliant, head-strong Toronto consultant engineer Winnett Boyd who rejected the Candu concept for a research reactor being designed by the C.D. Howe Company in 1954 where he was chief project engineer. Boyd ultimately ran as a Conservative candidate for Parliament but lost out. Other criticism in the early 1970s was mainly political. Ontario Liberal leader Robert Nixon railed against any Ontario Hydro expansion program as Liberals had done provincially since 1905. The federal Conservative leader Robert Stanfield was opposed to anything that C.D. Howe's socialistic Crown corporations, the AECL and Eldorado, were up to. "Only the New Democratic Party members tend to support nuclear policy, presumably because it's largely government operated and financed," *The Star* noted at that time. Within a half-dozen years NDP members were joining the anti-nuke alliance which could always be sure of unedited space in the *Toronto Star*. The other critics who tilted *The Star*'s editorial desk against Hydro's nuclear progress were British and American nuclear-reactor makers who had eyed the Ontario market for years.

By 1978 *Star* stories by reporter Ross Howard were presenting the anti-establishment, anti-nuclear, environmentalist line without any attempt to balance or authenticate the claims of Hydro's critics. "HYDRO PLANS NUCLEAR PLANT IN QUAKE ZONE," Howard claimed in April 1979. In fact Hydro didn't plan any kind of generating station in that part of the province. A month later Howard told *Star* readers, "NUCLEAR SAFETY ISSUE EXPLODING. Radiation and Information Leaking as Cover-Ups Charged." This story was an element in Opposition leader Stuart Smith's anti-nuclear, anti-Hydro campaign. It was based on several "abnormal event reports" leaked to Liberals by an unhappy nuclear operator at the Bruce nuclear complex. Such reports were mandatory for any non-routine occurence. The select committee examined the claims and counter-claims but found neither coverup nor hazardous practices. Hydro did, however, substantially improve poor staff communications in its nuclear-generation division which had provoked the unhappiness at Bruce.

"CHEAP ELECTRICITY IS $12 BILLION FOOL'S PARADISE," screamed a *Toronto Star* headline on May 11, 1981. Ross Howard quoted Energy Probe economist Jack Gibbons. At that time Energy Probe counted sixteen oil and gas companies — Ontario Hydro competitors — among the corporate sponsors supporting its quarter-million-dollar annual budget. Howard, Gibbons, the socialist New Democratic Party and the private gas and oil companies were agreed that government-owned Ontario Hydro had an unfair advantage over free-enterprise energy companies. "Hydro pays no taxes, is supposed to make no profit and borrows money for expansion at specially low rates because its debts are guaranteed by the Ontario government," said *The Star*. A year later *The Star* returned to the attack on the government-run nuclear industry with a new series by Ross Howard under the collective heading of "The Nuclear Fizzle." The headline type was even bigger. "SALES SLUMP SOURS CANADA'S CANDU HOPES, Ottawa Sticks By Fading Nuclear Goals," the paper said. "Seven years ago Ottawa's high hopes for the nuclear industry seemed fully attainable. Candu was booming with 31,000 direct jobs and 85,000 related jobs. But now the bottom has fallen out with sales reduced to zero." *The Star* seemed jubilant.

That *Star*, NDP, Energy Probe, oil and gas industry, anti-nuclear, anti-Hydro campaign waged for nearly a decade before Chernobyl and was an update on a much older story. It was first told in September 1922 by publicist William E. Murray who had been hired by the National Electric Light Association, the American power-companies' lobby. These private utilities were appalled by the success of "the most notable government-owned utility in the Western Hemisphere, i.e. the Hydro-Electric Power Commission of Ontario." Ontario Hydro had developed water power at Niagara Falls and was accomplishing in North America what Lenin could only promise for the future for the Soviet Union — cheap electric power for homes, farms and industry. William Murray's

220-page report concluded that, "The advocates of government or municipal ownership of electric utilities claim reduction in the cost of power by virtue of elimination of taxes, dividends and high-salaried executives." But taxes were not eliminated, Murray said and all the people paid the bill. Moreover, "government ownership would throttle initiative." In fact, when Ontario Hydro consumers paid their power bills they still bought electricity at a considerably lower price than Americans getting Niagara power via private utilities in 1922. Contrary to the Energy Probe-NDP-oil and gas lobby arguments, nuclear power proved significantly less expensive. By 1986 Ontario Hydro was meeting about half of its electricity demand from nuclear-power plants. Customers were paying less than a third of what New Yorkers did; half as much as in Boston or Detroit. Ontario industry was paying 30 per cent as much as industry in New York City; less than half as much as in Chicago, Detroit or Boston.

By June 1982 *Toronto Star* editors were beginning to realize that the vested interest was not Ontario Hydro. When a $900-million deal to supply a New Jersey utility with power by submarine cable fell through, Energy Probe economist Jack Gibbons said it was a "great victory for the environment movement in Canada" because it would reduce Hydro's need for coal-fired generation. Hydro estimated it would have meant a net benefit to Ontario electricity users of about a billion dollars over a ten-year period, and Canada's environment minister told *The Star* he didn't share Energy Probe's acid-rain concerns. The paper was beginning to see the absurdity of Energy Probe's arguments. Its editors and publishers were beginning to realize, as well, that this "watchdog" group with its American orientation was certainly not acting in either Ontario's nor the national interest.

The *Globe and Mail* was not uncritical over the dozen years that Ontario Hydro's nuclear-power plants were taking shape. But *The Globe* put Lydia Dotto, a first-class science writer, then Tom Claridge, an evenhanded and resourceful reporter on the nuclear beat. *Globe* stories were flatly objective and tediously detailed; neither Lydia Dotto nor Tom Claridge were into discotheque journalism. *The Globe* built national circulation on objective coverage. Bemused members of Parliament would read a *Globe and Mail* story on a nuclear issue then turn to the *Ottawa Citizen* for an alternative view. "TRITIUM IN RIVER COULD CAUSE MUTATIONS," *Citizen* readers were told one summer day in 1981. "Tritium, the radioactive material dumped into the Ottawa River this week could cause mutations to fetuses of pregnant women who drink the contaminated water," the paper said quoting Dr. Gordon Edwards of the Canadian Coalition for Nuclear Responsibility. "Edwards said laboratory tests have shown tritium causes serious genetic and developmental mutations in unborn mice. 'It tends to stunt the growth of the fetus and various organs.' " Worse, it might kill the unborn child, said Edwards, a Montreal mathematics teacher. *The Citizen* published an editorial the next day retracting that story. "I regret the tone of the article and I don't think people should be frightened. I agree with the Atomic Energy Control Board that there is no cause for alarm," Edwards apologized.

A dozen weeks after that *The Citizen* carried a Southam News story quoting US nuclear regulatory commissioner Victor Gilinsky. He said the diversion of nuclear fuel from peaceful to weapon use was "more difficult to detect" in Candu reactors because of the on-power refuelling facility that Canadians had built into its design. That was "a lot of bull," said a nameless external affairs official. "The US has been trying for years to say our reactors are inferior to help the sales of US-built models." The Southam story speculated that "of the ten countries believed to be seeking nuclear-weapon capability today, five of them — India, Pakistan, Taiwan, Argentina and South Korea — are now or have been nuclear customers of Canada." That studiously misleading piece of foreign propaganda was supplied by Southam News Service to sixteen member papers. Some used it but none phoned Atomic Energy Control Board officials to check its accuracy. In March 1985 Southam newspapers carried a four-part "SPECIAL REPORT showing how Canadians pay a price for such slack regulation." It was a vicious assault on the AECB who pointed out that neither the "price" nor the regulatory quality was "explored nor explained in factual detail." The AECB specifically disputed thirty statements made by Southam writers Peter Calamai and Margaret Munro. Neither *The Citizen* nor any other Southam paper carried a word of the AECB response. Having heard the sensationalized viewpoint of two reporters, *Citizen* readers deluged the editor with angry letters. "Nuclear industry out of control. . . . scandal. . . . already killed thousands. . . . expensive board members. . . . negligent attitude," they wrote.

Post-Chernobyl invective, however, provoked one ninety-two-year-old *Citizen* reader to protest. J. Stuart Smith of Port Hope was so incensed he took his complaint to the Ontario Press Council, a solemn panel of citizens with the publishers' mandate to make innocuous comment. "Fear of Chernobyl Creeps into Port Hope," a *Citizen* columnist claimed. "The psychological gap between Port Hope and Chernobyl is so narrow that instant terror in Chernobyl caused immediate panic in

Port Hope." There was neither fear nor panic in Port Hope said Mr. Smith. The paper admitted the remark was a bit hyperbolic but columnists did that all the time, they said.

A few weeks after Three Mile Island the *Halifax Herald* carried a byline story by Berton Robertson on the editorial page entitled "Nuclear Power Issue: Who Can You Believe?" He quoted one British and six American authorities but not a single Canadian. The November 1982 issue of *Canadian Business* admitted that 46,000 jobs "would be in some trouble if Canada's nuclear industry was thrown to the wolves of free enterprise." But said writer Robert Andrews, "the answer seems to be something much more ethereal than industrial economics or political job creation — it's *pride*. A sort of stubborn patriotism has been nurtured in Ottawa circles for more than two decades since the Avro Arrow was scrapped by Prime Minister John Diefenbaker, sending a torrent of Canadian technical talent to the US space and aeronautics industries." That story epitomized the Canadian psyche. Where else on earth would "pride" be italicized and patiotism questioned as a motive?

In the ten-day period following Chernobyl several major dailies carried reports from ethnic groups who feared for the safety of relatives in the Ukraine. Given the scarcity of Soviet information in the first four of those days, the exceptional nature of the accident and the historic background of some Slavic minorities in Canada, those stories were understandable. Less evident, however, was the motive of External Affairs Minister Joe Clark in permitting — or ordering — a series of highly publicized moves to remove embassy personnel from Moscow and Warsaw and Canadian students from Kiev despite authoritative advice they were not endangered by the Chernobyl fallout. Unexplained was his failure to use his ministry's facilities to actually help Canadian families contact kin in the Ukraine; to provide them with reassurance based on factual reports he was getting from both Canadian and British embassies or to correct dangerously provocative statements being made in right-wing media.

More sinister and treacherous were a series of Cold Warfare stories carried by a small number of Canadian daily newspapers and the CBC's international service in an orchestrated campaign in the fall of 1986 to combat Mikhail Gorbachev's move towards *détente* at the IAEA. "Thousands of Estonians face radiation contamination as they perform slave labour at the Chernobyl disaster site. . . . Twelve have been reported shot for refusing to work in late July," said a typical propaganda story in the *Toronto Sun* on October 29. "Nuke reports rebuked," said *The Sun* the following day citing the Soviet Embassy in Ottawa and Norman Rubin who admitted he had "heard nothing about forced labour in the cleanup effort." A week later *The Sun* pursued the Estonian slave-labour story with NDP leader Ed Broadbent who rejected it in the absence of any corroboration. The Estonian story, incidentally, was available in wire-service printout form at the IAEA pressroom in Vienna the last week of August from a "Voice of America" reporter there. It was studiously rejected by most news people.

Justifiably proud of their scientific and technological achievement since World War II, Soviet leaders were humiliated by Chernobyl. Their embarrassment quickly turned to resentment in the face of sensational reports by reactionary foreign news media. Deputy prime minister Boris Shcherbina was furious when he addressed a Moscow press conference on May 6. "Time will confirm the irresponsibility of those who have taken advantage of this misfortune to whip up a campaign of ill will and downright slander." A week later Mikhail Gorbachev told the Soviet TV audience that, "The accident at Chernobyl and the reaction to it have become a kind of test of political morality. . . . An attempt has been made to show the world that talks, let alone agreements, with the USSR are impossible. . . . We perceive this tragedy quite differently. We understand that it is yet another ringing of the bell, yet another stern warning that the nuclear era calls for new political thinking and new policy."

In mid-November the CBC used an article by *Toronto Sun* writer Lubor Zink in a broadcast beamed at the USSR which was studiously designed to create tension and hostility between various ethnic groups in the Soviet Union. Canadian Ambassador Vernon Turner told *Globe and Mail* correspondent Lawrence Martin in Moscow that the Soviets considered the personal attack on Gorbachev defamatory.

In a world where 7,500 multiple-weapon-tipped missiles are poised to deliver 700,000 times the genocide demonstrated at Hiroshima what purpose is served by such Red-baiting? What policy governs Prime Minister Brian Mulroney and External Affairs Minister Joe Clark's silence, if not their private aquiescence, in the face of perilously inflammatory propaganda aimed from Canadian localities at a foreign nation?

Is Canadian foreign policy being written by foreigners, by a war-mongering minority who can promise their vote *en bloc* in certain constituencies of key cities or by the majority of us who prefer to think as Canadians, peacekeepers in a perilous world?

13

The Rain on Tunney's Pasture

"We are not going to allow anything radioactive into Canada."

— THE HONOURABLE ARTHUR JAKE EPP, HEALTH MINISTER,
INSTRUCTS STAFF ON MAY 1, 1986

WHEN CANADA'S HEALTH MINISTER Arthur Jake Epp advised his staff after Chernobyl that, "We are not going to allow anything radioactive into Canada," his injunction ranked in futility with King Canute's decree that the tide should not ebb.

Each of us generates about twenty millirems of radiation annually, mainly from the radioactive potassium in our bones. More than three times that much radiation still pings from the sun and earth, mementos of the nuclear fury that marked our creation. X-ray machines beam fifty millirems or more at the average Canadian in a year. About a millirem still drops in annual rainfall from the Bomb tests of the 1960s; a little less than a millirem a year comes from mining and using uranium to make electricity. As Jake Epp's own ministry noted a half year later, "No group in the Canadian population received more than one millirem from the Chernobyl fallout. An exposure of several sieverts [several hundred, thousand times that much] is required to produce acute radiation sickness."

Yet in the first ten days of May the health minister's response to the Soviet nuclear accident and the media's mindless treatment of Health and Welfare bulletins exemplified the reckless reaction of politicians and the press to nuclear reality. The constant cataclysmic climate maintained by the interaction of TV, radio, newspaper and magazine editors

162

with ego-driven politicians to tittilate, amuse and distract the populace may seem a harmless social extravagance by a nation who never had it so good. But where it exploits the Hiroshima complex of awe, fear, misapprehension and guilt to fill the camera lens with woe and to harrow by headline, it does great damage in three respects.

Firstly, in the aftermath of Chernobyl it sowed mental anguish; the same real emotional trauma with which anti-nuclear zealots seeded the McClure Crescent home sites half a dozen years earlier. Secondly, it was one more assault on a high-tech field of endeavour in which Canadians have achieved world renown — everywhere except at home. Thirdly, it once again diverted the attention of sane and fearful men and women from the real nuclear danger — 7,500 multi-weapon missiles poised in silos, submarine tubes and bomb racks around the northern hemisphere, slicked to slip through supersonic air faster than sound, faster than recall, to snuff out humanity in a cloud 700,000 times more awful than Hiroshima.

At the outset local winds, born in the Mediterranean and Black Sea, distracted the weather watchers. They carried the Chernobyl fallout north to Scandinavia, west to Poland, then southwest through Romania. But in the first week of May westerly winds again prevailed. They blew out of the North Sea and the Baltic carrying radioactive fallout from the burned and broken Chernobyl reactor east across the Ukraine, across the Kirgiz steppe, across Mongolia and Manchuria. A week since explosion and fire sounded alarms in the Soviet Union, the westerly wind carried the fallout across Japan.

The rain dropped radioactive iodine at the rate of 150 becquerels per litre on Yokohama. The Japanese were not disturbed; Bomb tests in the 1950s caused 250 times that much radioactivity in their rainfall. The World Health Organization has said that people should not *consistently* drink water or milk containing 2,000 becquerels per litre of iodine-131. The IAEA has recommended half that limit; the European Economic Community said 500 becquerels were enough. Canadian health authorities decided in 1978 that drinking water should not contain more than *one per cent* of the radioactivity which the International Commission on Radiological Protection considered safe for nuclear workers continuously exposed to it; that was ten becquerels per litre. This ultra-cautious number, *a half of one per cent* of what WHO thinks safe, was blessed with acronym status by Jake Epp's ministry in the week following Chernobyl. Ten becquerels per litre were now a big MAC for maximum allowable concentration of radioactivity in drinking water. People who drank two litres per day of such water would increase their risk of fatal cancer by about two chances in a million each year, said Canada's dean of radiation experts, David K. Myers.

The Honourable Arthur Jake Epp was a high-school teacher in a little Manitoba town when the electors smiled and sent him to Parliament in 1972. Seven years later he was a cabinet minister in Joe Clark's fleeting government. Half a dozen years after that Brian Mulroney made Jake Epp minister of health and welfare. He had been eight months in office when the Chernobyl fallout brought him fame. Who could say worse of Jake Epp than that he was zealous, so anxious to succeed in the show business of politics that he leaned too far into the footlights and fell into the orchestra pit. From the first word of the nuclear disaster he kept the nation posted. "The best information we have at the moment is that Canadians are not at risk," he reported on April 29.

Nonetheless he invoked nuclear-emergency measures. Weather personnel at twenty-eight airports across Canada who normally check air filters weekly and rain content monthly for radioactivity were now alerted to do so on a daily basis. Phone 998-3624, the minister told the populace. "Any Canadians can use that number if they want to have further reassurance." During May about five thousand did.

Health and Welfare public relations director Carol Peacock installed three phones, then six. She had them staffed around the clock. "The phones just kept ringing constantly here in Ottawa just as the hot lines did all across the country. We had no idea how much interest there was out there." Nor were the people reassured. "It seems we were the victims of our own goodwill. The more information we gave out the more people wanted to know. We were damned if we did and damned if we didn't," said the PR lady in retrospect. "If you don't give out the information they think you are hiding something. If you give it all out then people read it in the paper or hear it on radio and they call and want to know if it's true." Carol Peacock demonstrates goodwill and there is no doubt she exercised it with the public, with the news media, with her bosses and especially with Jake Epp. Queried a half-year later she was politic and protective of the minister. I think she was still dazed by the ringing of phones, the clamor of news folk, the mass hysteria and the demands of political ego.

The minister operates from a lofty suite in the Confederation Building, centre stage on Parliament Hill. Most of his ministry, including Ms. Peacock's run and the lead agency in the post-Chernobyl activity — the Environmental Radiation Hazards Division of the Radiation Protection Bureau of the Environmental Health Directorate of the Health Protection Branch of Health and Welfare Canada — are located on Tunney's

Pasture four kilometres to the west. So theoretically the radioactive rain fell on Tunney's Pasture before it reached Confederation Square. The pasture, incidentally, is four hundred acres that sustains the Health and Welfare and Statistics Canada herds in a dozen monumental buildings on a bucolic stretch of downtown Ottawa where even the little Chaudiere Rapids are shushed to assure bureaucratic quietude.

Health and Welfare was the logical choice to be lead ministry when westerly winds wafted the bellwether ions of Chernobyl radiation eastward across this nation. Even if it had not been, Jake Epp would have prevailed upon the prime minister to make it so. The health minister, said the *Globe and Mail* was "a politician who could smell troubled waters" and knew where it was safe to fish for headlines. "It is not daring, after all for Canada's minister of health and welfare to battle the evils of booze and the weed," the paper observed. What more reprehensible thing could you target that Chernobyl summer than nuclear fallout from Russia? In any case External Affairs Minister Joe Clark, Environment Minister Tom McMillan, Energy Minister Pat Carney, Agriculture and Food Minister John Wise and both transport ministers wanted no part of nuclear stuff. If they opened their mouths on the subject they might be expected to do something about it. Jake Epp had been called "Mr. Clean" in newspaper headlines and he loved it. Now he was up front from the very first Chernobyl news report. For the next four weeks he was awash in a sea of rainy-day journalism, doomsaying activists and his own fundamentalism. "We are not going to allow anything radioactive into Canada," he promised.

Toronto Star readers might have wondered how Jake Epp could possibly exclude the great swath of radiation headed their way. A day earlier a *Star* artist's front-page drawing depicted how Chernobyl fallout might cross the top of the globe into Canada in a broad-tipped swipe at our atmospheric purity. That was the first-edition version. *The Star*'s final edition had a revised illustration. Now the fallout arrow circled the earth above the forty-ninth parallel. It seemed to be holding altitude and was heading back to dump on the Soviet Union. "Mr. Epp said the radioactive material that triggered atmospheric warning devices in Sweden on Monday will be off Canada's Atlantic coast within days heading for the Maritimes. For the moment he said no precautions were contemplated for Atlantic Canada," the *Globe and Mail* reported on April 30. Two days later it advised: "Mr. Epp said weather patterns are not expected to propel the radioactivity *directly* from Kiev toward the Atlantic coast of Canada but the material will *eventually* work its way into the prevailing winds that circle the globe and flow across

Canada from west to east." Some perceptive observers must have recalled that winds are westerly in the northern hemisphere and that Chernobyl fallout had a world to go round before it reached Canada's *west* coast first. Newspaper artists can revise their drawings from one edition to the next to meet such meteorological reality but cabinet ministers must be briefed on which way the wind blows. That takes longer.

While Canada waited, *The Globe* queried authorities, scientific and sublime. Their environmental reporter concluded that "upwards of a million curies of radiation could have been emitted" from Chernobyl. The Soviets said it was more like fifty million. The paper reported Rosalie Bertell's complaint that radiation guidelines were too high. The annual five-rem exposure for nuclear workers and a tenth of that for the public had not been changed since US, British and Canadian physicists established those levels in 1945, she said. (A rem measures the damage a roentgen of radiation can do under any circumstance.) Sister Bertell was wrong. The international standard for nuclear workers adopted in all countries had been cut by two-thirds in forty years. In fact, the average Canadian nuclear worker actually gets less than one rem exposure in a year, not five.

By May 5 the Canadian news media were losing their grip on the Chernobyl story. There is only so much you can say about a disaster seven thousand kilometres away. Even Canadians close by in Kiev were not cooperating. Among forty-five students being hassled by a Canadian Embassy official to go home, two flatly refused and another dozen couldn't make up their minds. "Canadian Embassy officials in Moscow said the bodies and clothing of nineteen-year-old Edmonton students registered measurable levels of radiation when tested," said the press. The bodies were alive and well; humans normally emit a measurable amount of radioactivity.

Meanwhile, Prime Minister Brian Mulroney and world-shaker Joe Clark were on the other side of the earth at a Tokyo conference of Western world leaders. The heads of the seven nations expressed concern about Chernobyl, sympathy for the casualties and they offered aid. They said smugly that they would have informed the world promptly had it happened in their countries and they hoped the Soviets would speak up now. In fact IAEA director-general Hans Blix had already arrived in Moscow at Soviet invitation to be briefed on Chernobyl. Politburo member Boris Yeltsin had told reporters in Hamburg two days earlier of the casualties and the Kremlin's US-Canadian spokesman Georgi Arbatov had updated British audiences via the BBC. The Soviets acknowledged the outside offers of aid but they were outraged by "faked reports spread on a death toll running into thousands, panic among the population, etcetera." Neither Brian Mulroney nor Joe Clark suggested any initiative or manner in which Canadian expertise might be dispatched to the USSR. In Ottawa External Affairs and the energy ministry covered their black holes of ignorance with rhetoric and evasion.

In this environment Jake Epp had the podium and the media's attention, but no story. "Canadian officials, who stepped up monitoring at twenty-eight radiation-testing stations, said none of the radioactive debris from Chernobyl has drifted over Canadian territory," *The Globe* reported on May 5. "If any did drift to Canada it was expected to show up over the [past] weekend. As prevailing winds blow west to east it is believed that material will first be detected in western or northern Canada. At worst the government expects fallout will raise normal background levels by only one or two per cent, not enough for anyone to worry about, officials say." That kind of talk wasn't helpful to troubled-water fisherman Jake Epp. He wanted to be pictured as a shark slayer and they were saying there were only minnows out there. He could dearly use some trouble for his ministry to deal with.

As if on cue it turned up on the west coast that day. Customs officers at the Vancouver airport seized 275 kilograms of what the Health and Welfare PR ladies described as "radioactive salad fixings" from Italy. Cynics might query the coincidence of this discovery when the minister needed it most. However, it was the result of concerted protective action. "We arranged with customs people and other federal agencies to notify us of any food products coming from areas of Europe affected by fallout. This was the first shipment we were told about. One reason we sampled it was there were definite media reports about contaminated vegetables in Italy," Barry Morgan explained. As the ministry's chief food inspector in Western Canada, the hot vegetables fell on Morgan's plate.

Jose Valagao of Vancouver, who imports fresh food specialties for the west coast gourmet-restaurant trade, was suddenly bereft of the classy fixings. They included Rosso radishes, curly endive, fennel, sun-dried tomatoes and two varieties of mushrooms. Twelve kilos of Pleurotus mushrooms contained 2,300 becquerels of iodine-131 per kilogram. That was nearly ten times the level international radiation health authorities think is safe for human consumption; it was thirty-three times more radioactive than Health and Welfare would allow. But as of May 5, by Jake Epp's decree, any radiation was too much, so the whole shipment of Italian produce was ordered destroyed. "Our original instructions were to use the zero factor. When we seized the vegetables it was not based on health, it was based on the fact that if they contained any level of radioactivity whatsoever they were considered to be adulterated. Section 4(d) of the Food and Drug Act says you can't sell adulterated food," Morgan explained.

The samples had to be air shipped to Ottawa for examination and it was two days before they made news. Pleurotus mushrooms were featured in Health and Welfare's Chernobyl briefing memo on the morning of May 7. This was the first of daily bulletins to alert the Canadian media to the impact of Chernobyl. "Fresh produce from Italy was found to contain radioactive iodine-131 at levels exeeding the safe limits set for food of ten becquerels per kilogram. This produce will be destroyed today," Health and Welfare officials said. That statement was less than accurate. No safe level had been set. The limit was raised from zero to seventy becquerels per kilogram the following week when rainfall on the west coast perceptibly dampened British Columbia produce and pasture land with a minimal amount of radioactivity. "If we continued to consider any amount of radioactivity to be adulteration all food production in Western Canada would have been eligible for seizure," Morgan observed. Nor was destruction of the seized shipment immediate. Vancouver had been tidied up and sanitized for Expo 1986 and municipal works officials told Mr. Valagao he couldn't leave radioactive vegetables in their garbage dump. It took ten days for Ottawa to say how radioactive the mushrooms were. Only then would the guardians of Vancouver's disposal grounds let him dump there.

Unofficially the produce importer had known on May 7 what the radioactive content was. Reporters for the *Financial Post* and the *Globe and Mail* read him the figures from the Health and Welfare news bulletin. Jake Epp's officials knew what should get priority. That May 7 bulletin was the first newsworthy evidence that Chernobyl fallout had reached Canada. Getting it to the media was terribly important. Mr. Valagao's disposal problem could wait. A day earlier Oregon officials advised state residents not to drink rain water because of its radioactive content and the news media reported similar rain in the state of Washington. Curious about Vancouver rain, University of British Columbia physicists sampled local showers. Sure enough the rain contained fission products, those radioactive elements produced in a runaway reactor.

World Health Organization experts meeting in Copenhagen that day advised European members that while the Chernobyl fallout "has now been diluted and most short-lived radionuclides have decayed," they should continue to monitor raw milk because there was still a chance heavy rainfall would wash an unhealthy amount of radioactive iodine into drinking water and onto dairy pasture land. Headed for a WHO meeting in Geneva that week Jake Epp had no such experience to report. His ministry people redoubled their vigilance. "The department is collecting rain in Vancouver. The results will be provided as soon as available," news editors were promised on May 7. From Vancouver to Moosonee and from Windsor, Ontario to Churchill on Hudson Bay, however, the rain content was normal — a disappointment for fallout watchers. From the Maritimes the only word was that Nova Scotian officials were letting Ottawa worry about Chernobyl. Then on May 8 rain fell on Tunney's Pasture and sure enough it was detectably radioactive; it contained sixty becquerels per litre of radioactive iodine. That was just 3 per cent of the level most WHO countries consider significant but it was six times what Jake Epp's ministry considered safe to drink. People who only drank rainwater should switch, Health and Welfare said. Their advisory was based on two days sampling in Ottawa but they said flatly, "This advice is for all Canada."

Nuclear stuff had alarmed Employment and Immigration Minister Flora MacDonald long before Chernobyl. Just what were Health and Welfare people doing about it now? she wanted to know. Was milk being sampled? Yes and the first results were expected the next day. It took another week but their intentions were good. Was the radioactivity in the current air samples higher than when the Chinese were testing nuclear weapons? No, but the radiation in some rain water was. What level of radioactivity in rainwater or milk would be considered hazardous to health? Ms. MacDonald wondered. It would have to be about ten thousand times worse before it warranted a health advisory, Health and Welfare admitted. Then what did the MAC number mean? It meant that if you drank two litres of over-MAC rainwater a day for a year you might increase the likelihood of cancer by one in a million, she was told.

Suspecting there were other worried people out there, Carol Peacock had her staff provide the questions and answers to the media coast to coast. On the one hand she wanted to be reassuring. On the other hand one could not ignore news editors' interest in radioactive rain that had circled the globe before it fell on Tunney's Pasture. Fallout in air samples did not warrant precautions, she advised the media, but habitual rainwater drinkers had better switch. It was okay to wash in the rainwater, however. On May 8 Jake Epp spoke to the nation's news people by satellite phone from the WHO conference in Geneva. "There is absolutely no danger in people taking a bath in rainwater or children playing in the rain," he declared. Still it was all very regrettable. "All of us were hoping that we Canadians would not be affected by the fallout from Chernobyl." The health minister sounded like Mackenzie King announcing the start of World War II.

Dorothy Meyerhof, chief of the radiation hazards division at Health and Welfare, advised Canadian Press reporter Warren Caragata that the iodine-131 in Canadian air was about twenty times higher than normal. "That's just twenty times a little wee number," Mrs. Meyerhof explained. CP told it exactly like it was but for general readers unfamiliar with nuclear numbers and concepts the headlines were frightening. "HIGH CONCENTRATIONS OF RADIATION DETECTED IN OTTAWA RAINWATER," *The Globe* reported. "SOVIET REACTOR RADIATION FOUND IN OTTAWA RAIN," declared the *Toronto Star* on page one. Chief of radiation services at Health and Welfare, Ernest Letourneau assured *Ottawa Citizen* readers that well water and municipal water supplies were okay. The rain would be well diluted and filtered before it got into the tap. None of the newspapers mentioned the MAC number or how small it was. They simply told people that the radioactivity in rainwater was "*six times over federal drinking water standards.*" Let people think what they will.

The most newsworthy report came from the west coast. "VANCOUVER'S WATER HIT BY FALLOUT SCARE," said the *Toronto Star* on May 11. The Coquitlam reservoir is one of three which supply Greater Vancouver. When it had been routinely tested the previous day a waterworks employee reported radiation readings fifty times higher than normal. Tests of a second Vancouver area reservoir showed only "slight traces" of radioactivity, a normal finding. The third reservoir had none. Pending a re-check of such an anomalous result, waterworks officials switched over to an alternate reservoir. The fifty-times too much radiation was apparently an arithmetic error because it never showed up again but Greater Vancouver Region spokesman Bud Elsie had already alerted the news media. "I suppose some will question why we told the public so quickly. But it could have been serious and we just didn't want to take a chance," he said. Since the Greater Vancouver populace couldn't drink water from the shut-off reservoir what chance was involved? The unmissed chance was what the PR folk call a "picture opportunity." They kept the Coquitlam reservoir shut for two more days. By then the media had their news pictures, the report had blown east and fallen like hot rain on Tunney's Pasture. Government flacks, particularly at local levels, are paid to keep editors happy. From Elsie's viewpoint it was better to be wrong with bad news than miss a deadline; better to delay re-sampling than kill a good story.

The psychological fallout from Chernobyl had circled the globe, swept down from Resolution Island, spanned the prairies, blown into the nation's capital. Once across the St. Lawrence River it seemed to recover equanimity. "Radiation level increase to be slight," said the *Moncton Times Transcript* quoting people at New Brunswick Power's Point Lepreau nuclear station. "NB Radiation Levels Within Normal Range," said the *Fredericton Gleaner* citing the provincial environment minister. "Official Sees No Health Risks from Radioactive Iodine in Province," said the *Saint John Times-Globe*. "Official: No Health Risks From Radioactive Iodine in Province," said the *Saint John Tele-graph-Journal* the following week. By then central Canada's big newspapers had recaptured reality. On May 10 the *Toronto Star* advised, "Radiation moving away from Canada," while *The Globe* reported, "Tests continue; rainwater alert remains in effect."

NB Power spokesmen had kept the Maritime papers posted. NB Power operated one nuclear plant in the Maritimes and wanted to build another. It had no interest in building small radioactivity levels to alarming news. In Jake Epp's paper warfare against the demons of Russian fallout the reverse was true. Disconcerting radiation levels got his picture in the news. The health minister would be outraged at any suggestion he courted publicity at the expense of public anxiety. Nor is there any suggestion he did so consciously. But each and all of us are victims of our own rationalizations. And the facts are that while Jake Epp was publicized as a health protector, guarding Canadian health from Soviet fallout, nuclear anxieties were raised in the public psyche by the flurry of reports about radioactive rainwater and irradiating vegetable fixings in the second week of May.

By then Jake Epp's people were getting a lot of feedback from across the country. Airport baggage handlers, postal workers, garbage collectors were refusing to handle anything they believed was contaminated from the Chernobyl fallout. Radiation hazards chief Dorothy Meyerhof is neither a politician nor publicist. She is a hard-headed, scientifically oriented administrator who reports the real world as it actually turns. Like most people in the physical sciences she is not big on the social sciences. She had the mistaken notion that people are rational. The transportation workers' fears were groundless, she said. "Even if something is contaminated you could touch it at these low levels, wash up and you would not be affected at all." In a directive to her field staff across the country advising them on how to detain and sample fresh produce shipments, she emphasized that "no health hazard is associated with the handling of potentially contaminated products. That might occur only with eating it."

Carol Peacock was astounded at how many people depended on rainwater cisterns for their drinking supply. "We had calls from Natural Resources people, forest-service workers out in the boonies, coast guard crews, people running lighthouses in remote coastal places, on oil rigs, people who would only get fresh water if it was flown out to them from the mainland," she said. "We ended up telling them that if their cistern had been partly filled before the Chernobyl fallout, the rainwater would be so diluted it would pose no problem." Still Jake Epp was not letting go of the tiger's tail. The government would continue to warn people against drinking rainwater, he insisted, because they wanted "to err on the side of prudence." There were authorities in Health and Welfare who could have told him that if you know what you are doing there is no need to err on either side. The mandarins don't bother correcting their ministers, however; a new one will be appointed next week. But the health minister's no-radioactivity-whatsoever edict confounded his ministry people following the Italian vegetable seizure. Carol Peacock seemed to have been the first to recognize their problem. Astonished by the Canada-wide news coverage accorded the Vancouver shipment she noted that, "There are currently no tolerances in the Food and Drug Act for radioactive elements in food." They were simply prohibited. The minister had not considered that even the mildest rainfall was likely to wash some trace of radioactivity from the sky somewhere over Canada to wet pastures and vegetable produce, adulterating them within the strict definition of the act. At home farm output was threatened by regulatory adulteration. Abroad some European food exporters were beginning to scream about the absurd Canadian embargo.

The Canadian government policy was "scientifically correct and defensible," Carol Peacock assured. However, she told the press, "it may raise the issue that Canada is being more stringent than necessary to protect Canadians" and that could lead to international complications. As Ms. Peacock noted, health authorities in a dozen European countries were trying to establish just what level of radiation was permissible in foodstuffs. "In these countries radiation levels may be predicted on the fact that some level of radiation is not avoidable." Translation: European officials faced reality; all foods contained some radioactivity. If you don't accept some minimum level you don't eat. Canada Health and Welfare policy was adjusted accordingly. Henceforth "foodstuffs contaminated with radioactivity will be considered unacceptable based on *reliable* levels of detection," they said. "Reliable" is a bureaucratic term said to be incapable of translation into English.

By May 9 Carol Peacock reported that the radioactivity in rainfall had dropped "substantially" in Ottawa and Toronto and that rain sampled elsewhere from Goose Bay to Vancouver contained no radioactivity at all. "It is assumed that radioactivity in Ottawa rainwater represented fallout from a particular segment of the debris. The advice to refrain from drinking rainwater still holds but it must be appreciated that this provides an *exceptional* measure of safety to the public. The level of iodine-131 would have to be 10,000 times higher before a health advisory was issued," said a Health and Welfare release. The survival of politicians and public relations people depends on a set of forensic skills: the ability to reverse direction without turning the head, to mumble without saying anything contradictory, to kick outmoded decrees under the rug without moving the foot.

By the time of Chernobyl, Nes Lubinsky had been a dozen years guarding Health and Welfare's Metropolitan Toronto outpost against media assault. Like a Roman centurian or Hudson's Bay factor he was on the frontier a long way from the decision makers. By nature he tended to deny catastrophe and discount the entertainment value in disaster. This made his job difficult. Lubinsky also coped with the distraught victims of hype, hyperbole and hysteria when they could penetrate the switchboard jungle to reach him. That made his work rewarding. There was one memorable call in May; the lady was hysterical. She had been caught in the Toronto rain without an umbrella the previous day. Would she get cancer? Should she burn the clothes that got wet? she wanted to know. Lubinsky tried to explain. He wondered how many other distraught people there might be out there.

Carol Peacock remembered a similar call. A woman wanted to know where she could travel right away to get away from radiation. "Every time we talked to journalists we tried to emphasize that people were not in danger, that there was never any risk to health posed by anything that was detected in Canada. Levels were so extremely low," she said. Editors were not inclined to use such news-killing comment as "never any risk." Such negation does not sit well beneath a heading that proclaims, "HIGH CONCENTRATIONS OF RADIATION IN RAINWATER." Did she get the feeling as time wore on that she was not getting her message across to the media? "I don't think the media were the problem," Ms. Peacock said. "It was people's understanding. Some of the public are just totally suspicious, skeptical, scared about the prospect of radiation and of nuclear energy in general," Ms. Peacock said. "There were intelligent people who wouldn't go out of their houses because it was raining. No matter how many times you tried to tell them it wasn't a problem they still perceived it as a problem."

Ms. Peacock is a woman filled with good will just as her minister Jake Epp abounds in good intentions. They didn't understand why intelligent people still perceived nuclear problems once the Chernobyl fallout had blown over. In mid-May the health minister sighed with relief. "Possibly the worst is over," he told the press. What worst? Well in Red Deer, Alberta pharmacist George Kondrat said panic consumption of liquid iodine got so bad druggists had to take the antiseptic off their shelves. In Calgary two people were reported in intensive care after swallowing the brown fluid formulated to sterilize cuts and scapes. A pharmacist is a professional practitioner. He has gone to university and learned that there are several different kinds of iodine compounds. One of them is potassium iodide, a combination of two chemicals in similar proportions to those normally found in the human system. The iodide part fills the thyroid appetite for iodine, closing it off from consumption of iodine-131 which is the radioactive kind. If there was a real risk of people in proximity to nuclear plants getting a sickening dose of iodine-131 from fallout, emergency services would distribute potassium iodide pills. Chernobyl created no such risk in Canada.

But on May 16 Rosalie Bertell suggested that perhaps the radioactive rainwater on the west coast had resulted from a US nuclear-weapon test that went wrong a month earlier at the Nevada test site. Greater Vancouver waterworks spokesmen had long since admitted their mistake in sampling the Coquitlam reservoir. Nonetheless, Sister Bertell told a Vancourer newspaper, "I'm suspicious that the radiation you're getting in Vancouver came from a major accident in Nevada." Jake Epp's people responded quickly to that one. The trace amounts of radioactive elements detected in Canada after Chernobyl came from the USSR accident site. Radiation protection chief Ernest Letourneau advised news editors to repudiate the Bertell story. Exploding nuclear bombs give off other radioactive elements, he explained.

Like the Swedish and Finnish networks of radiation monitors, the twenty-eight stations manned by Environment Canada's airport weather personnel were put on emergency alert less than forty-eight hours after the Chernobyl accident. That meant that they collected air filters and sampled rain content and air expressed them daily to Tunney's Pasture

174

for Health and Welfare analyses. Milk was sampled weekly at eighteen other cross-Canada locations during the summer. "Milk showed slight traces of radioactive cesium from the Chernobyl accident and several rainfall samples exceeded federal drinking water guidelines for continuous annual consumption. Limited testing of caribou at the peak of the crisis showed no increase in radioactivity levels and this meat is fit for human consumption," the health ministry said in retrospect in December. "In all cases the radiation doses to Canadians were extremely low. No group in the population received more than one millirem."

The health ministry noted that at the IAEA post-mortem meeting in Vienna, "Soviet experts provided information on radiation doses and possible long-term health effects to the population of the Soviet Union. Information gathered by the OECD allows similar estimates for Western Europe." The ministry added their own estimates for Canada and provided this table:

HEALTH & WELFARE ESTIMATES OF CHERNOBYL'S LONG-TERM IMPACT

	Within 30 km	European USSR	Western Europe	Canada
People affected (millions)	0.135	74	400	25
Average dose (millirems)	1200	280	1.4	0.023
Eventual cancer deaths	200	2,600	700	<1
Increase in cancer rate	1.6%	0.3%	0.001%	nil

These figures are the statistically predicted, theoretically calculated, professionally estimated Chernobyl casualties. The deaths shown are "notional or statistical, not real deaths," as one British publication put it. In presenting this tabulation Jake Epp's people stressed their hypothetical nature. "It must be emphasized again that all estimates of projected cancer deaths are based on a hypothesis that the risk is proportional to the exposure at any level," the Health and Welfare radiation experts reiterated. "There is no direct experimental evidence that the radiation doses in the table [above] will, in fact, lead to any cancer fatalities." They would like to be more definitive than that but they are scientists practicing their craft in the traditions ordained by the medieval monk Roger Bacon; they are voluntarily bound by the discipline of their profession, subject to review by their peers, as Francis

Bacon advocated they should be three centuries before. They do not guess nor speculate, nor make unfounded statements to please the press.Their vested interest is in analyzing reality, reporting how the real world turns. That is what they were trained to do in a high-tech world. That is what the government pays them for with taxpayers' money.

They do make comparisons hoping that they will be meaningful. One of the authors of the hypothetical Chernobyl casualty numbers has estimated that a 5,000-megawatt coal-fired power station, for example, will create enough sulphurous and nitric oxide fallout in a year to eventually cause at least one cancer death. In recent years about eight times that much coal-fired electricity has been generated annually in Canada to cause at least eight cancer deaths a year or some 560 cancer fatalities over a seventy-year lifetime span. Pro rata that would amount to 1,680 cancer fatalities over the life-span of the seventy-four million European Soviets or nearly nine thousand cancer fatalities in the normal lifetime of four hundred million Western Europeans. These, too, are notional or statistical — not real — deaths. They are but another way for mortal men to approach the reality that there is a cost to the generation, movement and application of energy here on earth.

A decade before Chernobyl, nuclear engineer Herbert Inhaber did a statistical study for Canada's Atomic Energy Control Board on the comparative risks of energy production. He reviewed some 150 other studies that had been done in Canada, the US, Britain, France, Spain and India. Inhaber calculated the likely public risks and occupational hazards involved at every stage from mining materials to transporting the energy from coal, fuel oil, natural gas, uranium, solar and wind power to the consumer. He concluded that over the normal lifetime of the average Canadian there was fifty times more chance of a premature or accidental death from relying on solar panels or windmills than from using electricity generated in either nuclear or natural gas-fired plants. In dollar or human terms there was no free lunch, said Inhaber.

The people in Health and Welfare labs, on Atomic Energy Control Board inspections and at Environment Canada monitor stations — they and their directors — are the scientists, engineers and technologists whom those with a vested interest in doomsday dialectics still decry. The alchemy activists, the doomsayers, the metaphysicians, the nostrum peddlers and pseudo-scientists promise "renewable energy" alternatives — the free lunch — if they can just drive the technologists from high places, if they can just get a few bucks from the guileless.

"Unnecessary radiation creates unnecessary risks," Energy Probe tells me. "Radiation Alert is the authoritative guide to what's tolerably safe and what's intolerably dangerous." Energy Probe provides an easy reply form for my "tax-deductible donation for $150, $100, $60, $35, $25. Also send me your new blockbuster Radiation Alert."

"Dear friend," Rosalie Bertell wrote me from the International Institute of Concern for Public Health a month after Chernobyl. "We are much in demand for providing scientific and medical assistance to the victims of environmental pollution. Normally professionals are available only to industry and government. . . . Please share with us what you can. . . . Your donations are tax exempt."

"I'm worried," Friends of the Earth executive director Ray Vlies wrote me in 1985. "In the last year I've seen some alarming trends. . . proposals to build a hundred-mile dyke across James Bay. . . to build a second nuclear generating station on the New Brunswick coastline. . . . We're fighting for a conserver society. . . . help us by making a generous donation."

I tell them that I have already given. I help support the experts whom I trust when I pay my taxes.

14

I'd Get Fired

"Ask a guy, 'Suppose you wanted to operate the regulating system a little different than approved procedures?' The guy would say, 'I'd get fired for doing that.'"

—ZYGMOND DOMARATZSKI, AECB DIRECTOR-GENERAL,
AUGUST 22, 1986

A HALF-YEAR AFTER CHERNOBYL no responsible nuclear authority would say that a reactor accident like that was impossible in Canada. The people who designed safety into Candu reactors, who regulate nuclear plants and those who train the people to operate them, never speak in absolute terms. They are realists working in a world of imperfect humans and machines that can go wrong. "In designing the Candu system we were required to look at multiple failures — failure of humans or of a process system and the coincident failure of a safety system," Ontario Hydro's vice-president for design and development, William R. Morison explained.

"We had a similar but smaller-scale accident at Chalk River back in 1952. The NRX research reactor failed to respond properly to its controls and we had a runaway reactor," AECL vice-president and chief engineer Gordon Brooks recalled. "It taught us the need for incorporating a very fast, very powerful and very reliable shutdown system. Actually Candu reactors rely on two separate shutdown systems today." Morison and Brooks were co-designers of the Candu nuclear-power plant; a generation later they went to the IAEA post-mortem at Vienna to compare notes with their Soviet counterparts. Morison had been following nuclear technology in the USSR since 1966. "That's when we decided to start using a zirconium-niobium alloy for pressure tubes based on the Russian experience."

Director-general of reactor regulations at the AECB, Zygmond Domaratzski would make no categorical pronouncement before or after the Vienna meeting. But he was clearly astonished by the litany of operator errors that Valery Legasov described. "It is not the kind of thing I would expect to see in my lifetime," he said softly. Canada's chief nuclear regulator is a tall, sparse man, quick-moving and perceptive as a wading bird in his native Manitoba. When he sees trouble his voice rises to summon attention. "I've seen people do things with regulating systems to by-pass them when they shouldn't have. When that happens the system catches them," he said. "It was like Three Mile Island. Everything that happened at TMI we have seen happen in Canada. But we just never saw them all happen at the same time. One has to be damn careful not to be categorical but I'm hellishly confident we've got the right process. We have a redundancy of safety devices and training and operational procedures and a general policy towards things to prevent such a chain of mistakes."

Like his boss AECB president Jon Jennekens, the director-general has taken an engineer's course in role playing. In trying to explain complex situations they both tend to break them down into simplified scenarios and folksy terms. "Go into a nuclear control room and ask a guy, 'Suppose you wanted to operate the regulating system a little different than approved procedures, what would happen?' He would either stare at you because he had never thought of doing anything like that, or he would just be aghast. The guy would say, 'I'd get fired for doing that.' It's that mental attitude which gives me a helluva lot of confidence. But one can't be categorical."

Larry Woodhead is another veteran of the Canadian nuclear industry. Like both Morison and Brooks he joined the AECL/Ontario Hydro development team in 1952. As director of six thousand men and women operating a dozen nuclear power plants in 1981 he was asked to write the definitive manual on how to operate a safe and efficient nuclear-generating system. He summarized his 50,000-word book succinctly. "A nuclear-electric program is fully successful," he said, "if electricity is reliably produced, cost is minimized, if workers and the public do not get killed or injured and emissions to air, land, and water do not seriously affect people, animals, objects, etc."

Canada's nuclear pioneers began thinking about occupational and public safety nearly a decade before Morison, Brooks and Woodhead joined the system. "The operation of the plant may entail hazards of a nature and scale beyond all previous experience," C.D. Howe told the builder of Canada's first reactor. Howe and Dean Mackenzie had George Laurence draw up the site specificiations. "Isolation was desirable to avoid the supposed hazards to population from possible explosion or release of radioactive dust into the atmosphere and to simplify secrecy control. It was suggested it not be less than ten miles from a town or village," Laurence said.

By the time power utilities began planning to build commercial nuclear plants there were compelling reasons to locate them within proximity of urban centres. Like all steam plants, nuclear-generating units require a lot of cooling water. That tends to put them on sea coasts or major lakes and rivers which is where the big cities were established long before. Transmission losses become great with distance so efficiency dictates putting electric-generating plants as close as feasible to where the power is required. In some parts of the world, the northeastern United States or northern France, for example, it would be hard to find a location more than fifty kilometres from a major city. And at some point in the Industrial Revolution societies opted for work within easy distance of where people lived. The trade-off between occupational and public risks on the one hand and employment and the benefits of an industrialized society on the other had been established long before commercial nuclear-power plants were first sited in the 1960s. What distinguished nuclear plants from other industries, however, was the degree of safety planning that went into them. By the time Ontario Hydro located its nuclear stations on the Great Lakes' shoreline — as a dozen American nuclear plants are — safety planning was an integral element at every stage.

Prodded by C.D. Howe's chief trouble-shooter Lesslie Thomson, National Research Council people moved in to make working conditions substantially safer for uranium miners at Great Bear Lake and for refinery workers at Port Hope at the war's end. "Eldorado directors ordered a mine ventilation survey to be made in 1945 and installation of a new mine-ventilation system in 1946," Thomson reported. "Dangers to health in the Eldorado refinery were, until late in 1945, extremely serious. The basic facts were reported at a meeting in Toronto on September 27 and 28 [1945]. On completion of the radiation surveys it was agreed that the hazards were far above recognized or accepted tolerances. Consequently, the Eldorado board authorized construction of new facilities to reduce the hazards to safe and accepted limits." That marked the transition in Canada from prewar radium operations, based on casual traditions born in sixteenth century Joachimsthal (Agricola's efforts notwithstanding) to responsible nuclear industry developed by government-owned and operated Crown corporations in the postwar period.

A decade later in August 1955 when nuclear engineers from about twenty nations met at Geneva for the United Nations' first International Conference on the Peaceful Uses of Atomic Energy, AECL's director of radiation hazards control Andre J. Cipriani confidently told participants: "Experience at Chalk River shows that exposure to radiation can be controlled within acceptable limits even under emergency conditions." The experience to which he referred was the 10 per cent meltdown of NRX three years before. In the susequent cleanup the Canadians dealt with only a small fraction of the radioactivity that got loose from Chernobyl. The NRX structure had kept it in the basement. But they had still to decontaminate a very radioactive reactor, to remotely dismantle and bury it. Chalk River work places had to be cleaned of radioactive pollution.

Most important, cleanup workers had to be protected. Cipriani detailed the radiation-safety training and careful control of working time in contaminated areas. In the two-year period following the NRX accident some eighteen hundred AECL employees worked at the station. "Despite work in high-radiation fields, in several cases higher than fifty roentgens per hour, only one person received more than the recommended fifteen roentgens per year upper limit." That one exposure was 16.1 roentgens. "There have been no significant radiation exposures [to workers] at Chalk River since operations started. Constant surveillance and strict control are largely responsible," Cipriani told the conference. "An independent radiation-hazards control organization with well-trained personnel in critical positions is considered essential. It is the practice to consider radiation hazards in the early planning of operations." Thirty years later the Canadian experts at Vienna could say virtually the same thing.

An international radiologists committee recommended a fifteen-roentgen annual maximum exposure for nuclear workers but it was calculated in different ways from one country to another. Canada was concerned with the annual total; the US and Britain allowed up to three-tenths of a roentgen per week. The Soviets kept track daily to assure that their workers did not sustain more than 0.05 roentgens to any part of their bodies in a working day. "In assessing the maximum permissible dose of irradiation one should bear in mind that this dose still exceeds the natural radiation background more than a hundredfold," the Soviet delegate A.A. Letavet told the UN Conference in 1955. "So from the viewpoint of maximum concern for the health of people subjected to the action of ionizing radiations it is advisable to resort to a reduced working day, longer vacations, and measures aimed at further reduction of radiation in the work place."

From the outset the Soviets considered nuclear workers' off-time or reduced hours as a preventive health measure, not a labour-management bargaining chip. Rest and relaxation were already a basic element in maintaining worker health in the USSR and Letavet cited a unique facility, night sanatoriums. At these preventive-medicine facilities, "a worker, while pursuing his occupation, is provided after work with the necessary regimen and medical treatment such as dietetic food and physiotherapy which would be impossible under conventional out-patient conditions." Night sanatorium accommodation was free and available for two to four-week periods. "People working under radiation conditions are advised to spend their annual vacation at sanatoriums and rest homes. Experience has shown such visits are very effective in eliminating the changes which might be ascribed to ionizing radiation," Letavet said. In describing the care and treatment of Chernobyl casualties and those evacuees who suffered emotional trauma, Leonid Ilyin, chairman of the Soviet national commission for radiation safety, cited the role that sanatoriums, rest homes and vacation resorts still play in maintaining occupational and public health in the USSR.

"Primary responsibility for overall safety at a Canadian nuclear power plant is clearly assigned to the utility. Only basic safety criteria and fundamental principles have been laid down by the AECB. We have avoided detailed design requirements," Jon Jennekens emphasized. AECB philosophy has been to set standards to protect the public and nuclear workers but to let the utilities decide how they meet those requirements. The AECB does not regulate detail, Jennekens insists. Ontario Hydro assumed the major role in training nuclear workers to safe and healthy practice. New Brunswick Power and Hydro-Quebec have been dependent on Ontario Hydro in this regard. The Ontario Hydro approach mirrors the AECB philosophy. Nuclear operators are not programed to go by the book; they are trained to know what they are doing and to act on the basis of experience. "A shift supervisor must be stable and decisive when unusual problems arise; he must not lose his normal good judgment under stress. To ensure that serious in-depth judgment, two management people must observe the candidate over some years of on-the-job experience," Larry Woodhead said.

"In an emergency it is the shift supervisor who must evaluate the scene and decide how serious it is, how he is going to regain control in that particular situation," said Robert Popple, manager of radioactivity and environmental protection services. Hydro has its own ideas on training its people to be self-reliant in such an event. There was a period when the AECB's licensing procedure required that operator trainees write "closed-book" examinations. "We didn't consider that was necessarily a good test of the on-job skills and knowledge needed at a new station," said Popple. "We encouraged the AECB to use more representative testing methods that would put a candidate in a position more like his everyday job." Michael Williams, assistant to the director of nuclear generation, cited other evidence of Hydro's emphasis on self-reliance with its nuclear staff. "We insist that every employee should be fully qualified in radiation protection; that he be able to look after himself and measure the exposure he is getting. We don't rely on health surveyors to baby-sit operational or maintenance people."

1985 was not a good year for Hydro's nuclear personnel. They were decommissioning the seventeen-year-old Douglas Point prototype reactor on the Bruce site and replacing nearly eight hundred fuel-carrying pressure tubes that had been irradiated for a dozen years in Pickering reactors 1 and 2. Decontaminating and immobilizing Douglas Point subjected workers to their yearly exposure quota quite quickly. At Pickering when tradesmen cut the six-metre-long tubes from the reactor face radioactive carbon dust was released into the work environment. The carbon dust was a fission product formed when reactor neutrons converted nitrogen atoms in the insulating gas; it was totally unexpected. Personnel monitors failed to detect this dust on nearly forty workers who tracked some of it home on shoes and clothing. Seventeen of them sustained some exposure and one tradesman received four times the annual five-rem limit. The contamination was quickly discovered and cleaned up; new tooling and a vacuum system to remove the dust were designed. More effective personnel radiation monitors were installed. Yet despite this setback the 168 people working on the retubing of the two Pickering reactors accumulated less than half of the three hundred man-rems that Hydro engineers originally estimated the tube removal would involve. Moreover, among nearly thirty-five hundred workers exposed to radioactivity in operational and maintenance work at Bruce and Pickering stations, including Douglas Point, in 1985 the average accumulated dose was one-third of a rem. That was about half of what the average exposure rate had been in the previous half-dozen years.

Since 1977 the average exposure of Hydro nuclear personnel has been well below one rem — less than a fifth of the annual level internationally recommended. But Hydro's health and safety people say they learned the hard way. "We were shocked by the excessive radiation exposure during the early years of Douglas Point operations," said Gary A. Vivian, the man who audited occupational exposure at Hydro. Averaged over the whole nuclear work force, the figure peaked in 1974 at just under two rems per person. This was less than 40 per cent of the International Commission on Radiological Protection's annual guideline but it was considerably too much for Ontario Hydro management. They saw it reduced by nearly two-thirds over the next three years. Because Ontario Hydro represents a vertically integrated nuclear operation it can effect changes from design to operational stages and it did. Feedback from nuclear operators to Candu designers has been a major element. The self-protection policy whereby all operational personnel and maintenance tradesmen are trained to monitor their own exposure and keep it minimal is another big factor in cutting radiation exposure. The Douglas Point experience prompted AECL and Hydro research engineers to develop Candecon, a decontamination fluid which soon went into worldwide use to cleanse a major amount of radioactivity from nuclear pipes, pumps and vessels during annual maintenance.

About 25 per cent of the radiation to which Ontario Hydro nuclear personnel are exposed annually is from tritium. Tritium is a triple-atom molecule of hydrogen created by the irradition of deuterium or double-hydrogen in the heavy water moderator. It is unique to the Candu reactor and the AECL and Hydro collaborated to control its accumulation. At Darlington a $150-million heavy-water upgrading and tritium-extraction plant has been built. While sharply reducing this source of radiation exposure to nuclear personnel the tritium plant was designed to provide $12 million worth of tritium annually for luminous sign makers, other commercial users and for fusion research. Anti-nuclear critics claimed the tritium would go into nuclear-weapon production. When this was denied by Ontario and federal authorities the critics switched their media campaign to alleged hazards in its transportation. Hydro then built a special 5000-litre container to move tritiated heavy water from Bruce and Pickering stations to the Darlington plant. Described as "a giant accident-proof stainless steel thermos jug" with foam insulation for both thermal protection and to absorb impact, the $200,000 containers were tested to withstand a hundred kilometre-per-hour crash into a bridge abutment. Still critics complained. The safe conversion of tritium from an on-site radiation hazard to a marketable product was yet another target for the peril pedlars.

"It's just as important to be seen to be doing well as it is to be doing it. Nuclear power has a pretty high profile thanks to Three Mile Island," said Ontario Hydro chairman Hugh Macaulay in the summer of 1979. Macaulay had been trained in politics and public relations. He appreciated the growing pressure being applied to both the AECB and Hydro as self-styled "public interest groups," anti-nuclear activists and political opposition exploited TMI anxieties. The resultant hassle was a "sophisticated form of gamesmanship," said science writer Leonard Bertin. "Hydro engineers working under deadline pressures felt that they had met legal requirements and they were exasperated by countless requests for additional information from an AECB staff that had expanded rapidly. For its part, the control board — which had no problem of deadlines or costs — often persisted in trying 'to make Hydro walk the extra mile' to meet additional safety requirements." Jon Jennekens ultimately reduced the friction. "We do not need an adversarial situation to ensure that the public interest is being served," he said.

Chairman of the Ontario select committee probing Hydro affairs, Donald C. MacDonald saw it differently. A former NDP leader in Ontario, author and historian, he had looked into nearly four hundred volumes of AECB-Hydro correspondence occupying twenty-four metres of shelf space. "It revealed something of the power conflict that up to now has been a standoff. The public perception was that the AECB has been unduly influenced by Hydro," MacDonald said. Whatever the public thought, the committee had waded through three years of euphemistic Hydro-AECB dialogue on upgrading the nuclear-safety systems at Douglas Point, Bruce and Pickering stations. When the polite obscurity was stripped away a "target" came to mean an enforceable standard; a "request" was really a directive and ultimately an order. "AECB is the boss. When they say the dialogue is over then we do it," Macauley agreed.

Jon Jennekens is an engineer, not a semanticist. He was not interested in merely enforcing regulations but in setting guidelines that made sense to all concerned. "You can have a licensee who is completely humbled and prepared to do what he's told without any argument. But if you do that you're talking about a situation such as Three Mile Island. The operators there knew they were working by rules but they couldn't ask, 'What do all these rules mean?' There isn't any single body, government or otherwise, that is totally competent. If you're going to have a nuclear industry in this country you can't have those turn-key operations that exist in other countries. You have to make sure that the operators know what they are doing; that they are confident and capable of understanding the intricacies. Then if a regulatory agency says, 'Jump in the air,' they will want to know the basis of that request, which for us means an instruction or directive."Nonetheless the AECB president told reporters as the hearings ended, "The big stick is that Hydro knows we can amend their license to limit their power if there is a risk of imminent danger or a very apparent increase in public risk." At issue was the availability of safety systems at Hydro nuclear stations. They were available only 99.7 per cent of the time and the AECB was demanding more reliability than that. Still Jennekens made it clear that, "There is no immediate safety risk associated with any Ontario Hydro nuclear-generating station." A year after Chernobyl, AECB president Jennekens was to become deputy director-general of safeguards at the International Atomic Energy Agency. The IAEA, beefed up to undertake an expanding role in the nuclear world, could utilize the judgment, integrity and understanding that the AECB president had given for so long to fellow Canadians.

In the aftermath of TMI back in 1979 both the AECB and Ontario Hydro leaned backwards to demonstrate safety concerns commensurate with public expectations. In the event of a malfunction or an operator error that might trigger a runaway reactor there are three separate systems which Canadian nuclear operators can use to take corrective measures. First, there is a fast-acting shutdown system that instantly thrusts neutron-absorbing rods into the reactor core and simultaneously either injects a gas to snuff out the nuclear reaction or dumps the heavy water moderator (which is necessary to sustain fission) into the reactor-building basement. Then there is an emergency core-cooling system which would supplement the normal cooling-water supply that transfers heat from the fuel to the steam drums. Thirdly, there is a containment system unique to Ontario Hydro nuclear stations. This is a giant vacuum system that would suck any and all dust, water or gases from a disabled reactor into a vast tank-like, reinforced concrete structure. The three safety systems are independent of each other which means that even at 99.7 per cent availability for each system at any given time, the chances of the two others not working would be nearly zero. Still it provided three separate installations to hassel about.

Soviet nuclear engineers had provided somewhat similar, though less elaborate and not triplicated, safety facilities for operators at Chernobyl. But these had been by-passed while the cooling pumps were allowed to run down apace with the reactor. "The test they were doing was a bit like cutting all the engines on an aircraft," said Zygmond Domaratzski. "When they pulled out too many control rods it was equivalent to letting an aircraft drop right out of the sky. By-passing the safety systems was a major contributor to the accident because it allowed the power to increase at a very fast rate and it dictated the amount of damage that would be done once the accident did occur. Withdrawal of so many control rods led to the runaway reactor. Other things they did with the system led to an incredible power surge once the reactor went out of control."

About a year before the Three Mile Island accident, a scientist associated with Canada's control board, Herbert Inhaber did an exhaustive study of the comparative risks involved in providing various kinds of energy. "There is no free lunch. For each type of energy production there is a risk. This risk is part of the social cost which includes air and water pollution, land abuse, depletion of resources and other factors," he said. Inhaber analyzed some 150 studies by energy-research scientists in six countries and guess-estimated that sun power and windmill systems would be three times safer than coal or oil-fired plants in terms of public and worker health and safety. But he said the sun and wind systems would be possibly thirty times more hazardous than to build and operate energy systems based on ocean thermal currents, natural gas or nuclear fuel. In light of the TMI accident Inhaber might have recalculated the odds to find that sun and wind systems were only ten or twenty times as dangerous as nuclear power.

The public, however, would still not have bought Inhaber's comparison. Nuclear energy was fixed in that section of their minds where the Bomb demons lurked. Sunshine and windmills conjured up safe and happy scenes from first-year school readers. The environmentalists and anti-nuclear activists reinforced those images, of course. Beyond all this, scientists and engineers, regulatory officials and politicians kept talking about risk. Risk is an engineering tool and a scientific or mathematical concept which everyone glibly refers to but few comprehend. The risk concept tries to compare a number of different dangers by multiplying two factors. How often is a particular kind of disaster apt to happen? And how many people will get killed if and when it does? Home computers have made such risk compilations possible but those who are inclined to play star-war games on the screen are not likely to enjoy the mathematical skills to make risk calculations. Even habitual chess players, numbers-game addicts and race-track bettors are unlikely to appreciate the statistical science involved.

NDP energy critic Evelyn Gigantes, one of the brightest of the fourteen select committee members back in 1979, noted that the leakage of tritium from AECL's small NPD (Nuclear Power Demonstration) reactor at Rolphton was 582 times worse than a tritium leak from one of Hydro's Pickering reactors. The AECB confirmed that the Pickering plant was only leaking 0.0004 per cent of what the control board said was a safe level while Rolphton reactor leakage was 0.233 per cent of the AECB guideline. Ms. Gigantes' arithmetic was right, if somewhat irrelevant. One might say with equal accuracy that a hummingbird was 582 times larger than a mosquito. The Porter Commission decided that, "Within reasonable limits the Candu reactor is safe"; the subsequent select committee came to the same conclusion. "There are no hidden disasters as critics suggest," the committee's long-time consultant James Fisher told the committee. "The plants don't always work perfectly, equipment and instrumentation fails, operators and maintainers make errors, incredible events occur. But when incidents happen the reactor shuts down safely and there is enough leeway in the systems to absorb malfunctions," the committee's counsel Allan Schwartz advised the legislators. Nobody talked about risk in numerical terms.

A few days before the Chernobyl disaster, the president of AECL Research Company, Stanley R. Hatcher reminded a business-management group that, "The real risk associated with any endeavour appears to be subordinate to society's perception of the risk." Hatcher compared the public response to Three Mile Island where there was neither death nor injury to a dam failure at Gujarat, India in 1979 that killed 1,500 people. TMI had "enormous" media coverage in North America, the Indian dam collapse was virtually unnoted. At that point there had never been a death due to radiation at any of some 375 nuclear-power plants in twenty-six countries over the previous generation yet more Canadians — 29 per cent — were absolutely opposed to nuclear-power plants than favoured them — 24 per cent. While the US National Academy of Sciences, the United Nations, the International Commission for Radiological Protection and the World Health Organization had all concluded that nuclear energy was the least hazardous way to generate electricity, 80 per cent of Americans and a like number of Canadians thought it was safer to use coal. Not only did public opinion run counter to reality but the AECL president pointed out that comparative risk statistics "can't even be used as a communication strategy."

"The gap between society's perception of risk and the real risk is shocking. A nuclear physicist was recently booed at a public meeting when he recited some figures to a group concerned about a proposed nuclear-waste site," Hatcher said of one of his own Whiteshell research staff who was addressing a Manitoba audience. Public fears of radio-activity were mainly due to "the idea that radiation is unnatural and any amount is likely to result in adverse health effects," he told the business managers. Where did Canadians get such ideas about nuclear radiation? Three in four got their knowledge — or lack of it — from radio and TV; three in five from newspapers; two in five from magazines. Stan Hatcher might have mentioned that the same viewers, listeners and readers not only thought solar radiation was natural and good for them but that they followed the advertisements that urged them to get a lot more of it.

In this psychological climate Chernobyl seemed to confirm prevalent opinions without significantly changing them. There was a little more opposition to nuclear power than support for it, a 29:24 ratio, before the world's worst nuclear accident occurred. A month after the ratio was 33:19. Before Chernobyl four in five North Americans thought it was safer to generate electricity from coal than from uranium fuel. Four months later the same percentage of people in Ontario throught the same. How upsetting was the Chernobyl disaster to Canadians? Before it happened 78 per cent were concerned; afterwards 85 per cent. But the number of people "very" concerned had increased. Two in three Canadians told pollsters they were more concerned about nuclear-power production in the summer of 1986 than they had been two years earlier, yet the same percentage felt Canadian nuclear plants were safe. Fifty-five per cent believed there was a likelihood of a Chernobyl-type disaster happening in Canada. Those were not significant shifts in public opinion. On the one hand there was a substantial part of the population who agreed with the doomsayers who said, "we told you so." But there appears to have been as substantial a number of people who observed that the worst imaginable nuclear-power plant accident had happened, that the sky had not fallen; that even within thirty kilometres of the Chernobyl station not one resident had shown any evidence of harmful radiation despite the most rigorous examinations by Soviet authorities. They had been painfully dislocated from lifetime homes and communities, farmlands had been contaminated perhaps for a number of years and there had been a significant blow to the Soviet economy. Still it hardly compared in human suffering with Bhopal, with the World War I explosion in Halifax harbour.

Much more surprising was the response to one pollster's question a fortnight after the Chernobyl accident. Did Canadians think their government was "telling the full story on the safety of our nuclear industry" or were they withholding information? Four in five respondents across Canada thought government authorities were withholding information; in Ontario three in four thought the same. Perhaps the question was ambiguous. My experience as a newsman seeking governmental response in the week after Chernobyl was that the federal energy and external affairs ministries were evasive, uninformed and lacking ministerial direction. Conversely, Jon Jennekens, Zygmond Domaratzski and Hugh Spence at the AECB were readily available and informative but unwilling to jump to conclusions. As a member of the press gallery in the Ontario legislature, I found Premier David Peterson and Ontario Hydro's top brass accessible and candid as ever. I found the Ontario energy minister Vince Kerrio and solicitor-general Kenneth Keyes covering ignorance by evasion after Chernobyl just as they had done before.

At the AECB Spence was angered by the public's lack of confidence in government authorities. He is the third generation to play a constructive administrative role in the development of nuclear energy from an Ottawa post. He takes his responsibilities seriously. "That poll reflects a perception created by the media," he told me. "They have reiterated the myth of secrecy and the criticism that we are withholding information so often that people actually believed it." Yet the AECB had made all significant event reports — which Ontario, Quebec and New Brunswick nuclear-station management must file promptly for any irregularity — available to any inquirer for six years prior to Chernobyl. In that time there had been less than ten requests to see them; just three from the news media, he said. "It seems that people wouldn't make inquiries themselves, but they have been told so often that things are being withheld I can understand them answering a survey question in that way."

At Ontario Hydro there was an unprecedented response to Chernobyl. It came from the chairman, from management and from union members. "We have well over 100 million man-hours of experience with high-performance nuclear operations without a single fatality from radiation. However, we are not complacent," they said, responding to the "intense public interest about nuclear safety here in Ontario." Ontario Hydro pointed out that nuclear-station personnel were trained not only to provide safety operations but also to cope with emergencies. "We spend about $40 million a year on nuclear training. It normally takes ten years to rise from entry level to first operator and just as long from junior engineer after university graduation to shift supervisor or technical superintendent. At every level there is both classroom and on-the-job training, Ontario Hydro exams, then five Atomic Energy Control Board exams for first operators and shift supervisors." Moreover, Hydro currently had four $40-million training simulators in service to test their response to any conceivable accident scenario, they said. That statement was signed by Hydro chairman Tom Campbell, by Kury Johansen the head of Hydro's professional and management association and by Jack MacDonald, president of the 16,000-member Ontario Hydro Employee's Union.

From New Brunswick Power's Point Lepreau nuclear station there was a similar, if unpublished response. One got the same reaction in nuke towns like Chalk River and Port Hope; in uranium-mining communities like Elliot Lake, Rabbit Lake, Key Lake and Cluff Lake, Saskatchewan. They felt great sympathy for the people of Pripyat and Chernobyl, but no fear.

15

Tea and Sympathy

"The minister advised the Soviets that Canada was offering any assistance we could provide. . . . If Canada has got some unique equipment or technology or capability they would like to draw on the minister has said we would do our best to make it available."

—MARK MOHER, EXTERNAL AFFAIRS CANADA,
MAY 6, *1986*

"We are not involved in any cooperation with the Soviet Union in the nuclear field at this time."

— ROBERT J. ROCHON, EXTERNAL AFFAIRS CANADA,
SEPTEMBER 18, 1986

THERE IS A LEGEND THAT Prime Minister Brian Mulroney and External Affairs Minister Joe Clark, a former prime minister himself, never really existed. People say they were radio-controlled robots devised by Dalton Camp and Senator Keith Davey in an effort to revive public interest in Canadian politics. Brian Mulroney was fashioned from an effigy of US president Franklin Delano Roosevelt, they say, citing the remarkable similarity of leonine heads, teeth-studded smiles and jaunty jaws. Only Roosevelt's long-stemmed cigarette holder was discarded in deference to the Canadian non-smokers' lobby. No one knows just who Joe Clark was meant to resemble. He was apparently built before robot technology was perfected. As evidence, they note that the word sounds were never synchronized with the lip movements and what they describe as "a mechanical gait."

The legend gained credibility after Chernobyl. The PM and Joe Clark were both quoted as offering all possible help to the Soviets. Yet the government was decidedly unhelpful when Ontario Hydro moved to provide such expertise. Why would External Affairs Canada try to block the supply of fast shutdown rods to prevent the recurrence of a Chernobyl-type accident? Why would the minister refuse to discuss technological transfer of non-weapon expertise with the Soviets? Why did the Mulroney government frustrate the AECB, tighten the screws on Eldorado Nuclear and allow perhaps five billion dollars worth of Candu reactor sales to die of attrition? I asked these questions in the months following the Soviet nuclear accident. Answers were pried from the jaws of silence, dug from bureaucratic depths. But nobody — I was not alone in my quest — got an answering word from Prime Minister Brian Mulroney nor External Affairs Minister Joe Clark nor Trade Minister Pat Carney nor Energy Minister Marcel Masse on post-Chernobyl nuclear policy in Canada. If the nation's leaders really existed they were out of town after Chernobyl. Only Jake Epp was left to mind the store.

Four days after the Soviet accident the prime minister said he was unhappy about the Russians' failure to warn their neighbours promptly about fallout. Still Canada would respond to any Soviet request "on humanitarian grounds." Joe Clark's comment was as curt: "We have specified a range of technical areas in which we would be prepared to help. We have so far not been asked." What was Canada's position on beefing up the IAEA's role? "We're working on it," said an External Affairs official on the following day. By then the PM and Mr. Clark had departed for a summit meeting in Tokyo leaving Health Minister Jake Epp to deal with nuclear issues. An interdepartmental task force had been set up in Ottawa, Epp said. Its role was to evacuate Canadians from Kiev, Moscow and Warsaw and to steer travellers away from the Ukraine. It would also contribute to any international assistance being offered to the Soviets. Liberal critic, Douglas Frith, hoped that Canada would take the lead in pushing the IAEA for a better monitoring service but he was not heard from again.

In the next few days Clark's ministry was preoccupied trying to persuade Canadian students to leave Kiev and warning our Moscow embassy people not to drink tapwater or local milk. At the embassy in Warsaw a diplomat said there was no certainty about the radiation risk from Chernobyl but women and children were to leave anyway. "You don't play around with kids' lives," said the first secretary. By then Brian Mulroney and Joe Clark were attending the Tokyo conference. A joint statement from the seven Western leaders said they, "remained ready to extend assistance, in particular medical and technical, as and when requested."

I queried Mark Moher, an External Affairs veteran in handling nuclear issues. Like Jon Jennekens, Moher believed Chernobyl might mark a turning point towards greater nuclear accord through the IAEA. "There has been a great deal of international cooperation and information exchange through the International Atomic Energy Agency over the past five or six years," he said. "We are now hoping that with Soviet coopertion, IAEA will move forward in the coming months to make the Tokyo declaration on cooperation for nuclear safety into a formal agreement." What was Canada doing about Chernobyl? I asked. "The minister advised the Soviets that Canada was offering any assistance we could provide. There has been no response beyond acknowledgment but my feeling is that the Soviets have enough on their plate right now," Moher told me. "If Canada has some unique equipment or technology or capability they would like to draw on, the minister has said we would do our best to make it available." Moher may have read better intentions into Joe Clark's brief comment than the Mulroney government intended. He was promoted out of the nuclear advisory post shortly after and I was never able to contact him again.

Two federal government agencies had marshalled services they thought the Soviets might find helpful. "If we are asked what Canadians can do in the short term it is to assist the Russians in determining the extent of the contamination problem. We have about a dozen people at the AECB and in the Canadian Geological Survey who proved their expertise in the Cosmos-954 cleanup," said AECB president Jon Jennekens. "We've got a lot of equipment, a whole variety of instruments for checking contamination," said AECL's research company president Stanley Hatcher. He had already advised the Soviets through our embassy that the AECL and Ontario Hydro had a range of remote handling equipment available for the asking. Private firms had phoned Ottawa from as far afield as Vancouver to offer equipment and expertise to the Soviets. No record of these offers was kept.

In Ontario where about half the electrical generating capacity was now nuclear, where his government was under continuing pressure from the NDP to scrap the half-built Darlington nuclear station and where some 25,000 wage earners were dependent on nuclear industry and uranium mining, Premier David Peterson refused to be panicked by Chernobyl. Like all Liberals during their long years in opposition, Peterson had been anti-Hydro and he had opposed the utility's nuclear expansion, especially the $11-billion Darlington project. But the premier was neither opportunistic nor evasive. On April 29 he told the legislature about the Chernobyl accident in measured tones. "There is no question this accident is a very major one," he said. Opposition leader Larry Grossman, a Conservative, urged that Ontario Hydro and the AECL, "offer the Russians any and all expertise they may have at hand."

NDP leader Robert Rae concurred that the Soviets should be offered "profound sympathy and expertise." However, he wanted everyone to realize that only Ontario, the Soviet Union and France were developing "a very serious dependence on nuclear power." He made it sound like drug addiction. "We entered it with almost limitless optimism. We now realize there are limits to man's knowledge and expertise."

"There is going to be a very strong reaction to Chernobyl both intellectually and emotionally. I think it is going to put the nuclear industry under some siege," said the premier. "There will be fear in some quarters. There is no reason for fear in Ontario. There are major differences between nuclear plants in Canada and in the Soviet Union. I'm assured by everybody in the industry that there are layer upon layer of safety apparatus and certainly I have no fear of the system. If we thought there was any risk in our nuclear reactors we would close down the ones we have." Darlington, Peterson said, would be judged on economic grounds alone. It was, and the government confirmed that it would be completed. The premier of Ontario did not consider it his role to fear monger nor did he make grandstand gestures of help to the USSR. "If we can make a constructive offer, we will," he said. Within a week NDP leader Rae and two of his caucus shifted their anti-nuclear attack. They wanted the government to stop building a tritium extraction facility at Darlington. The premier ignored that, too.

A week after Chernobyl, Yuri Shymko, elected to the Ontario legislature by fellow refugees from Eastern Europe, milked the Soviet nuclear disaster for venom. "Tonight we will demonstrate our condemnation of a regime which for thirty-six hours exposed some 50,000 citizens to such doses of radiation that today they have a mere 50 per cent chance of survival," he told fellow MPPs. They let it pass. A day earlier Jon Jennekens deplored press reports that said Chernobyl was a thousand times worse than TMI. "What purpose is gained by that? If they are trying to embarrass the Soviets, to suggest that they are really very backward, they are incorrect."

Late in June — while the IAEA (the UN nuclear agency) planned a post-mortem meeting in Vienna with the complete cooperation of the USSR, when the IAEA's director-general had already toured the Chernobyl site, and Ontario radiation health services director Harry Aitken had been to Poland under IAEA auspices to advise them on fallout protection — Shymko introduced a resolution urging that, "the United Nations form an international investigative team to enter the Ukraine; that Canada declare its preparedness to contribute emergency aid such as medicine, food and technical personnel to help in treating the Chernobyl disaster victims either in the USSR or in Canada."

The resolution was seconded by NDP MP Michael Breaugh who two years earlier had called for civil disobedience to declare Ontario "nuclear-free." He had sent a copy to every provincial legislature in Canada. "Food in grocery stores in Toronto, on the west coast and the east coast, has had to be removed from store shelves because of the radiation contamination. It is here on our front door as well," Breaugh told the legislature on June 26. Ontario citizenship minister Tony Ruprecht supported this resolution with a wry twist. "It is obvious we should try to do whatever we can to support the government of the Soviet Union and, directly, the people of the Ukraine. Ontario Hydro is willing, ready and able to supply as much expertise as possible," he said.

Ontario Hydro chairman Tom Campbell's response to Chernobyl had been as prompt and emphatic as Premier Peterson's. Within three days of the Chernobyl accident he had contacted External Affairs in Ottawa to offer the Soviets technical assistance. "At this time little is known about the emergency shutdown systems in their plants. Candu reactors have two independent emergency shutdown systems. Although Ontario Hydro believes that Candu reactors are a better design and are much safer than the Soviet reactors at Chernobyl we are not complacent when it comes to safety," he said.

Hydro's development boss and co-designer of the Candu reactor, Bill Morison is a big, blunt, affable engineer who looks at people and machines alike, with a laser-sharp eye. "The validity of the Canadian response to Chernobyl is that we have fairly broad experience in handling matters of this kind," he said. The calandria cores of both the NRX and NRU reactors had been replaced almost routinely by AECL personnel over the previous quarter-century. Hydro's replacement of nearly eight hundred radioactively hot fuel channels in two Pickering reactors had taken them to the leading edge of technology. State-of-the-art robotics were applied to provide a series of self-propelled TV, electronic and ultrasonic probes that scanned the reactor's innards. Moreover, said Morison, AECL and Hydro health and safety officials had developed procedures based on rehearsals and extensive drills with mockup equipment that duplicated the actual facilities.

In the fall of 1986 the half-billion-dollar pressure-tube replacement project was nearing completion at Pickering but Bill Morison had two other programs demanding his attention. Hydro was just completing safety innovations that had been recommended following exhaustive studies of the Three Mile Island accident in 1979. They had incorporated an emergency core cooling system that worked by injection in new reactors at Pickering and Bruce. All but one of the eight earlier reactors would be back-fitted by 1987 and all Darlington reactors would be so equipped. By 1987 all Hydro reactors would be fitted with hydrogen igniters as well. "They work like spark plugs in car engines to ignite hydrogen as fast as it forms," Morison explained. Hydro had begun to install these preventive devices on the basis of the Americans' TMI experience where a dangerous hydrogen bubble formed in the dome of the reactor structure. The igniters were ordered for Hydro nuclear plants before hydrogen explosions destroyed the US shuttle *Challenger* and wrecked the Chernobyl-4 reactor.

The other program that involved Morison in the latter half of 1986 was tapping the utility's 100-million man hours of safe high-performance nuclear experience to help the Soviet's upgrade their own nuclear facilities in the wake of Chernobyl. This was in response to tentative queries which the USSR's science and technology ministry had made in June. Tom Drolet is Ontario Hydro's global salesman for radioisotopes, mainly cobalt-60. Eighty-five per cent of the world's supply of this gamma-radiation source used in cancer therapy and in sterilizing foods and drugs is a by-product of nuclear-power production at Pickering and Bruce. In June Drolet was moving through Western Europe marketing cobalt-60 and heavy water (Ontario Hydro is also the world's largest heavy water producer) when Soviet authorities queried the Ontario trade office at Frankfurt-au-Main about plastic protective suits.

Coincidentally, Drolet knew all about these suits; they had been developed to protect Hydro nuclear personnel from tritium radiation when he was involved in that phase of Hydro work. The suits were built to Hydro specifications by an Ontario manufacturer in the late 1970s. Made of heavy-grade propylene, they completely enclosed the wearer and were self-contained with respirator and phone connections. The Soviet query, passed along by Austroimpex, an import trading firm in Austria, Germany and the USSR, was urgent. Decontamination crews tunnelling under the razed Chernobyl reactor were being subjected to high radiation fields and intolerable heat. A sample quantity of the protective suits were quickly supplied. "It was no big deal. Depending on how many they might eventually want it could mean anything from a $10,000 to $3 million sale," Drolet said. At the year end the Soviets had not yet decided on the quantity. But by then Hydro-Soviet discussions had a multi-million-dollar potential.

Two months after Chernobyl Ontario Hydro and Soviet nuclear engineers met over lunch in Vienna during the IAEA review meeting. Newly arrived as a one-man nuclear trade mission to the IAEA, Ron Thomas arranged lunch to follow up on brief discussions Canadian nuclear experts had had at a scientific conference in Moscow earlier that summer. Later that fall External Affairs officer Larissa Blavatska dismissed the Vienna lunch meeting as unimportant. "Canadian and Soviet technical experts happened to be in Vienna at the same time and simply had a luncheon together," she told me. AECL vice-president and chief engineer Gordon Brooks described it in slightly different terms. "We had very informal discussions between technocrats to see if collaboration was possible," he said.

Gordon Brooks came away from that luncheon convinced that collaborative efforts were not only possible but had been well started in the week's review of Chernobyl. So did the other Canadian engineers. "We've been analyzing things that go wrong for the last twenty years and then deciding if changes should be made in training programs or operational procedures," said Hydro's nuclear training chief Larry Woodhead. "We keep in close contact with the Americans next door and we've had dialogue with the French, British and Swedes, all of whom do things differently. Now we'd like to know if the Russians have any bright ideas on operating procedures, policies and training."

There was a mutual interest in training nuclear operators and in the operating performance of zirconium-niobium pressure tubes. Then Brooks mentioned the fast-acting shutdown rods which AECL and Hydro engineers developed for Candu power reactors. "I told them how NRX had failed to respond properly to control and we had had a runaway reactor. It taught us the need to incorporate into the power reactor design a very fast, very powerful and very reliable shutdown system," Brooks recalled. The Canadian "scram-rod" system thrusts twenty-eight to thirty-two spring-loaded, gravity-dropping, neutron absorber rods the full depth of the reactor within two seconds. If this failed to counteract a nuclear excursion then sensors would immediately activate a second system. That would inject gadolinium gas under pressure to "poison out" the nuclear activity.

Because the Candu reactor and the Soviet RBMK units such as Chernobyl were both of pressure-tube design they were subject to what

nuclear engineers describe as "positive void coefficient." This charac-
teristic — which they shared to a very different degree — was a major
factor in letting the Chernobyl reactor run out of control. As the power
surge began the reactor heat boiled coolant water to steam. As the
coolant level was reduced so was its moderating effect. As the radioactivity increased the cycle quickly accelerated to runaway proportions.
The positive void factor could create two and a half times as much
nuclear imbalance in an RBMK reactor than it could in a Candu unit,
Bill Morison explained. But the Canadian scram-rod device would
counteract almost double the RBMK imbalance and the gadolinium
would cope with ten times the amount of negative void. The AECB's
Zygmond Domaratzski thought the scram rods might work even better
than that. Earlier in the week they had heard Rudolf Rometsch, the
Swiss nuclear engineer who was chairman of the post-accident review,
describe how the Chernobyl reactor had gone from 7 per cent of its
rated capacity to "a hundred times its nominal value in less than a
second and the power plant was destroyed in the following four seconds." Brooks, Morison and Domaratzski were convinced that the
Candu shutdown system would have worked at Chernobyl within a two-
second period to prevent the disastrous damage.

The Candu scram rods were of immediate interest to the Soviets because, as Gorbachev, Shcherbina and Legasov now stressed, industrial
and domestic electricity demands required all the nuclear-generating
capacity they could safely provide in the shortest feasible time. The
proven performance of the Candu shutdown system — it is partially
tested once every shift on every Canadian power reactor — might take
the Soviets a big step towards backfitting RBMK plants in record time.
There were other areas of interest as well. Two fields for potential
collaboration involved operational training programs with, or without,
computer-based simulators and Ontario Hydro's development of sophisticated controls to automatically regulate reactor operations.

The Soviets' inquiry, made through Austroimpex Export Trading
Company two months after the Chernobyl accident covered "the sup-
ply of engineering services, technology transfer and special safety
equipment." It confirmed Tom Drolet's hunch that the Soviet interest
was much broader than plastic suits and that there was some urgency.
The Vienna luncheon was on August 29. Within two weeks Ontario
Hydro had received an invitation from the Soviet State Committee for
Science and Technology for four "senior officials and technical ex-
perts" to go to Moscow. Hydro sent Tom Drolet, his boss Donald E.
Anderson who headed the utility's aggressive New Business Ventures

marketing division, Robert Popple manager of the radiation and health protection branch and Gerry Armitage, health physics manager at Pickering. All were nuclear engineers; together they took eighty-six years of nuclear-power industry experience to Moscow. "We sent people who could give an expert picture of Ontario Hydro's nuclear experience," said Hydro's executive vice-president Arvo Niitenberg. "We probably had the spectrum of nuclear services as well packaged and integrated as anyone but I didn't know what was going to come out of this Russian trip. It was quite possible nothing would."

In fact Hydro's sales engineering quartet were hustled through a hectic week starting on Tuesday, Sepember 22. Their first meeting was with eight officials of three Soviet agencies at the offices of the State Committee for Science and Technology (GKNT). It resulted two days later in the signing of a protocol by Don Anderson for Hydro and Ivan F. Rubzov, deputy director-general for GKNT. The committee's main interests covered nuclear-reactor materials, training simulators and radioactive waste management, they were told. Still conversation ranged over the tendency of experienced nuclear operators to become complacent, the zirconium-niobium alloy for pressure tubes, Hydro's philosophy for management control at nuclear stations and responsibility for worker radiation protection. On Wednesday morning they met with the director-general and vice-president of Sudo Imports, the largest trading house in the USSR. Sudo was interested in Canadian submarine technology to repair sea-bottom pipelines, in Hydro's laser technology for dam inspection, in their technology for handling PCBs, and in nuclear health physics that might be applicable to Soviet nuclear icebreakers. That afternoon they saw officials of GSK and Atomenergoexport, the Soviet foreign trade ministry concerned with nuclear energy. Atomenergoexport had not dealt outside the Communist bloc up to this time but had supplied nuclear-power plants in Bulgaria, Romania and Finland and was currently negotiating on projects for Finland, Yugoslavia, Syria and North Korea. Where GSK might be a competitor to AECL, Hydro would be unable to deal with it but they saw some limited potential in becoming a subcontractor for siting, environmental studies and the possible supply of training simulators. The ramifications for trade between the Ontario utility and the Soviet Union were unfolding in a fascinating sequence.

The Hydro-Soviet protocol visualized cooperation in six areas: 1) design of safety systems for reactors and other elements of a nuclear station; 2) operational staff training including simulator use to prevent emergency situations; 3) design of processing and storage systems for low and medium level radioactive waste; 4) design of operational and control systems; 5) design and development of "radiation detectors, safety equipment, devices, instruments and machines including robot devices for elimination of accidents"; and 6) development of materials for reactor components and other nuclear-station systems. The Soviet authorities said they would wait on an official proposal.

They never explained why they studiously pursued discussions with Ontario Hydro, a provincial Crown agency, rather than with the Government of Canada or its nuclear agency, AECL. Hydro made it clear that their expertise was shared with AECL and that Gordon Brooks would be a member of any expert team involved. Soviet Science and Technology people agreed with that but they wished to deal with Hydro, not with the Canadian government, they insisted. Why? Perhaps the distinctly anti-nuclear sentiments of the Mulroney government were evident as far afield as the USSR. Possibly, the folks in the Kremlin were appraised of Canadian newspaper reports. Whatever triggered the Soviet preference, they were right. In the backwash from Chernobyl the Canadian government found political and historic reasons to avoid nuclear discussion more compelling than any "humanitarian" concerns or abstract consideration of Mikhail Gorbachev's conciliatory step towards global nuclear accord.

There were two major reasons for federal government hostility to Ontario Hydro's nuclear trade overtures with the USSR. It would offend hate mongering minorities in key constituencies on whom the Mulroney government would count heavily for support in the next election. And it might prove to be a stopgap lifesaver for the Canadian nuclear industry in general which at least four Mulroney cabinet ministers hoped would die of attrition.

On May 2, Andrew Witer, MP for Parkdale-High Park, told the Commons, "Thousands are reported dead, tens of thousands may be suffering the effects of radiation sickness and the 2.5 million residents of Kiev are threatened by the contaminated water reservoir. Intelligence reports indicate there may be a second meltdown in process." Joe Clark's ministry knew on May 2 that what Witer was saying was untrue but no member of the Mulroney government then, or later, had the political courage or sense of common intellectual honesty to stop this dangerous hate mongering and correct the record.

"The Western world's repeated requests for an exact account of the disaster, detailed information concerning the affected population and a comprehensive, verifiable investigation have all met the usual Soviet benign silence. Such complacency... strains the boundaries of common human decency," John Reimer, MP for Kitchener declared on May 6. That was the day that Soviet vice-chairman Boris Shcherbina and first deputy prime minister A.G. Kovalyov held a lengthy press conference about Chernobyl at the Foreign Affairs Press Office in Moscow. Messrs. Witer, Reimer and Shymko were spokesmen for a virulent minority among Canada's seven hundred thousand citizens of Ukrainian ancestry. It is very doubtful that any member of the Mulroney cabinet shared the hate-filled sentiments of people who would rather be "dead than Red." Indeed, at least two of his ministers privately deplored them. But nobody spoke up on May 2, on May 6 or on any other day in 1986.

"What are the energy alternatives in the soft energy path? What about the $100 million of taxpayers' money that went to keep the Cape Breton heavy-water plants going?" asked Jim Fulton, the NDP member for Skeena, BC, leading off his party's renewed attempt in mid-May to destroy the Canadian nuclear industry. He demanded "a full public inquiry into the future of nuclear power" which the Conservatives, themselves, had urged two years earlier. Fulton quoted at length from the writings of Dr. Gordon Edwards whom he said, "long ago should have been given the Order of Canada for his work in relation to the nuclear industry." The debate he provoked in the Commons brought the only public response on record from Energy Minister Pat Carney with regard to nuclear matters. "Nuclear power in Canada is different from other countries and in many ways more successful. Nuclear-power reactors in Canada achieve a level of safety comparable to the best reactors in the world. They are licensed by an effective independent regulatory agency with expert staff, the Atomic Energy Control Board," said the minister, who refused during her entire tenure in the energy portfolio to meet with the presidents of either the AECB or the Canadian Nuclear Association. Nuclear power was a high-technology industry attracting other advanced industries to Canada with cheap and reliable energy. There was no need for any further nuclear inquiries. That said, Ms. Carney sat down hoping she would never have to rise again on a nuclear matter. The prime minister may have lip-read her prayer. He made her trade minister soon after that. Marcel Masse, her successor, proclaimed great interest in Canada's nuclear industry. On July 30 he held a joint press conference with Ontario energy minister Vince Kerrio at Queen's Park. What were either of them doing to help market heavy water? I asked. They didn't know. What was either minister doing to help the AECL sell two 300-megawatt Candu plants to Argentina? I wondered. Marcel Masse said the sales effort had his blessing; Kerrio said nothing.

The anti-nuclear attitude of senior Mulroney cabinet ministers was deep-seated. The twin nuclear agencies, Atomic Energy of Canada Limited and Eldorado Nuclear Limited, were part of a plethora of socialistic Crown corporations that the Liberal strongman Clarence Decatur Howe had implanted in the Canadian economy under his wartime authority. Diefenbaker eliminated one of them, A.V. Roe, even if he had to destroy the Canadian-owned aircraft industry and put blowtorches to the famed Arrow in the process. Joe Clark and Sinclair Stevens had personally tried to destroy Eldorado Nuclear and the government's uranium control secretariat even if they had to alienate Steven Roman, his Denison Mines and Rio Algom Limited in the process. Allan Lawrence, the member with more nuclear wage-earners in his riding than any other Canadian politician, had brought Tory vengence down on AECL's senior management in a bitter parliamentary inquiry that ran through 1977 and 1978. Pat Carney did not disguise a similar distaste for the Canadian nuclear industry. She refused to have anything to do with it long before Chernobyl. The hypocrisy of her brief post-Chernobyl remarks was only exceeded by her discomfort in having to recite them.

Seven years earlier as prime minister of Canada, Joe Clark had personally urged the Japanese prime minister to buy four Candu reactors and was bluntly rebuffed. Ross Campbell, Canada's former ambassador to Japan who then headed AECL, had persuaded Joe Clark to make the pitch and Clark never forgave him nor the industry. A fortnight later when AECL bid to sell the Argentinians four more Candu reactors, Prime Minister Joe Clark, External Affairs Minister Flora MacDonald and Energy Minister Raymond Hnatyshyn stood silent in shadow land. Not only was rejection possible but General Jorge Videla's military junta had already refused the Trudeau government's demands for satisfactory non-proliferation safeguards. Trade Minister Michael Wilson, a forthright man in dubious company, carried the Candu ball to Buenos Aires. Canada's price was a billion dollars; Germany's Kraftwerk Union wanted $1.5 billion for equivalent nuclear-power plants. Then Flora MacDonald, making her maiden speech at the United Nations, deplored the Argentinian junta's "crimes against humanity." The junta rejected AECL's bid the day after that. No one could fault Flora MacDonald's speech but several questioned its timing. The resultant feud between her and Ross Campbell was bitter and she hounded him till he resigned as chairman of AECL.

By the summer of 1985 the Falkland Islands War had made changes in Argentina. A civilian government found that the AECL's erstwhile Italian consortium partner had bribed a junta cabinet minister. Allan

Lawrence, the man from the Port Hope riding, demanded another RCMP investigation. He was ignored but the odour of rancor lingered. A year later when Argentina's President Raul Alfonsin sent his director-general for nuclear affairs and disarmament to Ottawa for three days talks on the "political dimensions" of further Canadian-Argentina nuclear relations, an iron curtain clamped down on Canada's capital. External affairs, AECL and Energy Minister Marcel Masse stonewalled queries while Joe Clark made an unannounced trip to Buenos Aires in September 1986. There he told a press conference that Canada remained "steadfast" in its demand for bilateral nuclear non-proliferation agreements. But in Ottawa his ministry would not even acknowledge that he had made a statement. A half-year after Chernobyl the Mulroney government was not talking about nuclear matters — at least not to Canadians.

With its Argentina sales hopes once again dashed, AECL had two other Candu prospects in 1986. In South Korea where a Candu plant had performed flawlessly, AECL bid to build two more reactors in a $3 billion project. By fall they had lost out to an American supplier because the US applied economic pressure and the Mulroney government did nothing. On a Far East business junket David Peterson minced no words. "Without a Candu sale we will have to find other ways to rectify some of the trade imbalances that exist," he told a South Korean business group. By December TEK, Turkey's electricity board, called off a proposed deal for a Candu plant because they said they were tired of waiting a year and a half for the Canadian government to decide if they would finance the complex arrangments. Canada had not even appointed a diplomatic representative to Ankara in more than a year, the Turks complained.

"The government won't overtly pull the rug from under AECL or Eldorado. They will let them bleed to death by attrition," I was told at the year end. I have repeated that comment to people in the nuclear industry, Crown corporations and the Ottawa millieu. They agreed with it and wondered when — not if — Ontario Hydro would take over the leadership of the Canadian nuclear industry. Meanwhile a federal-provincial clash was brewing over Hydro-Soviet business. The week the Hydro foursome were in Moscow I asked Joe Clark's ministry how they felt about Canadian-Soviet nuclear trade.

"We are not involved in any cooperation with the Soviet Union in the nuclear field at this time," Robert J. Rochon, director of the ministry's nuclear division said flatly. I didn't tell him different.

16

The Colonial Reflex

"You can't expect a young country like Canada to strike out and adopt a military aeroplane policy. It is too expensive a luxury at the present time."

— COLONEL EUGENE FISET, DEPUTY MINISTER OF
MILITIA AND DEFENCE, *OTTAWA CITIZEN*,
AUGUST 12, 1909

"Given the costs associated with a safekeeping corps and the Canadian government's current policy of fiscal restraint, it would not appear appropriate at this time."

— ROBERT J. ROCHON FOR RT. HON. JOE CLARK,
AUGUST 13, 1986

WHEN THE CANADIAN AERODROME COMPANY — Alexander Graham Bell, F.W. "Casey" Baldwin and J.A.D. McCurdy — tried to get the Canadian Army airborne in 1909 the government was not encouraging. "You can't expect a young country like Canada to strike out and adopt a military aeroplane policy. It's too expensive a luxury at the present time. We will probably follow in the footsteps of England," said Colonel Eugene Fiset, deputy minister of militia and defence.

When I suggested to External Affairs Minister Joe Clark after Chernobyl that Canada might package its nuclear expertise into a high-tech safeguard team under IAEA auspices a ministry official replied. "Given the costs associated with a safekeeping corps and the Canadian government's current policy of fiscal restraint, it would not appear appropriate at this time," Robert J. Rochon advised me. The minister did not say it was a foolish idea, which it may be. He just didn't think the government could afford to spend a lot of money on nuclear safekeeping in such tight times.

"While the Russians may yet utilize Canadian services and facilities," I wrote Mr. Clark a month after Chernobyl, "I deferentially suggest that you avail of the current climate for rapprochement generated by the Chernobyl nuclear accident to promote the concept of a Canadian nuclear-safekeeping corps that would operate at Canadian expense under the auspices of the International Atomic Energy Agency."

A fortnight earlier General Secretary Gorbachev had urged the IAEA's 117 member nations, "To declare for a serious deepening of cooperation in the framework of the IAEA to create an international regime for safe development of nuclear power. We must without delay embark on an international regime of safe nuclear-power development aimed at reducing to an absolute minimum the possibility of peaceful atoms causing harm to people," the Soviet leader said on June 3. "Worldwide 152 nuclear-power plant emergencies involving release of radioactivity have occurred. Thus a number of states have experience on which we can and must develop an international nuclear-safety regime." I thought that a safekeeping corps might be a dramatic way for Canadians to give the Gorbachev bid both substance and longevity.

There are half a dozen historical reasons for Canada to undertake such a safekeeping project. We are the only nation which from the outset has had the expertise, technology, resources, infrastructure and economy to build the Bomb and did not. Then Canada co-founded the UN Atomic Energy Commission and played a pioneer role in establishing the IAEA. We have been a major contributor of funds and expert personnel in the past. But Ottawa's interest in the IAEA notably declined in the years between Three Mile Island and Chernobyl. With a year's retrospection it is evident that the Chernobyl disaster evoked lip service and perfunctory platitudes but no new commitment from the Mulroney administration.

Yet Canada has traditionally undertaken major peacekeeping roles through the United Nations and humanitarian activities via such agencies as the World Health Organization. A safekeeping corps, I believed, would be in the tradition of the Canadian peacekeeping troops who manned the UN barriers of the world's incendiary frontiers in the Lester Pearson years. However, I thought it impolitic to mention that to Mr. Clark. When US President Ronald Reagan wanted to send American troops on a war-making mission to Central America in October 1983, Clark's Liberal predecessor Jean-Luc Pepin expressed Canada's contrary view. The country was prepared to dispatch a peacekeeping mission there, Pepin said. Nor did I think it prudent to remind Mr. Clark that the million dollars a year his ministry was spending to develop the technology to verify adherence to a Bomb-test ban had been previously pledged by Pierre Trudeau.

Looking back on recent history from the summer of 1985, William Epstein who had been a participant in the negotiations for the 1968 Non-Proliferation Treaty noted Canada's leading role in earlier days. "Canada was the first Western country to adopt in 1976 a policy of full-scope safeguards on all exports of nuclear material, equipment and technology to all countries. It would not agree to any nuclear exports unless the importing country accepted international inspection of its entire nuclear program to verify that there was no diversion of nuclear energy to military use," Epstein said.

In fact, Canada's requirements that Candu, uranium and nuclear-technology buyers sign bilateral agreements that are more restrictive than the Non-Proliferation Treaty demands cost the Canadian nuclear industry substantial sales and garnered for the country considerable ill will among European nations in recent years. Such zealousness at home might qualify our role to send monitoring teams abroad. The Canadian nuclear industry has not argued against either the NPT or Canadian bilateral demands. They would, however, point out that in the global effort to defuse the Bomb Canada has paid its dues.

Historically, geographically and strategically we are in a position to play a major role in the prevention of nuclear warfare. But I suggested to Mr. Clark that there were also four very pragmatic reasons for Canada to fund, develop and operate such a safekeeping unit. As the world's largest uranium producer for the foreseeable future Canada has a vested interest in sustaining a safe and viable nuclear industry. Canadian industry and technology produces the safest, most efficient nuclear-power system available. We have every reason to promote high standards of safe nuclear operations. The cost of a nuclear-safekeeping corps on an ongoing basis would be small in relation to Canada's nuclear investment and trade. Moreover, we might get more national security for our money this way than with an equivalent expenditure for a conventional armed forces corps.

In his June 3 address Gorbachev said: "Many states do not have the means and resources to deal with an emergency on their own. That is why we think an important component of safe nuclear-power development must be a well-designed mechanism for swift provision of mutual assistance. At the same time the main task is to prevent an accident from happening. It will be necessary to strengthen international verification of compliance to IAEA nuclear-power plant safety recommendations." A month earlier IAEA spokeswoman Marlene O'Dell said the agency was already being besieged with demands to establish an international watchdog team. Within a week of the Chernobyl accident she said some IAEA members had proposed, "that our agency should serve as a safety-monitoring organization."

I suggested seven functions that a nuclear-safekeeping corps would perform. 1) It would monitor nuclear-power facilities to enforce non-proliferation agreements. Canada has already developed electronic surveillance equipment for this purpose; that is, to prevent the diversion of plutonium in spent fuel to weapon making. 2) It would monitor and routinely inspect nuclear-power stations to assure that they were safe for operational personnel, for those living within proximity, and that there was minimal risk of contaminating the environment with effluent or fallout. 3) It would play a major role in the operation of a worldwide radiation-detection service, contributing Canadian expertise in aerial survey, gamma spectrometry, infrared detection and other airborne technology.

A Canadian safekeeping team, moreover would: 4) Provide direction, guidance and planning for the safe design of nuclear-power plants; either on a fee-for-service basis or with offset credits of international value. 5) Maintain as a Canadian Armed Forces squadron at the IAEA command a highly mobile response team on constant alert to move with airborne facilities to the scene of any nuclear emergency; there to act at the request and direction of the host country. 6) Monitor the reduction of nuclear stockpiles when and if accord is reached by the nuclear-weapon states. 7) Combat and counteract the dissemination of false, misleading and hyperbolic statements of nuclear dangers by providing the IAEA with statistical evidence, computerized data and electronic read-out of monitor findings.

"There are two compelling reasons to pursue this safekeeping concept," I told Mr. Clark. "It may be the most rational, viable way for any one nation to significantly advance détente and nuclear safety over the next two decades. And it would package Canadian expertise, excellence and enterprise in a high-profile global activity under the Canadian flag in the same way that our air force provided a focus for national pride in two world wars. It would stimulate Canadian youth to pursue high-technology careers while affording Canadians of all ages a sense of national worthiness," I suggested.

My words must sound quaint; I was born in one wartime and fought in the other. My commission in the Royal Canadian Air Force was signed by George VI as King of the British Dominions beyond the Seas. That was only forty-three years before Chernobyl. My generation was hardened off during the Depression years like spring-planted vegetables in cold frames. Then we went to war — *voluntarily*, eagerly. That was the terrible part of it; war then could still be fun for Canadians. But does it serve the global peace today to decry patriotism? What guns were stilled when the National Film Board denigrated Billy Bishop? Would we be more secure if those flyboys of World War I had not trundled our northern skies in their winged wheelbarrows of the 1920s? Would you have wished the Nazi regime we scourged with obscene eggs dropped from valkyrie flanks a gneration later? The paradox of my generation was that to defend humanity we morally desensitized the human race.

In post-Chernobyl Ottawa, the Mulroney government was silent about Canada's global role. Others were not so reticent. "We can't contract out. We may be getting a nuclear-free ride but we are not a nuclear-free zone. We have to influence our allies and we have to do it through the IAEA," George Ignatieff told me. He thought a safekeeper team under the IAEA aegis was "absolutely right, not absurd at all." But this veteran Canadian diplomat may be biased. He was a founder of the UN Atomic Energy Agency which evolved into the IAEA. He thinks every Canadian government since Lester Pearson's day has been dragging its feet on nuclear issues.

Jon Jennekens wouldn't phrase it quite that way but he thinks people should be reminded of Canada's earlier stance. "That delegation in 1946 — General McNaughton, George Ignatieff and George Laurence — not only provided a tremendous amount of the initiative and creative thinking that led to the UN Atomic Energy Agency but they were a stabilizing force when the Americans and Soviets argued about what the agency should do," he recalled. Canada in the post-Chernobyl world was still a stabilizer that Jennekens believed both superpowers would allow to exercise IAEA nuclear-safekeeping authority. "With the two superpowers, the developing countries, and to a large extent the nonaligned countries, Canadians are accepted as being people in whom you can place some trust. We're close allies of the States, of course. But it's significant that in February two months before Chernobyl, General Secretary Gorbachev instructed their ambassador here to begin a series of initiatives to enhance Canadian-Soviet Union relations — not just in narrow areas but overall. There is probably a greater foundation of trust between the Soviets and the Canadians in the nuclear field. My experience at the IAEA has been that the Soviets believe Canada doesn't have an overriding bias; we don't have an axe to grind."

"The way the Russians have responded to Chernobyl is going to have a beneficial effect, not only on their relations with other countries and the IAEA but it is going to be helpful in the long term in counteracting negative public reaction to nuclear reactors. They have been more frank on this than anything before," Gordon Robertson observed. "I think the Canadian government should encourage them. Whether we like it or not we have to establish some means of cooperating with the Russians, particularly in the nuclear field." As privy council and cabinet secretary, Robertson was Canada's senior mandarin through the Pearson and Trudeau years.

It is noteworthy that Joe Clark's predecessor in the Diefenbaker government, Howard Green, uttered a global cry in 1963 for a treaty to ban the Bomb. "Stop tests, period," Green demanded. As the Americans provocatively continued Bomb-testing in the face of Gorbachev's post-Chernobyl test-ban overtures, the Mulroney government was mute.

Indeed, having signed the seven-nations' cautious concurrence with Gorbachev's bid to strengthen the IAEA a week after the Chernobyl disaster, Mulroney and Clark clamped the lid on any further government plans or policy to: (1) assist the Soviet recovery program at Chernobyl; (2) to facilitate the offers of help volunteered by Canadian nuclear agencies and industry; (3) to increase Canada's participation in the IAEA; or (4) to update, revise or even review Canadian nuclear policies at home and abroad. Information sources I had regularly contacted on nuclear issues in recent years at the External Affairs, International Trade, or Energy, Mines and Resources ministries suddenly became non-communicative or unavailable within the week after the Chernobyl disaster. While Prime Minister Mulroney made mighty-mouse noises about American trade policies, he was not prepared to second guess what direction the elephant might take on its war path. The government of Canada was once again genuflecting to imperial powers in foreign policy matters. The Mulroney administration was not talking about nuclear safekeeping and/or peacekeeping until Washington trumpeted the North American line. Just prior to the outbreak of World War II, the Brits sent the King and Queen to Canada to get our attention. In January 1987 the Americans dispatched Vice President George Bush to tell Canada's prime minister what was what.

By the fall of 1986 Ontario Premier David Peterson, with or without federal government encouragement, intended to do nuclear business with the Soviets. Had the Hydro team gone to Moscow with his support? Absolutely. "Hydro's new business-ventures people are working in a lot of countries around the world and they've got my blessing. We've got some world-class nuclear techology here so let's sell it." He said Soviet interest ranged from fast-acting scram rods to operator training.

Despite the Ontario premier's blessing, Hydro was running into a federal wall of disinterest in doing business with the Soviets. By November ongoing conversations between Tom Drolet at Hydro and Robert Rochon at External Affairs Canada had reached an impasse. To observe Drolet and Rochon is to anticipate some measure of conflict. Drolet is a graduate of the Royal Military College of Canada with a doctorate engineering degree from the University of London. Robert Rochon is a learned diplomat in waiting; a political science graduate of universities in Ottawa, Louvain and Lille as well as law at Harvard. Rochon is flawlessly bilingual, bureaucratically doctrinaire; a gloved mortician to bury killed ideas. Drolet personifies the hard edge of pragmatic inquiry begun by Roger Bacon; Rochon speaks with the metaphysican's voice, uttering the two-sided words that have clogged gears, broken spokes and dulled steel blades for half a millenium.

Tom Drolet and I both dealt with Rochon, the nuclear division director in the special trade relations bureau of director-general Howard R. Wilson, all under assistant deputy minister Anthony T. Eyton's control. Eyton reports to the deputy minister for international trade. He, in turn, speaks to the under-secretary of state for external affairs who is said to converse with Joe Clark. I met with Rochon the same day the Hydro foursome flew to Moscow. He was flanked by Larissa Blavatska, an ambassadress in training. Ms. Blavatska speaks the cultivated nuances of Canada's current-day diplomacy. Yet I could picture her as a Tolstoy anti-heroine toying with words at a ballroom window as the snow fell on St. Petersburg a hundred years ago.

"We are not involved in any cooperation with the Soviet Union in the nuclear field at this time," Rochon told me. So what was the framework in which the Canadians and Soviets had lunched? "Canadian and Soviet technical experts were at Vienna at the same time and simply had a luncheon together," Ms. Blavatska explained. "Official exhanges were suspended after Afghanistan but not all conversations. There have always been contacts between Canadian and Soviet scientists though not necessarily involving AECL," she said.

If, for example, AECL or Ontario Hydro or Canadian Aviation Electronics, who make training simulators, or any other Canadian industry wanted to pursue nuclear business with the Soviets were they free to do so, must they go through External Affairs, or what? "We would need a bilateral agreement with the Soviet Union to do that," said Rochon.

So what were the steps to arrange a bilateral agreement? "They would have to satisfy our non-proliferation, safeguards policy in terms of nuclear cooperation." Canada had such agreements with the US and with Euratom which covered the nuclear weapon states of Britain and France. "We don't have one with China but we are prepared to look at that if the Chinese are prepared to accept our non-proliferation policy," Rochon told me.

So was External Affairs Canada prepared to look at a bilateral safeguards agreement with the Soviet Union? "For the time being I don't think that question arises," the division director advised. Would it arise when Soviet foreign minister Eduard Shevardnadze came to Ottawa in a few days? He didn't know. "They would also have to satisfy other Canadian requirements and safeguards. We would want to look at re-transfers, reprocessing, all sorts of issues," Rochon continued. "In addition to that, a political decision would have to be taken as to whether or not we wanted to have such cooperation with the Soviet Union. It's not limited to nuclear questions. You have a whole realm of politics involved."

Was he talking academically or stating government policy? "I am speaking academically. There is no policy," he told me. Nearly a half-year after Chernobyl and a week before the Soviet foreign minister arrived in Ottawa the Canadian government had no policy, no decision, on whether they wanted to do business with the USSR. But Clark's ministry had marshalled an array of reasons not to deal with the Reds. Canada's External Affairs minister met the Soviet foreign minister in Ottawa at the end of September. But a bilateral safeguard treaty or a Canadian-Soviet trade and technology exchange were not mentioned. Mulroney's foreign trade negotiators were too busy being rebuffed by the superpower to the south to consider market queries from the superpower on the north.

Tom Drolet met with Rochon, Ms. Blatvaska and David Sinden of the Atomic Energy Control Board on October 21. The AECB are advisers to External Affairs on what trade is possible in the nuclear field. Hydro's initial draft which covered their Moscow discussions with the Soviets embraced $18 million worth of shutdown devices for twenty-two RBMK reactors, automated reactor-control systems which could represent up to a $100 million worth of business and about $4 million worth of

Hydro engineering time. No dollar figures were put on the remote-handling equipment developed to retube Pickering reactors but Soviet interest was sparked by a panoply of robotic devices: COSTURD, a computerized, ultrasonic system for turbine drives; CANSCAN, a minicomputer-based eddy-current probe to inspect boiler or reactor tubes; CAVIAR, a calandria vault inspection arm; CIGAR, a channel inspection and gauging apparatus.

If COSTURD, CANSCAN, CAVIAR and CIGAR were considered to reflect Hydro "expertise in replacing reactor-core pressure tubes," then the AECB's export authorization would have to wait on a Canadian-Soviet nuclear agreement, Drolet was told. If these devices represented Hydro's "expertise in robotics" they might be a "sensitive COCOM issue." COCOM, the Coordinating Committee on Export Controls, is the NATO-inspired, Paris-based, US-dominated clearing house that decides what Western-world technology might give aid and comfort to the Communist bloc. Theoretically COCOM prevents the Soviets from acquiring the advanced technology needed to target their nuclear weapons on Western Europe and North America.

COCOM is another mechanism to apply the sort of American economic pressure that required Korea Electric to buy nuclear reactors from Combustion Engineering in the US rather than from the AECL in Canada. Regardless of what Hydro considered the training simulators to be that they had developed jointly with Canadian Aviation Electronics or the computerized nuclear-reactor control systems developed with other Canadian firms, COCOM would rule out such technology transfer, Drolet was told. External Affairs and COCOM could — and would — declare computerized boiler-tube probes and safety shutoff devices to be instruments of war if Hydro persisted, Drolet was implicitly warned. On the basis of this advice Hydro submitted a preliminary proposal covering just $4 million worth of engineering services.

While Hydro sought help and guidance from the Mulroney government in mid-October Valery Legasov took a Kurchatov Institute deputation to Helsinki to talk with officials of STUK (Finnish Centre for Radiation and Nuclear Safety) and the Finnish government research institute, Valtion Teknillinen Tukkimuslaitos. They discussed nuclear monitoring and safety equipment, including a training simulator. "A final decision will be made within the next two months," Legasov said. "We are also talking with French, Canadian and US companies."

In mid-November while Canada's External Affairs officials were stalling Ontario Hydro's negotiations with the Soviet Union, Westinghouse, Bechtel Engineering, Stone and Webster and two other

American companies met with the US State Department, the US Department of Energy and the US Nuclear Regulatory Commission to discuss similar business with the USSR. They were told that if the nuclear technology was strictly safety related —*as the Candu fast scram rods were* — it should have no problem clearing the COCOM hurdle. While Hydro was being hassled by the Canadian government at the year end, the US Department of Energy was preparing guidance material to help the US competitors of Hydro and AECL meet COCOM requirements.

Robert Rochon walks the corridors of the Lester B. Pearson Building where the Nobel Peace Prizewinner's name has been obscured by NATO, NORAD and sundry secret arrangements which they say it is not "in the national interest" for the public to know about. Rochon didn't say it like that. He spoke of the "whole realm of politics involved." Ms. Blatvaska explained that "any nuclear cooperation with any country is only entered into after a whole range of considerations that would involve looking into a series of questions." What Rochon and Blatvaska were really talking about was the colonial reflex — instant genuflection to the south.

The disdain for federal authority shown by Ontario Hydro in unilaterally dispatching a marketing team to Moscow infuriated External Affairs mandarins, if not the minister himself. Hydro proposed to invite Soviet officials and engineers to visit Canadian nuclear facilities. It was told by federal functionaries that "Ontario Hydro is not in a position to invite senior USSR officials to visit power stations, research facilities or institutes other than those of Ontario Hydro." But in the hushed corridors of the Pearson building where the shredders hum behind padded doors and people avoid attribution with paranoic ploys, the bureaucracy is skilled in verbal billiards — the carom play of one's message out of another's mouth. The federal injunctions were issued by David B. Sinden, the AECB safeguards and security manager, to Robert Rochon at External Affairs after he had "discussed these comments with Mrs. Isabelle Massip of your division. I will pass them to Mr. Tom Drolet if he so requests." If billiard balls were identified by names, that play might be described as X to Rochon to Massip to Sinden to Drolet to Y, where X was an unidentified pooh-bah in External Affairs and Y was the president of Ontario Hydro.

In the first week of November Hydro's new business director Don Anderson formerly requested that External Affairs start thinking about a Canadian-Soviet agreement to allow the utility to do business in the USSR. "We feel that major efforts by the Soviets in the areas of nuclear-safety systems and operations training would significantly improve the level of public and worker safety in their nuclear system. Ontario Hydro would pursue further cooperative ventures if a bilateral agreement could be reached between Canada and the USSR. This is an important step in achieving worldwide vigilance and cooperation in the field of nuclear safety," Anderson told Rochon. Seven weeks after he received that letter Rochon told Hydro that External Affairs was "still thinking about it."

By January Hydro's executive vice-president Arvo Niitenberg was involved. "We realize that the final decision lies with the federal government but we feel this is a very responsible and desirable exchange of technology. It's important to the Soviets but we can also learn from it," he said. Niitenberg is the soft-spoken trouble-shooter for a $30-billion corporation that puts $5 billion annually into Canada's economy, employs thirty-one thousand Canadians and has brought utility leaders from around the world to tour its showcase Pickering nuclear station in the interests of the Canadian nuclear industry. Hydro is also the major business instrument in a province that accounts for a third of Canada's population and two-fifths of its economy.

Hydro president Robert C. Franklin is not hesitant to cite these statistics in the utility's worldwide bid for business. A half-year after Chernobyl he wrote Soviet Prime Minister Nikolai Ivan Ryzhkov: "All countries where nuclear power is used should share their accomplishments, not only through the IAEA at Vienna but directly with each other." Following on the Hydro-Soviet meeting in September they had hoped to proceed immediately in five areas. These were: 1) training of nuclear operational staff, including emergency planning; 2) nuclear-waste storage; 3) research on radiation-detection equipment and instruments to eliminate accidents such as the discharge of a radioactive plume; 4) research and development of reactor materials; 5) evaluation of sites for nuclear-power plants.

The Hydro president proposed that a joint team of Canadian and Soviet nuclear engineers should work on problem-solving for alternate months-long periods in Canada and the USSR. "Later we should consider a more permanent association which would operate on a continuing basis," he suggested. The nuclear engineers whom Hydro proposed were their design and development vice-president William G. Morison, technical and training director Larry W. Woodhead, health and safety director Robert Wilson, Don Anderson and Tom Drolet, as well as AECL's vice-president and chief designer Gordon L. Brooks.

Franklin explained to the Soviet prime minister that there were a half-dozen areas of Soviet interest which involved technology transfer.

These included a new emergency shutdown system that would work in a half to one and a half seconds; advanced training simulators to condition operators to emergency situations; use of Canada's patented Candecon decontamination fluid; technologies developed by Hydro to destroy such hazardous materials as PCBs; specialized transmission facilities and materials especially developed for nuclear reactors. The Canadian government had advised Hydro that "more extensive cooperation in these high-technology areas would require a bilateral agreement." Franklin was unable to be more specific than that. "Mr. Prime Minister," he told Nikolai Ryzkhov, "I hope that you will understand that this proposal is generated not only by the desire to sell products and services to the USSR but also by a collective sense of international responsibility for the safe generation of nuclear energy for peaceful purposes." That "collective sense" was precisely what nuclear scientists and engineers had experienced in the week-long IAEA review of the Chernobyl accident in August.

In the fall of 1983 IAEA director-general Hans Blix told me, "Canada plays a very active role thanks to the many people you have who are knowledgeable, due to the fact that you have a reactor design of your own, due to your uranium resources and the research going on in Canada; these things plus a strong government interest in non-proliferation. I don't think anyone would suggest that Canada is second rate at the IAEA." Not then. But shortly after that the government of Canada changed and its interest in nuclear issues at home or abroad notably waned. How long would the Mulroney government maintain Canada's status at the IAEA or even a low profile at home?

Why did the Mulroney government turn its back on the Soviet's post-Chernobyl bid for collaboration when every public and private element in the Canadian nuclear field was prepared to respond? There were three reasons. Firstly, they were frightened of the backlash from a virulent minority of Canadians who wish to perpetuate the Russian Civil War in our country. Hate mongering means votes in certain urban ridings of Canada and both the Liberal and Conservative parties have wooed those votes for a generation. It is time more rational elements in both of these political parties faced the awesome reality of 700,000 Hiroshima Bombs and ceased the hyphenated-Canadian game, that is the incitement of ethnic and racial groups for political gain. Secondly, the Mulroney government like the NDP, like Energy Probe, like the earth children with their feet dug into primal clay to turn back the wheel, suffered the colonial reflex. They were waiting on the White House and the Pentagon for direction. Thirdly, this government's leaders suffered the Hiroshima complex which beset us all. They repressed the twin nuclear genies — Candu and the Bomb — believing that both could be wished back into the dissolution of smoke from the lamp of knowledge. But one twin had no bearing on the other and neither would lie down in the dark recesses of the public psyche forever.

In 1984-1985 McMaster University professor of pediatrics and family medicine K. Ross Parker probed the feelings of more than 7,500 school-age Canadian youngsters from Inuvik to St. John's. What concerned them most? he asked. A third of these young Canadians said the threat of nuclear war did. Concerns about getting work or getting by in school didn't bother nearly as many. Then he asked the question in a different way. When they thought about the future what three things worried them most? More than half (55 per cent) queried in 1984 said the threat of nuclear war did. There was slightly less anxiety (49 per cent) the next year.

In June 1984 four Toronto public school children presented a play they called "Our Story May Yet Be Told." They wore ghost-white masks and shroud-like costumes. They were labelled, "Hope," "Home," "Love" and "Reason" and they appeared to be pointing to a sunless sky. They said they were trying to show "what the world would lose in a nuclear war." These children are the third generation since the Bomb was dropped. We perpetuate our fear but we pass along no wisdom on how to relieve it. These are the children of the baby boomers who were conceived while my generation lay awake in awe and guilt at what we had created.

The technology of annihilation followed such a slow curve for so long it went unnoted. Two million years elapsed between the use of wooden clubs and flint-tipped arrows, ten thousand years between the stone axe and iron weapons. Yet it is only 2,500 years ago that armies were first marshalled into infantry, cavalry, archers. Gunpowder was invented seven centuries past. Nitocellulose and nitroglycerine were produced in the mid-nineteenth century. Before Queen Victoria died her empire was equipped for war on a grand scale. A dozen years after her death warfare was airborne. It began inauspiciously enough; German zeppelins and airplanes killed 1,400 Britons and the Royal Air Force killed twice that many in World War I. The Luftwaffe bombed 60,000 British civilians to death in World War II. The RAF Bomber Command killed 200,000 German people in 1942-1945. Half that many Japanese people were killed with two Bombs in seconds on two August days of 1945. Today's arsenals hold 700,000 times the killing power of the Hiroshima Bomb.

217

But the nuclear-weapon tests persist. There had been 1,580 Bomb tests before the Chernobyl accident. That accident exposed Canadians *once* to a fraction of the fallout they still get *every year* from past nuclear-weapon testing.

John Macpherson speaks softly but with a sharp, clear edge to his words, a gift of mild sea air in his native Hebrides. He taught there, gained a measure of note on the BBC, came to Canada to tout heavy water and the Gaelic in Cape Breton. He speaks now for Atomic Energy of Canada Limited. "It is estimated that nearly half a million people each year receive treatment on cobalt-60 cancer therapy machines in eighty countries that were designed and built by AECL," he notes. "Cancer specialists say that these units have added more than thirteen million person-years of extended life to cancer patients. I have no estimates on how many people worldwide benefit from medical and surgical supplies that have been sterilized in cobalt-60 process facilities; I only know that AECL provides 80 per cent of these facilities worldwide. This company produces a range of radioisotopes — elements made radioactive in Canada's NRX and NRU reactors. Physicians estimate that they use these isotopes for ten to twenty million diagnostic procedures in hospitals and clinics across Canada each year."

There is a Greek myth that Prometheus, god of fire, stole flame from Mount Olympus to give earthlings comfort and humanity. But did he tell us that the fire must always be tended? Controlled in furnaces, fire warms the living place, cooks food, raises steam power. Unattended or violently released it generates fire-storms, razes cities, commits genocide. Turning off the furnace will not disarm a single Bomb. And there is such a multitude of Bombs to be defused.

Illustrated Glossary

AECB (ATOMIC ENERGY CONTROL BOARD)
Canada's regulatory agency, established in 1946 by the Atomic Energy Control Act. The Board licenses all nuclear facilities and operations, uranium mining and refining, and the domestic use and export of nuclear materials.

AECL (ATOMIC ENERGY OF CANADA LIMITED)
A federal Crown corporation established by C.D. Howe in 1952; operates the NRX and NRU reactors and research facilities at Chalk River Nuclear Laboratories; Whiteshell reactor and underground research facilities at Whiteshell (Manitoba) Research Establishment; Candu design and development at Candu Operations, Sheridan Park, Ontario and Montreal; radioisotope production at AECL Radiochemical Co., Kanata, Ontario, and at the University of BC cyclotron; cobalt-60 production in Ontario Hydro Pickering and Bruce and Hydro-Quebec Gentilly reactors; and cancer therapy equipment at the medical products division, Kanata, Ontario. In 1986 AECL had assets of $1.1 billion, sales of $260 million and employed 5,540 prople.

ATOM

L. Cook

Atoms are the smallest fragment of an elemental substance to retain that element's characteristics. The Greeks considered them solid little balls that rolled together to form various chemicals. Rutherford changed that with his concept of an atomic nucleus (protons and neutrons) like the sun around which electrons orbited as planets do.

CANDU (CANADIAN DEUTERIUM URANIUM REACTOR)

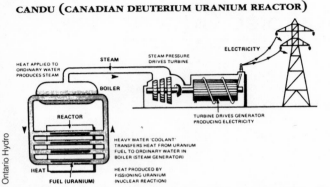

Ontario Hydro

The diagram illustrates horizontal pressure tubes in which heavy water "coolant" transfers heat from hot fuel bundles to a steam system which drives a turbine to generate electricity.

CHAIN REACTION

L. Cook

A neutron bullet shatters a uranium-atom nucleus that contains 235 neutrons and protons, creating three new neutrons in the process. One or more of these new neutrons causes the fission of another uranium atom, releasing more neutrons to cause a chain reaction. It requires about 375 million, billion fissions to generate one kilowatt-hour of electricity.

CONTAINMENT

These diagrams compare structures that contain Candu and Chernobyl-type reactors. Canadian experts say the top of the Chernobyl structure was not strong enough to withstand an explosive force and was not pressurized to retain radioactivity even with a lesser accident. The

Candu containment and secondary vacuum system are designed not to leak more than one per cent per day "under any conceivable accident condition; time enough to let fission products decay and let us decide on action," said an Ontario Hydro engineer.

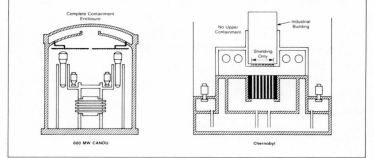

CONTROLS

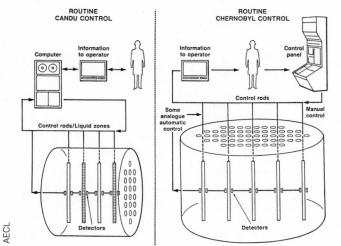

These diagrams compare the computer-based control system of Candu with the *partially* automated control of the Chernobyl reactor. In the Candu operational control rods respond to computer signals based on detectors in the reactor. The Chernobyl operational control rods respond to both analogue calculators and manual application.

ELDORADO NUCLEAR LIMITED

A federal Crown corporation with sole authority to refine and convert Canadian uranium to compounds for use in reactor fuel. Eldorado is one of five companies worldwide which provides such services. It operates refinery and conversion facilities at Blind River and Port Hope. Eldorado is also a major uranium producer; it owns and operates a uranium mine and mill at Rabbit Lake and has a one-sixth share of Key Lake mine, both in Saskatchewan. The company was founded as Eldorado Gold Mines by Gilbert and Charles LaBine in 1925 and developed the Port Radium pitchblende mine for radium in 1932. C.D. Howe nationalized the company as Eldorado Mining & Refining Ltd. in 1943 to produce uranium for the Bomb project.

EMERGENCY SHUTDOWN RODS

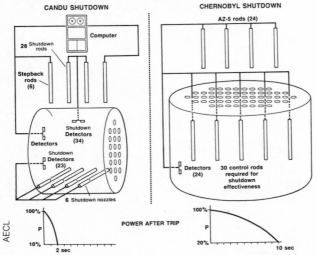

The diagrams compare the two shutdown systems in the Candu with the Chernobyl system. First the Candu system inserts twenty-eight rods to soak up neutrons and stop 90 per cent of a nuclear reaction in two seconds; if this fails detectors would activate a discharge of gas through six nozzles to "suffocate" a reaction. The Chernobyl reactor relied on thirty rods which were 80 per cent effective in ten seconds.

ENTOMBMENT

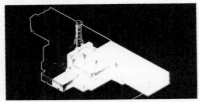
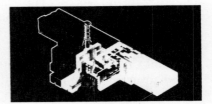

222

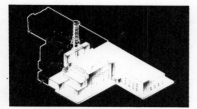

The Soviet drawings of Chernobyl-4 illustrate the structure around the reactor before the accident, after the accident and after enclosure in a concrete "shroud" which has been designed to provide cooling and containment for decades to come.

FALLOUT

FALLOUT FROM CHERNOBYL

	Population in Thousands	Collective Dose in Million Rems
Town of Pripyat	45	0.15
Kilometres from accident		
3– 7 km	7.0	0.38
7–10 km	9.0	0.41
10–15 km	8.2	0.29
15–20 km	11.6	0.06
20–25 km	14.9	0.09
25–30 km	39.2	0.18
Total	135	1.6
Average		12 rems per person

Radioactive fallout consists of the atomized fission products produced in a nuclear reaction which are windborne from the site and literally fall out of the plume or cloud, either dropping by gravity or in rainfall. The fallout is generally measured in terms of the radiation dose or exposure, in millirems per hour, that it produces at a given location.

FISSION

L. Cook

The spontaneous disintegration of a uranium atom was described by nuclear scientist Leslie G. Cook this way: "The neck of the bag bursts open and a bridge foursome of alpha particles goes flying out followed quickly by an electron fragment (beta ray) and a bolt of lightning (gamma ray). Of the ninety-two electrons in the bag, two break off and go along with the alpha particle to make a new two-electron baby atom of a different element."

FUEL CYCLE

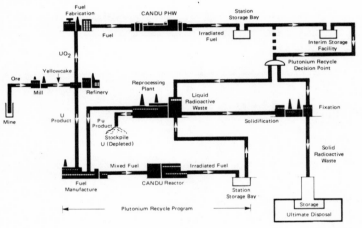

Possible CANDU Fuel Cycle

A nuclear fuel cycle covers the system from the mining of pitchblende or uranium ore through conversion, refining and fabricating to fuel bundles, production of electricity in a power reactor, storage of spent fuel and ultimate reprocessing to extract plutonium as additional fuel and burial of non-usable nuclear waste. A possible Candu fuel cycle is illustrated in this flow diagram from a 1970s publication. It was dropped from circulation when the Trudeau and Davis governments both decided that reprocessing was too political a subject to be discussed in the twentieth century.

224

HEAVY WATER

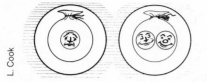

L. Cook

Heavy water or deuterium contains twin protons in each hydrogen atom which makes it twice as heavy and more effective in slowing neutrons to atom-smashing velocity. Heavy water looks, feels and tastes like tap water but only one molecule in every seven thousand of fresh water has a double-hydrogen atom in it.

NRX AND NRU

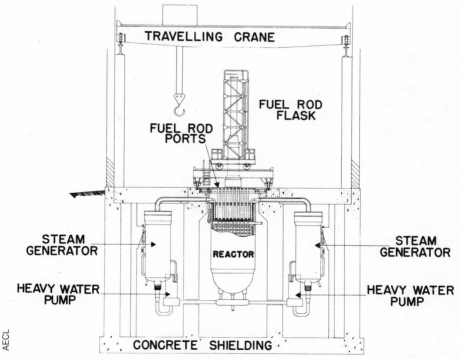

AECL

The NRX (Nuclear Research Experimental) and NRU (Nuclear Research/Uranium) reactors went into operation at Chalk River in 1947 and 1956 respectively. The NRX was forty megawatts; the NRU was two hundred megawatts; both had vertical pressure tubes. The diagram of

225

the NRU showing a fuelling machine resembles the basic design of the Chernobyl reactor.

ONTARIO HYDRO

Ontario Hydro is a Crown corporation, administered by a twelve-member board of directors appointed by the provincial government. It evolved in 1906 from a royal commission headed by Adam Beck to investigate development of hydroelectric power in Ontario. With assets over $30 billion, Ontario Hydro is one of the top three corporations in Canada. It is second only to Electricité de France in the operation of an integrated nuclear-power system. A joint AECL/Hydro project team began the design of a prototype Candu reactor, the NPD (Nuclear Power Demonstration) at Chalk River in 1953. NPD was built by AECL, Hydro and Canadian General Electric at nearby Rolphton in 1962. The federal-Ontario cost-sharing plan to build the first two Pickering power reactors was signed in 1964.

RADIOISOTOPE

A radioactive isotope is any chemical element (cobalt, sodium, etc.) made radioactive in an atomic pile. Neutrons in the pile knock the atoms of the chemical out of balance; make them radioactive. Thus a radioisotope is a source of energy. Like an electric lightbulb it shoots off rays which can be photographed, measured, reflected or recorded. Isotopes *per se* are atoms of the same element with the same number of protons and elements which makes them chemically identical; they look, feel, smell, taste the same. But isotopes differ in the number of neutrons at their core. That makes some of them radioactive and some not so. Some isotopes are naturally radioactive, for example uranium-234, uranium-235 and uranium-238. Others get that way in a reactor, for example hydrogen-3, which is called tritium.

RBMK

The Reactor Bolchoie Molchnasti Kipiachie means cooled by water and moderated by graphite. Developed from a five-megawatt prototype at Obninsk in 1958-63 to four 950-megawatt units at Chernobyl and Smolensk from 1971 to 1975. Ten more 950-megawatt and one 1,450-megawatt units were built prior to the Chernobyl accident at Kursk, Leningrad, Smolensk and Ignalina.

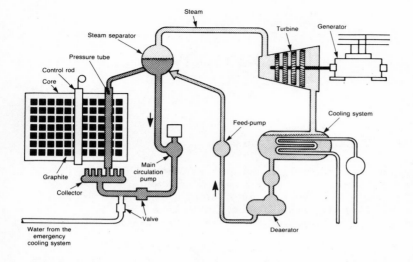

URANIUM ATOMS

The nucleus of the common uranium atom contains 146 neutrons and ninety-two protons which makes it both a good source and a good target for neutrons. There is a rare (less than one per cent) form of uranium with three less neutrons but much more response to the fission process. This uranium-235 is used to enrich fuel in American and European reactors.

URANIUM FUEL

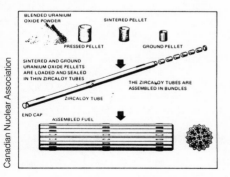

Canadian Nuclear Association

Uranium oxide is powdered, pressed and sintered to pellets which fill finger-thick tubes. Twenty-eight to thirty-seven tubes form a fuel bundle which is loaded by a fuelling machine into a pressure-tube channel.

Bibliography

BOOKS

Bertin, Leonard. *Atom Harvest*. London: Secker & Warburg, 1955.

Bothwell, Robert. *Eldorado*. Toronto: University of Toronto Press, 1984.

Bothwell, R., and W. Kilbourn. *C.D. Howe*. Toronto: McClelland & Stewart, 1979.

Calder, Angus. *The People's War*. London: Panther Books, 1971.

Calvocoressi, Peter, and Guy Wint. *Total War*. Harmondsworth, U.K: Penguin, 1972.

Canning, John, ed. *Great Disasters*. London: Treasure Press, 1984.

Churchill, Winston. *Hinge of Fate, Closing the Ring, Triumph & Tragedy*. Boston: Houghton Mifflin, 1953.

Clark, R.W. *Greatest Power on Earth*. London: Sidgwick & Jackson, 1979.

Dunning, John R. *Glossary of Terms in Nuclear Science & Technology*. New York: American Society of Mechanical Engineers, 1953.

Eayers, James. *Defense of Canada*. Toronto: University of Toronto Press, 1972.

Eggleston, Wilfrid. *Canada's Nuclear Story*. Toronto: McClelland & Stewart, 1965.

Eve, Arthur S. *Rutherford, Life & Letters*. Oxford: Oxford University Press, 1939.

Ford, Daniel F. *Three Mile Island*. New York: Penguin Books, 1983.

Fuller, G.A., et al. *125 Years of Canadian Aeronautics*. Willowdale, Ontario: Canadian Aviation Historical Society, 1983.

Glasstone, Samuel. *The Effects of Nuclear Weapons*. Washington: U.S. Atomic Energy Commission, 1957.

Glasstone, Samuel. *Sourcebook on Atomic Energy*. Toronto: D. Van Norstrand Canada, 1950.

Goldschmidt, Bertrand. *The Atomic Complex*. LeGrange, Illinois: American Nuclear Society, 1984.

Gowing, Margaret. *Britain & Atomic Energy, 1939-45*. London: Macmillan & Co., 1964.

Gray, Mike, and Ira Rosen. *The Warning, Accident at TMI*. Chicago: Contemporary Books, 1980.

Jay, K.E.B. *Britain's Atomic Factories*. London: Her Majesty's Stationery Office, 1954.

Jones, Michael W. *Deadline Disaster*. Newton Abbey, U.K: David & Charles Publishers, 1976.

Jungk, Robert. *Brighter Than a Thousand Suns*. Hammondsworth, U.K: Penguin Books, 1964.

Lapp, Ralph E. *The Radiation Controversy*. Greenwich, Connecticut: Reddy Communications, 1979.

Bibliography

Leclerq, Jacques. *The Nuclear Age*. Paris: Le Chene, 1986.

Roberts, Leslie. *Life & Times of Clarence Decatur Howe*. Toronto: Clark Irwin, 1957.

Rutherford, Ernest. *Radio-Activity*. Cambridge: Cambridge University Press, 1905.

Sanger, Penny. *Blind Faith*. Toronto: McGraw-Hill Ryerson, 1981.

Schubert, Jack, and Ralph E. Lapp. *Radiation*. Toronto: Macmillan Co. of Canada, 1957.

Smythe, H.D. *Atomic Energy: A General Account of the Development*. Washington: U.S. Government Printing Office, 1945.

Solomon, Lawrence. *Breaking Up Ontario Hydro's Monopoly*. Toronto: Energy Probe, 1982.

Stacey, C.P. *Arms, Men and Governments*. Ottawa: Queen's Printers, 1970.

ARTICLES, REPORTS, SCIENTIFIC PAPERS, SUBMISSIONS

Aaltonen, H., et al. "STUK-B-Valo 44: Interim Report on Fallout." Helsinki: STUK Finnish Centre for Radiation & Nuclear Safety (May 1986).

AECB. "The Nature of Reactor Accidents." Ottawa: Ministry of Supply and Services (1981).

Agra Europe. "Chernobyl Unlikely to Make Major Impact." U.K: Tunbridge Wells (May 9, 1986).

Aikman, Major Wm. R. "Operation Morning Light." Ottawa: National Defense Department (1978): 2:14.

Anderson, Donald, and Thomas Drolet. "Proposal for Joint Work to USSR State Committee for Science and Technology." Ontario Hydro (November 1986).

Andrewes, P.W. "Final Report: Select Committee on Energy." Toronto: (July 1986).

Canada Health & Welfare. "Impact of Chernobyl Nuclear Reactor Accident on Canada." Ottawa: Canada Health & Welfare (December 9, 1986).

Cipriani, A.J. "Health & Safety in Reactor Operations." New York: International Conference on Peaceful Uses of Atomic Energy, United Nations (1956): V. 13.

Cook, Leslie G. "Homo Sapiens and Uranium." University of Toronto (1956).

Dakers, Ronald G. "Eldorado Nuclear." Toronto: submission to Ontario Select Committee on Hydro Affairs (September 1980).

Driscoll, D., et al. "Eldorado Occupational Health Control." National Research Council: field notes and report. Public Archives of Canada (1946).

Edwards, Gordon, and Ralph Torrie. "Myths and Metaphors." Toronto: summary argument to Porter Royal Commission on Electric Power Planning (1979).

Eldred, V.W., and K. Saddington. "Post-Irradiation Examination at Windscale." London: U.K. Atomic Energy Authority (February 1962).

Fritz, Charles E., and J.H. Mathewson. "Convergence Behaviour in Disasters." Washington: National Academy of Sciences – National Research Council (1957).

Gray, J.L. "Reconstruction of NRX Reactor." New York: National Industrial Conference (October 1954).

Greenwood, J.W. "Contamination of NRU Reactor." Chalk River, Ontario: AECL publication (May 1959) CRR-836.

Gummer, W.K., Campbell, F.R., Knight, Geoff B., and J.L. Ricard. "Cosmos-954." Ottawa: AECB publication (May 1980) INFO-0006.

Howe, C.D. "Howe Papers." Public Archives of Canada (1940-57) series RG 28A and MG 27.

Hurst, Donald G. "The Accident to NRX Reactor." AECL publication (1953).

Inhaber, Herbert. "Risk of Energy Production." Ottawa: AECB (1978).

Jensen, M., and J-C Linde. "Activities of Swedish Authorities After Chernobyl." Stockholm: Statens Straklsky (May 12, 1986).

Knight, Geoff B. Correspondence regarding 103 Church Street, Toronto. Ottawa: AECB (1975-76).

Kupsch, W.D. "From Erzgebirge to Cluff Lake." Saskatoon: University of Saskatchewan (1978) The Musk-Ox, #23.

Lawson, Patricia. "Mismanagement of Radioactive Waste Point Hope & Point Granby." Submission to Porter Royal Commission on Electric Power Planning (June 1977).

Legasov, Valery, et al. "The Accident at Chernobyl Power Plant and Its Consequences." Vienna: USSR State Commission on Utilization of Atomic Energy (August 1986).

Letavet, A.A. "Health Protection of Workers from Ionizing Radiation." New York: Proceedings of International Conference on Peaceful Uses of Atomic Energy, United Nations (1956) V.13.

Lewis, W. Bennett. "The Accident to NRX Reactor." Chalk River, Ontario: AECL Report DR-32 (1953).

McCullough, C.R., Mills, M.M., and E. Teller. "Safety of Nuclear Reactors." New York: Proceedings Atomic Energy, United Nations (1956) V.13.

Morgan, J.R. "A History of Pitchblende." London: UK Atomic Energy Commission (March 1984).

Morison, W.G., and O.J.C. Runnalls. "The Reality of Nuclear Accidents." University of Toronto (May 27, 1986).

Myers, David K., et al. "Carcinogenic Potential of Various Energy Sources." Ottawa: AECL (1981).

Porter, Arthur. "A Race Against Time." Toronto: Report of the Royal Commission on Electric Power Planning (September 1978).

Runnalls, O.J.C. "Radon Gas and Other Perils." Toronto: Canadian Energy Exposition (May 1982).

Rylsky, Maxim. "A Town Born of the Atom." Moscow: Soviet Life (February 1986).

Sievert, Rolf M. "Measurements of Low-Level Radioactivity." New York: Proceedings Atomic Energy, United Nations (1956) V.13.

Tatu, Michel. "La Sage de Tchernobyl." Paris: LeMonde (June 29-30, 1986).

Thornburgh, Dick. "Statement on TMI Cleanup." Middleton, Pennsylvania (July 9, 1981).

Tracy, Bliss L. "Fallout Over Canada From Chernobyl." Ottawa: Canada Health & Welfare (June 24, 1986).

United Kingdom Atomic Energy Office. "Accident at Windscale No. 1 Pile." London: Her Majesty's Stationery Office (November 1957).

United Nations Scientific Commission on Effects of Atomic Radiation (UNSCEAR). "Ionizing Radiation Sources and Biological Effects." Geneva (1982).

Bibliography

Vuorinen, A.P., et al. "Summary Report Post-Accident Review Meeting on Chernobyl Accident." Vienna: International Nuclear Safety Advisory Group (INSAG) (September 16, 1986).

White, J.M. "Decontamination of Radium from 103 Church Street, Toronto." Chalk River, Ontario (October 1976) AECL CRNL-1552.

Woodhead, Lawrence W. "A Nuclear-Electric Program." Toronto: Ontario Hydro (June 1981).

PUBLICATIONS

Ascent. Toronto: Atomic Energy of Canada Limited (1979-86).

Atom. London: UK Atomic Energy Authority (1980-86).

Bulletin. Vienna: International Atomic Energy Agency (1983-86).

Canadian Atomic Newsletter. Toronto: L. Ray Silver (1957-58).

Canadian Isotope Newsletter. Oakville, Ontario: P.J. Stewart and L. Ray Silver (1952-57).

Current Digest of the Soviet Press. Columbus, Ohio: PAIS Bulletin & Political Science Abstracts (1986).

Nature: Illustrated Journal of Science. London & New York: Macmillan & Co. (1871 et seq).

Nuclear Canada. Toronto: Canadian Nuclear Association (1980-86).

Nuclear Fuel. New York: McGraw-Hill (1978-86).

Nucleonics Week. New York: McGraw-Hill (1978-86).

Philosophical Transactions of The Royal Society. London (March 1667 et seq).

Index